Divining
the Body

Divining the Body

the Body

RECLAIM THE HOLINESS
OF YOUR PHYSICAL SELF

Jan Phillips

Walking Together, Finding the Way
SKYLIGHT PATHS Publishing
Woodstock, Vermont

Divining the Body:
Reclaim the Holiness of Your Physical Self

2014 Quality Paperback Edition, Fourth Printing

© 2005 by Jan Phillips

Library of Congress Cataloging-in-Publication Data
Phillips, Jan.
Divining the body : reclaim the holiness of your physical self / Jan Phillips.
p. cm.
Includes bibliographical references.
ISBN-13: 978-1-59473-080-1 (quality pbk.)
ISBN-10: 1-59473-080-6 (quality pbk.)
1. Body, Human—Religious aspects. 2. Spiritual life. I. Title.

BL604.B64P45 2005
202'.2—dc22

2004026591

Grateful acknowledgment is given for permission to reprint material from the following sources: Coleman Barks, *The Essential Rumi;* Judi Beach, "The Way Hands Bless the Self"; Toni Farkas, "After Ruth Krauss"; Kabir Helminski, *The Pocket Rumi Reader,* www.sufism.org; Daniel Ladinsky, *Love Poems from God* and *The Gift;* Myra Shapiro, *I'll See You Thursday;* Sandy Supowit, *Halves of Necessity.* Photos on p. 176 © I.H.M General Institute, from *Messages from Water* by Masaru Emoto, published by Hado Kyoiku Sha Co., Ltd.

10   9   8   7   6   5   4

Manufactured in the United States of America
Cover Design: Sara Dismukes

SkyLight Paths Publishing is creating a place where people of different spiritual traditions come together for challenge and inspiration, a place where we can help each other understand the mystery that lies at the heart of our existence.

SkyLight Paths sees both believers and seekers as a community that increasingly transcends traditional boundaries of religion and denomination—people wanting to learn from each other, *walking together, finding the way.*

SkyLight Paths, "Walking Together, Finding the Way," and colophon are trademarks of LongHill Partners, Inc., registered in the U.S. Patent and Trademark Office.

Walking Together, Finding the Way®
Published by SkyLight Paths Publishing
A Division of LongHill Partners, Inc.
Sunset Farm Offices, Route 4, P.O. Box 237
Woodstock, VT 05091
Tel: (802) 457-4000   Fax: (802) 457-4004
www.skylightpaths.com

To the Divine in each of us

Contents

Introduction

Many of us are told as children that our bodies are temples of God, houses of the Holy Spirit, and that within our very beings exists a spark of the Divine itself. Following this joyful pronouncement, we also learn that our bodies are dirty, shameful, not to be touched, enjoyed, played with. We're taught to deny ourselves pleasure, to fight temptation, to hold back, to go without, to resist carnal connection.

The Imitation of Christ, attributed to Thomas à Kempis, was first published in Latin over five hundred years ago and remains in print today. It has been translated into dozens of languages and has a reputation as being second only to the Bible as a guide and inspiration to Christian believers. In a modern translation, we read: "Sometimes you must use violence and resist your sensual appetite bravely. You must pay no attention to what the flesh does or does not desire, taking pains that it be subjected, even by force, to the spirit. And it should be chastised and forced to remain in subjection until it is prepared for anything and is taught to be satisfied with little.... You must know that self-love is more harmful to you than anything else in the world. You should give all for all and in no way belong to yourself."

It was this contradiction, this kind of training, that kept me confused and disembodied for the better part of my life. I grew up reading *The Imitation of Christ* every night before bed, from age eleven through thirteen. I was trying to be as good a Christian as I could be, and I thought if I read that book, I'd end up being more Christlike. But its message only helped me sever my soul from my body, kept me from tuning in to its urgent, loving messages, fortified a fear that all light was outside me and all darkness within.

The great tragedy of Western religion is that it elevates disembodied love over embodied love, leading us to believe that it is better to be *out of* our bodies than in them. Even in the dictionary, the definition for *carnal*, which simply means "of the flesh," is charged with the added connotation: "usually stresses the absence of intellectual or moral influence."

It's not specifically a Roman Catholic upbringing such as mine that will create this division from the body, for this mentality has pervaded our cultures and religious traditions for thousands of years. Cultural anthropologists tell us that there was a time when humankind honored its oneness with the natural world and lived in peaceful, full-bodied harmony with nature. But as broader social organization developed, as religion became codified in language and in hierarchy, and as the intellectual became dominant over the physical, we began to separate our souls from our bodies. We forgot we were sparks from the same flame, waves of the same sea, that as much as the Divine is around us, the Divine is within us, experiencing itself through every sense in our bodies. The journey of our lives is a journey of remembering and reconnecting. It is a journey of joy and discovery, a chance to feel and reveal the radiance within. The spiritual path leads inward, for the beloved dwells there in every cell, like the oak in the acorn, the jewel in the mine. The great secret within us is waiting to be told through the living of our lives, waiting to be shared through the pleasures of our senses.

We need to climb back into our bodies and honor them as instruments of our souls. They are the means through which the Divine takes shape in this world, crucibles in which the raging blaze of spirit is transformed into luminous thought, radiant creations, enlightened action. We are the word made flesh, and through our bodies, we are continuing the creation of the universe, physically and metaphysically. It is not happening *to* us, but *through* us—and the meaning we're seeking, the deep joy and passion we're after, the enlightenment we long for, all this arrives as we begin to re-pair what cultures and creeds have torn asunder.

In the process of divining our bodies, we embody the Divine as the mystics did. We feel the beloved in every cell, sense the sacred one in every heartbeat, every touch, every image our eyes encounter, every sound our ears behold. Transcending duality, we shift from a sense of "self" and "other" to a sense of self *in* other. When we embrace the Divine within ourselves, it becomes natural to find and love the Divine in others. It is our nature to do this. If we love ourselves tenderly, that feeling of compassion and kindness will seep out of us and transform every relationship in our lives.

This book is an attempt to undo the damage we've sustained living in a culture that thrives on our self-hatred. It is a sanctification of our human bodies, a consecration of ourselves as hosts to the Great Beloved. It is a journey of awe and reverence through the sacred terrain of foot and hand, back and breast, heart and brain. The path to peace is the pathway through ourselves, starting with the inward step, the brave, gentle step toward the Divine within. Godspeed to us all.

A Deep Step into God

A secret turning in us
makes the universe turn.
Head unaware of feet,
and feet head. Neither cares.
They keep turning.

—Rumi

Our feet are our connection to Mother Earth. They ground us, balance us, take us wherever we choose on our journey to wholeness. They are the part of our sacred garment of flesh that allows us to move toward others in communion, toward nature in a quest for quiet, to other lands and cultures for adventure and learning. Our feet draw in energy from the earth every moment of our lives, as our lungs draw in air, our eyes draw in images, our ears draw in sounds. Heaven and earth converge in our bodies, entering in through the crowns of our heads and the soles of our feet. Our feet are sacred portals, thresholds over which great energy enters us from Mother Earth.

In different spiritual traditions, the feet have been a symbol in many teachings. It is said that from the soles of his feet the Buddha radiated a light that looked like a wheel of a thousand spokes. Some claim that this wheel symbolizes the respect that the Buddha had for his teachers and the actions he performed to show that respect. Some claim that Buddha's life was his teacher and that he followed in his own footsteps. Either way, temples around the world contain replicas of the feet of Buddha, and various Buddhist texts affirm that whoever looks upon the footprints of the Buddha "shall be freed from the bonds of error, and conducted upon the Way of Enlightenment."

Today, the footprints of the Buddha are venerated in all Buddhist countries, reminding followers to walk in his footprints by being present to the ordinariness of everyday life and alert to every opportunity for compassionate self-giving.

In the Hindu tradition, the word *Upanishad* (meaning to sit near) evokes an image of students or devotees sitting at the feet of a master. The spiritual texts of the Upanishads were composed over a time span of a thousand years, centuries before the birth of Jesus. They contain the highest wisdom revealed to illumined sages in the depths of meditation. Eknath Easwaran, a respected modern translator of the Upanishads, describes them as "ecstatic snapshots of supreme reality" and adds that unlike other great scriptures that look outward in reverence and awe, "the Upanishads look inward, finding the powers of nature only an expression of the more awe-inspiring powers of human Consciousness."

The wisdom of the Upanishads is a *realized* and embodied wisdom, felt in the marrow of the bones. Sitting at the feet of a master is a step on the way to self-mastery. By placing ourselves in the presence of one who has experienced the Divine in his or her own spaciousness, we can learn the practices that lead to deeper experience and higher consciousness.

As the Upanishads were transmitted to disciples at the feet of the masters, so were the teachings of Jesus. And so were his

One should worship with the thought that He is one's self, for therein all these become one. The self is the footprint of that All, for by it one knows the All ... so whoever worships another Divinity than his self, thinking "He is me, I am another," knows not.

—UPANISHADS, EIGHTH CENTURY BCE

teachings meant to be embodied. So, too, were they about the kingdom *within* us. When Jesus attempted to wash the feet of his disciples before his arrest, they were unnerved. "Never!" said Peter. "You shall never wash my feet." Jesus was the master, and this was not his role. But his gesture was an attempt to help them become their own masters. Jesus replied to Peter, "If I do not wash your feet, you can have nothing in common with me. If I am the Master, then do what I do. I have given you an example so you may do what I have done and wash each other's feet."

Washing another's feet symbolizes recognizing and honoring the Divine in the other. It's about deconstructing the separation between master and student and taking on both roles as we make our way through life. "Look within" is the message of all the masters. "Know that you are gods and love each other and yourself as God" is as simple as it gets. We are all teachers to someone, and we are all students of everyone. Every encounter has something to teach us when we become mindful observers of our own lives. Our lessons are in our relationships. Our life is the classroom field trip. Our bodies are the medium of our learning. And it is our feet that carry us forward on the path.

They ground us to the earth so we can feel in every cell of our body the mystical union of heaven and earth right in the center of our being. The Christian mystic Catherine of Siena said, "All the way to heaven *is* heaven." This is it. This is the holy event. Our bodies are the word made flesh, the Divine incarnate. Every child is the child in the manger. Every bush is a burning

> You are the light of the world. Your light must shine in the sight of men. —MATTHEW 5:14

3

bush. Every breath is a breath of God. We are walking our way through heaven day to day, whining and complaining all the way. "I'm afraid." "I don't have enough." "They don't treat me right." "I don't dare take the next step." Big as we are, we're full of fear, more afraid than toddlers to keep walking forward toward the love that draws us.

Toddlers are obsessive about walking. No fall deters them. No obstacles detain them. They are master learners—always falling, always climbing back up, always attempting more no matter what the challenges. Children's feet take them forward into the unknown, toward the ocean, up the hill, into the forest. They are close to the earth and love what it offers. They have not learned to be afraid. Their instincts are to explore, to seek out the new, to discover something they have not yet found. This is their nature, and they are true to it.

On the path to adulthood, many of us lose this connection. Education severs the threads connecting us to nature, and the quest slackens for the great unknown. We settle instead for the mediocre known; the stuff of life that weighs us down. Years go by, and we hardly notice the death of our wonder because it's happening everywhere and no one cares. Who asks you about the path you're on, the metaphoric wilderness you're here to explore? Who is reminding you to be true to your instincts, to walk down the path your heart calls you to? Who speaks of awe, of the God within, of our collaborative role to cocreate?

Messages of what we we're supposed to want bombard our mindscape, diminishing our capacity for original thought.

A journey of a thousand miles starts in front of your feet.

—KABBALAH

4

Even our feelings get numbed along the way, and we end up doubting our own perceptions, unable to access the passions within, if any are even there. Some feel a call to follow the path of the heart but haven't a clue how to discern it. How *do* we know the path to follow?

I worked once in a mall that sponsored a huge antique show. When I walked around to see the vendors' displays, my eyes landed on a pair of tiny black patent leather shoes lined with a stunning pink silk. They were just like *my* shoes, the ones I wore for Easter and dress-up occasions when I was three. My heart jumped when I saw them. Deep feelings stirred when I picked them up—not specific memories, but *feelings* from that time in my life. Cavernous feelings of wonder and curiosity about the world opening up in front of my eyes, ahead of me. Feelings of innocence, fearlessness, trust.

I bought those little shoes for the feelings they elicited, the joy that welled up when I imagined myself in the shoes of a child again. One day I took those shoes and my camera to the playground, to the lake, to the church steps—and I photographed them in every environment. I placed the shoes in front of the bottom step to the big slide, at the water's edge, approaching the huge golden doors to the cathedral. Each time I did this, new feelings would rise up and I could access something old and true about myself, something untainted, untouched by anything outside me. I felt my body as I had felt it as a three-year-old. I was fully present, completely embodied. Feelings from forty years earlier came to life like a waking dragon coming out of a long slumber. I felt fearless again, in awe again.

When I packed my backpack for a trip around the world, I slipped those shoes in at the last moment. It seemed like a ridiculous thing to do, but in some way, they were my vehicle to wholeness, what some might call a transitional object that kept me in touch with a part of me I didn't want to lose. It wasn't that I was afraid to go without them—it was that there were places I wanted to go *with* them to feel the fullness I sensed with them.

When I reached the base camp to the Himalayan Annapurna Sanctuary, I rose at dawn and placed the shoes on the ground before some of the world's most magnificent peaks. As the mauve tones of daylight crept over the horizon, a wild joy surfaced as I photographed those little shoes. I remembered myself. I was the little girl who had climbed the mountain. I was the one who had no fear, who was in the moment, who felt the breath of God in the blowing wind. I was safe, in the arms of the Great Mother, always safe, never alone.

In some strange way, those shoes helped me. They transported me to my deepest desires, my earliest knowing. They revived feelings I had learned to suppress, and once I learned the secret of finding my feelings, I was free to let go of the patent leather shoes.

Trekking down the mountain, I came upon a mother bathing her young daughter at the village pump. The girl looked small enough, I thought, for the shoes to fit her. I reached into my pack and pulled them out, offering them to the mother when the bath was complete. With smiles and sign language, I did my best to say: "Have her try them on. If they fit, she can have them."

The girl's face lit up like the morning sun. She put one on and it fit her perfectly. Then she pulled on the other one, buckled the shiny straps, and danced with delight. The mother bowed over and over with gestures of gratitude, and I bowed back, over and over, thanking *her* for the chance to be of use.

Every time I think of those shoes, it all comes back, and mostly what I cherish is knowing that I *can* reclaim my body. I *can* have

When I was at camp, at night, if I imagined there were eyes in the soles of my feet, I could walk in the dark. —DIANE GAGE those original feelings. I just need to remember what it feels like to be three, to be new to walking in the world. And to be conscious that the direction I move in is toward joy, toward nature, toward that desire throbbing in the middle of my heart.

In *The Teachings of Don Juan,* Carlos Castaneda writes, "All paths lead nowhere, but one has a heart, the other doesn't." Our one job in life is to find the path of our heart and walk that one. It's not the destination we're after—it's the experience of being true to our calling and nature. The deep step into God is a step of awareness. The path of the heart is a journey into consciousness. The steps go inward, the process is discernment, the question is: Am I being true to my heart's desire?

Do I wake up in the morning thrilled that my beloved is within and all around me, or am I heavy with resentment and blame toward others that my life is not turning out like it should? Am I walking on a path of fear and insecurity, draining my spirit with work that feels hollow and empty of meaning? Am I choosing matter over spirit, trading my precious hours for a paycheck that keeps the whole drab cycle spinning? The Persian poet Rumi writes:

> *Keep walking, though there's no place to get to*
> *Don't try to see through the distances.*
> *That's not for human beings. Move within,*
> *but don't move the way fear makes you move.*[1]

To be on the path of the heart is to move the way courage makes us move. It is to be light and unencumbered, emptied of

The power that you gain by pursuing your interest will give you the ability to take upon yourself a greater challenge than you have taken on so far. We gain in power by pursuing our purpose in life.

—HAZRAT INAYAT KHAN

debris and old illusions, knowing everything that ever happened to us got us to this moment, which is the only moment we have and the only place God dwells. If we are still dragging pieces of the past into today, we may need to turn around, back up, and revisit people or places to free ourselves from entanglements that keep us from our path. And this may take some time.

In 1967, I entered the religious community of the Sisters of St. Joseph of Carondelet to become a nun, but I was a little too radical and was sent home after two years in the novitiate. For years after being dismissed, I was a furnace of raging anger. The night my superior informed me that I was not to continue my novitiate, I was stunned into silence. When she said, "You know why, don't you?" I lied, trying to make this difficult job easier on her. "Yes," I said. "I guess so."

When my parents were ushered into the room next door, I asked, "What am I supposed to tell them?"

"Just tell them you don't have a religious disposition," she said, and that's exactly what I uttered as they walked toward me in that tiny parlor. But I was wondering why this had happened when I loved that life so deeply.

For months afterward, I'd go to the mailbox thinking maybe this was the day I'd get a letter from the convent saying it was all a mistake. But it never came. And I never forgave them. And I never found my heart's path, because *that* was it, and they ripped me away from it. Or so I thought.

I was so full of anger and resentment that it tainted everything. There was no space inside for joy. There was no way to

That visibility which makes us most vulnerable is that which is also the source of our greatest strength.

—AUDRE LORDE

carve out a new life because all my energy was going into the old one I wanted so desperately to have. I would not let go. Bad people had done bad things to me. I was a victim of a terrible wrongdoing. My whole life became this story. I joined the ranks of the walking wounded and stopped taking responsibility for the path I was on.

Eight years passed before I wrote to the community, asking for an explanation of why I was dismissed. I wrote about the hole in my heart and my inability to heal it without their help. Would they please just give me the reason so I could begin my process of recovering?

My novice director had died of stomach cancer, and I received a letter from the nun who had been director of the young professed sisters when I was there. She vaguely remembered me, and she was now the Mother Provincial, in charge of all the sisters in the Albany, New York, province. In her letter, she reminded me that according to canon law, the community did not owe an explanation to anyone who had been dismissed. But she'd gone to my file, and since it was so short, she sent along this passage: *Jan Phillips did not have a religious disposition and was dismissed because of her excessive and exclusive relationships.*

Finally. Something I could latch on to. It was a beginning, but only that. I had years to go to complete the process, to forgive them and move on. It helped me to have a reason, but the one they offered seemed ridiculous. They were just frightened by my passion, I told myself. No one was more inclusive than I when it came to relationships. And what did they mean by

If we were to abuse our children, social services would show up at our door. If we abused our pets, the Humane Society would come take us away. But there is no creativity patrol or Soul Police to intervene if we insist on starving our own souls.

—SUE MONK KIDD

9

"religious disposition"? That you never questioned authority? That you memorized maxims and ate everything on your plate? That you recreated with someone different every day and finished the Stations of the Cross before 5 p.m.? Was it my attachment to the *resurrected* Christ, my lust for life in all its abundance that was really the issue?

While my anger had dissipated over the years, I was still bound somehow, still resentful, still blaming them for banishing me from the one life that felt true to me. I could not find the path of my heart because my heart was locked up, and I could not unlock it on my own.

It was in 1991, twenty-two years after my dismissal, that I called the sister who was the Mother Provincial when it happened. I asked if she would just sit with me while I told her the story of how it felt. That was all I wanted, a witness from the community. She agreed and we set a date. When I arrived at her convent, we went out to the screened-in porch and sat down, knee to knee.

"I'm going to start when I was twelve," I said, "when I first decided to be a nun. I'll probably cry through the whole story, but I just want you to listen from the beginning to the end, all right?" She nodded her head yes. For the next hour, we both wept as I drained out all my feelings and despair over the whole incident. I was honest about my broken heart, my shattered faith, my inability to find another path for myself while I was harboring all this sorrow and resentment. "I just want to let it go, Sister. I want to let it go, and I need your help," I sobbed. "Can you help me get free of this?"

She took my hands in hers and said, "Jan, will you forgive me personally for the part I played in this deep and terrible pain of yours?" I nodded my head yes. "And will you forgive the community for the pain we caused you and for the mistakes we made in dealing with you while you were with us?"

"Yes, Sister, I forgive the community," I blurted out, and with that forgiveness came the release, the freedom I needed to go on with my life and find the path that was calling me. With that forgiveness came a surge of energy, a rush of tenderness I hadn't felt in twenty years. It opened me up, unlocked my heart. It was a step into God I couldn't make while I was clinging to my pain and anger.

Only after I forgave could I understand there was nothing to forgive. They did not cause me pain. They just did what they did. Pain was my response to it. Pain was me holding on to it. Pain was me refusing to accept the life before me. Once I released it, I could bless that time I had. I could see that my two years in the novitiate was all I needed to get my footing in a faith I was meant to live out more publicly. I was like a young eagle in a nest, peering over the edge, afraid to fly. And they nudged me out so I could soar. And I am.

Two years ago I returned to the motherhouse to give a workshop on Creativity as Sacrament. When I got to reconciliation, I used myself as an example. I told the story of my long journey to forgiveness and of how blocked I was for all the years I held on to my misery. In *A Course in Miracles,* the author Helen Schucman says that "forgiveness is the healing of the perception of separation." I only *thought* I couldn't have the life I wanted. Because my perception was of separation, I was living like something was being denied me, when I was free all along to construct a life that was like my life in the convent—a life that balanced silence and solitude with community and service.

I smile these days when I look at my life and see how much like a religious life it really is. I begin with morning prayers, work in solitude for the most part, give service by teaching and sharing what I know. And I've created a vital community of kindred spirits in my own town and across the country, so I have sisters around me everywhere I go.

There aren't that many steps to forgiveness, but sometimes it takes a long time to make them, or to figure out what we need to do to complete the process. The first step is to stop blaming others for our state of mind. If we feel someone is keeping us from being happy, then it's our responsibility to change the nature of the relationship. Clinging to a relationship out of habit or guilt or fear is a betrayal of our soul. Holding on to resentments weakens our immune system, steals our energy, and roots us in the past where there is nothing real, nothing to feed us, no sign of the Divine.

The step into God is a bold, clean step into now—this day with these people under these circumstances. If we sink our feet into the present moment and feel anything but joy, we're probably not on the path of the heart. It is time, then, to go inward, to ask our heart what it desires, and to move our feet in that direction.

REFLECTION

Where do your feet lead you every day? Into what environments do you walk, through what landscapes do you tread as you manifest this one life of yours? If you could retrace any steps, would you choose your path differently? Are you leading the way, or do you feel led by a force outside yourself?

EXERCISE

Try to do this every day, before you get dressed in the morning or before you go to bed at night: Rub lotion into your feet, massaging them one at a time, thinking of nothing but your feet. Think of every tendon and muscle, every cell and atom, every nerve and blood vessel. Massage each toe, one at a time,

Creating heaven on earth is the responsibility each one of us bears to make God a reality.

—PIR VILAT INAYAT KHAN

12

thanking every part of your feet for the ways they have stood by you, grounded you, and moved you through your days.

Exercise

Go through the shoes in your closet and take out every pair of shoes that does not make your feet feel loved. Make a decision to give them away or throw them out—and act on it.

Writing Exercise

Draw an outline of your bare foot on a piece of unlined paper. Fill in your blank foot with images or pictures of where you have been, what you have experienced during this lifetime. Start with your earliest memories and let your mind drift casually from one memory to another. As you look over all the images from your life's geography, choose one that has a particular appeal to you. What sense or senses were most engaged during this time or experience? What sights, smells, sounds, or feelings come to mind when you think of it? Write a few paragraphs or more about this, focusing on just one sense.

Love of the Dance

When you walk across the fields with your mind pure
and holy, then from all the stones, and all growing
things, and all animals, the sparks of their soul come out
and cling to you, and then they are purified and become
a holy fire in you.

—Hasidic saying

We're in a dance with the invisible force. The question we might ask is: Who's leading? This is how our minds work. We're immersed in duality, so our conditioning is to divide everything. If there's a dance, somebody leads and the other one follows. All we want to know is what's our part. But if we step out of duality for a moment and consider the dance itself, we see that it's not about leading and following. It's about flow.

This is the mystery of our lives. We're in a constant, ever-flowing exchange with the Divine. "We receive the light and we impart the light, thus we repair the world," says the Kabbalah. It happens moment by moment, in the form of insight, joy, community, service. Our bodies are the visible manifestation of the great invisible force. We are the shining of the diamond, the rainbow rays of the great light shot through the prism of this atmosphere. We are the vocal cords to the breath of God, and it is through us that the music of the beloved is heard.

A mystery as grand and humbling as this has trouble surviving in a culture bent on certainty. Instead of inspiring a theology of humility, a philosophy of unity, a sociology of spirit and communion consciousness, its magnitude frightens the weak of heart. We have a fear of intimacy with the one we belong to. Instead of dancing in the streets at this incredible chance to live in a body and hold heaven in our hearts, we put ourselves on simmer and get lost in thoughts that are miles away from our source and our joy. What rises in our absence is a fortress of fundamentalism, structures designed to silence us, and a pulling away from the great miracle of our own incarnation as the body of God.

In Psalm 82:6, we hear the voice of Yahweh trying to get through to us, "You too are gods, sons of the Most High, all of you." Why does it frighten us to take this in and let it source our lives? Heaven, in Aramaic, means the universe. It means our home. The dance of human and divine is the same as the dance of heaven and earth. One completes the other, is immersed in the other, has no life outside the other. "The Self is hidden in the hearts of all, as butter lies hidden in cream," says the Upanishads. "The kingdom of heaven is within you," says Jesus. "As above, so below," says the Tao Te Ching. This is good news. Why aren't we dancing? Why are we standing like wallflowers at the prom of our lives?

Several hundred thousand years ago, our ancestors danced. It was one of their main forms of communication—with each other, with nature, with the universe, and with the great force of life. Dance was their main medium to explore and express their search for meaning. In *Quantum Theology,* Roman Catholic priest and social psychologist Diarmuid O'Murchu refers to dance as the connecting link with the ultimate source,

Stress is the perception that we are separated from our divine source.

—BRIAN LUKE SEAWARD

15

the medium used to establish archetypal communication with the heart of reality.

"Dance emerged as the primary medium to make sense and meaning out of life. Dance is the first, most ancient, and most enduring form of religion," writes O'Murchu. "Long before religion was ever taught, preached, or codified in sacred texts, it was lived and celebrated in ritual play and dance."[1]

Moving our bodies to the sound of music, the beat of a drum, is a way of reconnecting ourselves, re-pairing the parts we learned were separate. In this ancient ritual act, our bodies become the medium through which the soul enacts itself. Once we are in the flow, entrained to the sounds, we have no thoughts of how to move. We are, in effect, danced by the music, twirled and dipped by the energies within.

In cultures around the world, dance is used to express emotions that are too deep or complex for words. In his book *Ritual: Power, Healing, and Community*, West African shaman Malidoma Somé describes the use of dance in the tribal funeral ritual. Elaborate steps are taken to ensure that the mourners fully express their grief in every way possible, not only for themselves but to help the dead souls go home. Relatives who come from afar often play the role of "containers," making sure the mourners stay in the ritual space and do not harm themselves. The whole village is there, not only to assist in the grieving of the mourners, but to complete their own unfinished business with their own deceased relatives.

Members of the immediate family of the dead are tagged with cords around their wrists, and people are assigned to look after

True spiritual practice springs from, but not toward, enlightenment. Our practice does not lead to unity consciousness, it is unity consciousness.

—J. KRISHNAMURTI

them during the ceremony. The caretakers mimic the actions of the mourners, doing exactly what they do, only two feet behind them. Musicians and cantors play and sing in a way that encourages the wildest expressions of grief. Xylophones weep the tune, drums dramatize the sadness and chaos, and the singers chant spontaneously about the life of the person who died. The whole group engages in a visceral dialogue with the music and chanters, and great wailing occurs in the grief ritual space.

> Sometimes, a large group of fifteen to twenty people will come out to join a primary relative battling with his sorrow. The whole group will end up as a line of dancers dancing exactly what the relative is doing in the front of the line. It is understood in the ritual that the feeling of the person in front of the line will be transmitted to every person as they dance together in one line.[2]

This is the potency of ritual, this understanding of oneness among everyone who enters into it. The village, in this case, becomes one whole unit dealing with the immensity of grief. The whole body is involved in the process, allowing the emotions to flow unselfconsciously and unrestrictedly through every part. This is the way to wholeness and healing. Divining the body and embodying the Divine is one complete act. Like yin and yang, light and dark, one is nothing without the other.

In the mid-1980s I was staying at a Gandhian ashram in Gujarat, India. It was monsoon season, hot and humid. Tribal

Carefully seek the heart of heaven and earth with firm determination. Suddenly you will see the original thing; everywhere you meet the source, all is a forest of jewels. —LIU I-MING drums played through the night, for this was the season of marriages, festivals, and nonstop celebration of life in all forms.

Bhai, the ashram's founder, had lived with Gandhi for many years and started this community after the Mahatma's death to help the tribal villagers reconcile their differences. These were India's indigenous people, the Adivasis.

One night, during a week when a group of teens from New Delhi were there, Bhai arranged for the Adivasi youth to meet with the city kids. The young men arrived by bullock cart, beating drums and playing handmade bamboo flutes. Decked out in festive wedding costumes, they gathered in two circles—girls in the middle and boys outside—and began rotating in opposite directions. The drums got faster and louder as the boys worked themselves into a frenzied pace. The girls tightened their circle, their backs to the boys, their arms entwined.

The well-dressed and sophisticated urban boys had never seen anything like this before, and their mouths hung open at the sight of their peers in feathers and loin-cloths, lost in the rapture of tribal dance. Suddenly one let out a whoop and jumped into the circle, dancing the latest steps from Delhi's discos. Then a few more joined and the circle grew, blue jeans and loincloths side by side. Without missing a beat, the villagers backed out, and the boys from the city took their place, dancing with abandon around the girls.

When the drums finally died down, the teens screamed out in wild applause, howling and hooting in sheer delight. While they couldn't speak each other's language, these two groups of teens merged two eras, bridged two cultures, with one dance that took them beyond their borders. There was a great power let loose from that circle, a light that arose from their love of life. Had I eyes to see, I'd be privy to the threads that bound them in oneness to each other and the stars. If I have ever seen the Holy Spirit, ever heard the laughter of God, it was there that night, in the middle of India, in that brink between cultures, when music and movement drew back the veil.

The voice of Seth in *The "Unknown" Reality* says: "Your religions in large measure have taught you to hate yourselves and physical existence. They have told you to love God, but rarely taught you to experience the gods in yourself."[3] The process we must go through to experience the divinity within is a process of subtraction, not addition, as we're told by Meister Eckhart. There is nothing to learn, but much to unlearn. It is not facts we need more of, but feelings. We need to return to our senses, to reenter our bodies and allow what is within to flow through and out of us.

I went to a national dance competition of hip hop teams recently and was brought to tears by the energy and joy these teens radiated. Many of them were youth-at-risk striving to rechannel their anger and discontent into an art form that was big enough to contain them. It was obvious from the imaginative choreography, the exquisite synchronization, and the soul-stirring blend of art and acrobatics that these teens had collaborated diligently, brilliantly in their efforts to be a team. Dance was their way to find themselves and each other. They are advancing this art form just as slam dunkers once advanced the art of basketball. Their moves were original, spontaneous, full of spirit and joy. The energy in that auditorium was palpable, electrifying. These teens were sharing the energy of their lives with us.

Until that evening, I was like a lot of middle-aged Americans who, out of ignorance, have nothing good to say about the whole hip hop culture. I was, in fact, worried about it, scared of it, because some of the lyrics I'd heard were full of violence. I

> Sometimes truth depends on a walk around the lake.
> —**WALLACE STEVENS**

needed to understand it more, so I tuned in. I went to a website where youth were discussing the importance of hip hop coming out of Africa. What a tremendous surprise to find words like these:

From one youth: "African hip hop is our own modern day unifying language. We constantly hear about the mortality rates of our young brothers and sisters in the West due to all sorts of unnecessary causes. But the lyrics coming out of the mouths of young Africans inject and infuse sounds of life, hope and perseverance in this morbid reality. We are our own CNN, MTV, BBC."

From another: "Africa, in a miraculous way, is very much unified, held together tightly by one strand, the strand of strength, courage, survival and struggle. It's an untapped and unrealized well, deeply imbedded within our psyche. And finally, we're starting to hear it come out of its hidden spaces, through the voices of the young hip hop heads of today! Hip hop in Africa is just continuing that ancient oral tradition that kept our people informed and guided. The youth are carrying on that tradition. So why is it important for these youth to know about each other? Because if they don't then they miss out knowing about themselves, about their purpose, and about their potential.

"We need a new gathering of ambassadors and leaders, and these gatherings are no longer going to happen in city or congress halls, they're not going to be in the press conferences, or huge round tables, business conferences.... They haven't worked, they didn't get the job done. The real movement will take place in the ciphers, indabas, street corners, dancehalls, battle grounds, and school yards, or wherever young boys and girls gather together to reason, rhyme, and revolutionize their minds, bodies, communities, and their people."

These kids are serious about the future that's coming their way. They see how this culture has failed them, and they, like our ancestors, are using dance as a medium of communication and communion. They know the power of ritual, the value of celebration, and they are not afraid of expressing it. They know this dance connects them. They perceive it as an art form and are perfecting their masterpieces.

The ritual of the whirling dervishes, known as the *semâ,* was founded by the great philosopher and writer Mevlana Jalaluddin Rumi in the thirteenth century. It is a serious religious ritual performed by Sufi Muslim devotees in a prayer trance to Allah. Rumi believed that during the *semâ* the soul was released from earthly ties and was able to freely and jubilantly commune with the Divine.

In the Middle East it is believed that the dervish is in prayer and that his body becomes open to receive the energy of God. The Turkish sultans often consulted the dervishes in difficult times. Their spinning created a relaxing and hypnotic effect in which the sultans could search for guidance.

Dervish literally means "doorway" and is thought to be an entrance from this material world to the spiritual, heavenly world. The dervish does not retain the power nor is he to direct it. He accepts that he is the true instrument of God, and therefore he does not question the power that enters and leaves him.

In the *semâ,* the ritual begins with a chanted prayer to the Prophet Muhammad, who represents love, and all prophets before him. Next a kettledrum sounds as a symbol of the divine order of the Creator, followed by haunting musical improvisation on the *ney* (a reed flute), which symbolizes the divine breath that gives life to everything.

You are the whole ocean. Why send out for a sip of dew?

—RUMI

21

The master bows, then leads the dervishes in a circle around the hall. As they pass the master's ceremonial position at the head of the hall, they bow to each other. This bow is a salutation of soul to soul concealed in bodies.

After three circles, the dervishes drop their black cloaks. One by one, arms folded on their breasts, they approach the master, bow, kiss his hand, receive instructions, then spin out onto the floor. Through whirling, the dervishes relinquish the earthly life to be reborn in mystical union with God. Opening their folded arms, the dervishes hold their right hands palm up to receive the blessings of heaven. They hold their left hands palm down to transfer the blessings to earth.

Eventually, the *semâ* reaches a point where all dervishes are simultaneously whirling. After about ten minutes, all stop and kneel. Then rising, they begin again. This combination of whirling followed by salute is performed a total of four times. Each of the four repetitions of kneeling is a salute, and it signifies humanity's birth to the truth of God as creator, the rapture of humans witnessing the splendor of creation, dissolution into the rapture of love and the sacrifice of mind to love, and termination of the spiritual journey, including return to everyday life and subservience to God.

At the conclusion of the whirling, the master reads from the Qur'an, especially the verse from Sura Bakara 2:115: "Unto God belong the East and the West, and wherever you turn, there is God's countenance. He is all-embracing, all-knowing." The *semâ* closes with a prayer for the peace of the souls of all prophets and all believers.

The dancers in these rituals use their whole bodies in this display of surrender and acceptance. They are enchanted, entranced in the process. They are not thinking up prayers to say, they *are* their prayers. It is through their bodies that they experience a complete and mystical union with the Divine. As St. Francis prayed, "Lord, make me an instrument of your peace," the dervishes become those instruments. While the Western way is to pray for oneness, the Eastern way is to *experience* it. Sensing this, knowing it in their bodies, they can't help dancing for joy.

Our legs are like the roots of a tree, grounding us, keeping us balanced. They are our means of movement from one mode to another, shifting direction as our brains shift consciousnesses. They carry us forward, into experiences that shape and direct us. They are what we use to stand up for something or someone, to take a stand. Doing the legwork means getting out of the mind and getting into the heart of the matter. With our legs, we walk our talk, run our lives, and carry out our commitments.

We are not here to transcend life, but to be fully immersed in it. Our bodies are not something we must triumph over. They are the medium of our transformation, the cauldron in which the elements of heaven and earth are steeped until they transmute one day into the being of which we are now the embryo. The journey we are on is a journey to fulfill this destiny, and we accomplish it through remembering our true nature, not through learning.

We accomplish it by being true to our instincts, by listening to the wisdom of our bodies, and by abandoning with absolute fervor all notions of separateness and other. The German mystic Meister Eckhart writes, "In the measure that the soul can separate itself from multiplicity, to that extent it reveals within itself the Kingdom of God. Here the soul and the Godhead are one.... The whole scattered world of lowered things is gathered up to oneness when the soul climbs up to that life in which there are no opposites."[4]

This is the great challenge upon us, and it is revolutionary work. It calls for extraordinary heroism in the realm of the

> Dancing is not rising to your feet painlessly like a whirl of dust blown about by the wind. Dancing is when you rise above both worlds, tearing your heart to pieces and giving up your soul. —RUMI

23

everyday. It calls for us to take a stand. To stop colluding in the darkness of duality, to stop trafficking in negativity, and to let out, once and for all, over and over, the light within. To see through the veil of multiplicity to the kingdom of God within, we must act on the basis of what we feel and know from our own experience.

We know we are connected—otherwise the terrorist attacks of September 11, 2001, wouldn't have brought us to our knees. We know, in our bones, that another's pain is our pain. If not, why are so many millions of us in angst over these wars, this hunger, this injustice throughout the world? If we cut our finger or break a bone, every cell in our body works in concert to bring about healing. As the cosmic body of God, it will take the whole of us, every one of us as a cell, to heal the wounds being inflicted so mercilessly out of greed and ignorance. By acknowledging our oneness with others and acting from this awareness, we enable the healing to take place at a faster pace.

The challenges upon us are huge, and the life on earth is in all our hands. The notion that the movement of a butterfly's wings in Japan can cause a hurricane in Argentina has become a cliché. How about a more direct statement? Driving an SUV in America causes the rivers to flood over a Bangladeshi farmer's crops. Failing to love our bodies *as they are* causes enough stress to harm our own immune systems. Refusing to create our lives with intention and attention hurts us in the long run.

Newspapers and television news overwhelm us. Statistics numb us. We feel impotent, angry, powerless. What can one

God created humankind so that humankind might cultivate the earthly and create the heavenly.

—HILDEGARD OF
BINGEN

person do? The voice in our head plays over and over: It doesn't make a difference what I do. They have power, I don't. The rich rule, the poor go without. Dualistic thinking.

A woman known as Peace Pilgrim walked penniless across this country seven times from 1953 until her death in 1981 at the age of seventy-three. She vowed to "remain a wanderer until mankind has learned the way of peace, walking until given shelter and fasting until given food." Her only possessions were a comb, a toothbrush, and a blue smock with the words *Peace Pilgrim* on it. "I didn't learn meditation," she'd say. "I just walked, receptive and silent, amid the beauty of nature."[5]

Her work has led to a network of thousands of people from around the world joining forces, being in personal contact, finding small ways to make big differences in their own lives and in the world. If you feel in need of inspiration, search the Internet for "Peace Pilgrim," and what you find will uplift you.

Jesus walked through the desert for forty days to prepare for his preaching. Buddha walked for years from cave to cave, village to village, before he reached enlightenment under the bodhi tree. Mother Teresa walked through the streets of Calcutta looking for people who needed her help. Mahatma Gandhi walked through villages in India, teaching the ways of nonviolence. When a villager saw him on a train once, he rushed to Gandhi's window, calling, "What can I take back to tell my people? What is your central message?" Gandhi wrote five words on a paper bag and held them up for the man to see: *My life is my message.*

I try to remember it is not me, John Seed, trying to protect the rainforest. Rather I am part of the rainforest protecting myself.

—JOHN SEED, DIRECTOR OF RAINFOREST INFORMATION CENTER

People know us by our walk, by how we use our energy. We're inspired by people who *do* something with their passion. And those people inspire themselves in the process of acting. Many of us feel paralyzed and impotent in the face of the massive systems breakdown we're undergoing. It's time for a funeral ritual, but we don't know how to grieve and let the old way go. Every day more and more images of death are strewn in our path, and it weakens us. We're lifted up by signs of hope, yet the media fails to give them to us. Outdated as it is, "blood sells" remains their mantra.

So *we* have to be the storytellers. We have to scour the environment for stories that can help us, strengthen us, remind us of the power of one to affect the many. When Dorothea Lange took the photograph called "Migrant Mother," she didn't know it would become an icon of the Great Depression. She had been a successful portrait photographer who was deeply moved by the breadlines of the homeless and unemployed gathering in the streets below her San Francisco studio. She decided to use her skill in the service of others and began to work for the Farm Security Administration to document the effects of unemployment, labor unrest, and drought.

Her images were seen by thousands of Americans, including John Steinbeck, who was so moved by them that he wrote *The Grapes of Wrath,* a book that in turn was read by thousands more. When a film producer read Steinbeck's book, he was so moved that he made a film of the story, which had a massive public audience. As a result of millions of people viewing this film, a new consciousness of compassion emerged on a national

Humanity is being taken to the place where it will have to choose between suicide and adoration.

—TEILHARD DE CHARDIN

26

scale, and legislation was put into effect that benefited the lives of these impoverished people.

A recent issue of *YES! A Journal of Positive Futures* includes two other accounts of small actions leading to big changes. When the freed slave Olaudah Equiano, founder of the Sons of Africa, published the story of his capture, transport, enslavement, and eventual release, it made its way into the hands of Cambridge University student Thomas Clarkson, who was aspiring to win an essay contest in 1787. Equiano's story and his work as an anti–slave trade organizer informed Clarkson's essay, which addressed the question: Is the slave trade morally defensible? By the time Clarkson won the contest with his meticulously documented treatise depicting the horrors of the slave trade, he'd become an activist with a mission. He became a spokesperson for the Committee of the Society for the Abolition of the Slave Trade, traveling through England and France, speaking and organizing chapters wherever he went. The transatlantic Quaker networks joined in, sharing organizing strategies and tactics.

A new genre of political poetry was introduced by female activists, shedding light on the subject, and pottery magnate Josiah Wedgwood was moved to produce what came to be must-have fashion accessories—pins and brooches with the image of a slave and the words "Am I not a man and a brother?" inscribed on them. Mrs. Aphra Behn's play *Oroonoko,* the tragic story of an enslaved African prince, became the most widely produced drama of the eighteenth century in England.

Politicians began debating the issue, and thousands more antislavery pamphlets and newsletters made their way to Scotland, Ireland, Wales, Canada, and the United States. By 1808, not only was the foreign slave trade banned in England and the United States, but each country's navy was used to intercept and search ships coming from Africa, sending Africans back to their homeland.

In a more recent example, when the British musician Peter Gabriel first saw the video footage of Rodney King being beaten by Los Angeles police officers, he realized that videotaping could be used around the world to record international abuses more purposefully. He joined with the Lawyers Committee for Human Rights and the Reebok Human Rights Foundation to start Witness, an organization that provided cameras and assistance to global activists recording human rights violations in action. They started with a budget of $150,000 and a staff of two. In 1996, they helped Global Survival network produce *Bought and Sold,* a documentary on the Russian mafia's involvement in the trafficking of women from the former Soviet Union. Footage of this was picked up by ABC, BBC, and CNN and became a front-page story in the *New York Times.* In response, President Clinton allocated $10 million to fight violence against women, with special emphasis on trafficking. Secretary of State Madeleine Albright put it on the agenda in her meetings with heads of state, and in 2000, the United Nations passed a transnational protocol to prevent trafficking. The U.S. Congress also passed the Trafficking Victims Protections Act that year.

This is what happens when we walk our talk. When we pay attention, act from our heart, move with our legs. We have these bodies in order to *be* the light of the world. And the irony is, it is only through action that we are acted upon, only when we're *in* the dance that we are danced. Let your legs carry you to a new place in your life, a new discovery of your own potential to be wildly moved, intimately swayed, carried away in the luscious, loving arms of the Great Beloved.

REFLECTION

Before you go to sleep tonight, ask yourself: How did I use my energy? Where did my legs carry me? Was my movement consistent with my truest beliefs? Did I cast a shadow or spread some light?

EXERCISE

Commit to a one-month discipline that involves the conscious use of your legs. It could be a dance class, tai chi, swimming, walking. Be true to it and notice your legs as you do it.

WRITING EXERCISE

Give some thought to the history of your legs. Consider your ankles, your calves, your thighs, your knees. Imagine that your legs would like to tell you something about this journey you've been on. In your journal, write a piece called "My Legs Are Talking to Me."

3 The Whole World in Our Hands

I could not bear to touch God with my own hand
when He came within
my reach,

but He wanted me
to hold
Him.

How God solved my blessed agony,
who can understand?

He turned my
body into
His.
—Meister Eckhart, "But He Wanted Me"[1]

When I was a toddler, we lived in a small village in upstate New York. My mother belonged to a women's group called the Home Bureau, and the members gathered weekly in our house to share skills in sewing, upholstery, and other crafts. My earliest memory is the joy I felt when these women came through the door, picked me up in their arms, and cuddled me close to their breasts. I remember the feel of their hands, those sweet arms around me, those extraordinary moments of being adored and cherished just for being alive.

It was their touch that said it all. Their hands on my face. The way they patted my cheeks, stroked my forehead. It was all I needed to feel safe, comforted, at home in the world. And it wasn't long before I learned that my touch could be of use to someone else.

By the time I was in first grade, my dad was paying me a penny a minute to sit on the back of his chair and rub his head, helping him relax after a hard day's work in his grocery store. He'd read his newspaper, and I'd climb up behind him, swirling my fingers through his hair, around his ears, and across his forehead, adrift in the luscious delight of giving him joy.

When I visit my mom, who's in her eighties and living alone, there's nothing she likes more than for me to touch her face, to massage her hands and feet while she lies back in her reclining chair, the candles burning, and music playing softly in the background.

Of all the gifts we can give to people, the gift of our touch is one of the most priceless. Through our hands we convey a kind of radiance. A warmth seeps out from our inner fire, a wrap for someone's chill, a light for another's dark. Hands have a power greater than words. When I lay my hands upon you, I feel more than your skin, more than your bones and muscles. I feel your

> Paradise is attained by touch. —HELEN KELLER

31

energy merging with mine. I sense our threads entwining, our cells connecting, our souls touching. I feel something that I cannot see.

Biologist Mae-Wan Ho describes this gift from a scientific standpoint in her article "The Entangled Universe": "Invisible quantum waves are spreading out from each of us and permeating into all other organisms. At the same time, each of us has the waves of every other organism entangled within our own make-up."[2] With the shift in physics from Newtonian mechanics to quantum theory, we are beginning to see that energy fields are the fundamental units of all matter, and since a human being's energy extends slightly beyond the skin, we are interconnected through this energy with everything in our environment.

According to Albert Einstein, this experience of ourselves as separate from the rest is a delusion of consciousness: "This delusion is a kind of prison for us, restricting us to our personal desires and to affection for a few persons nearest to us. Our task must be to free ourselves from this prison by widening our circles of compassion."

Although most of us have not evolved to the point where we can *see* these waves that connect us, mystics, sages, and artists have been referring to them for centuries. Painter Alex Grey's brilliant, transcendental art gives form and shape to the mystery of our oneness.[3] His books, *Sacred Mirrors* and *Transfigurations,* are full of images that illustrate the deeper dimensions of our beings, depicting those quantum waves radiating outward from our hands, our eyes, our centers of energy,

It is more blessed to give and receive than to have and hold.

—DOROTHY SOELLE

merging with the waves of others in a dance both beautiful and mystical. These paintings offer unforgettable glimpses of trans-figuration as they bring to light the energies of the soul and unveil the intimacy between our finite self and infinite spirit. In Grey's hands, a brush becomes a tool for conveying one of the most profound mysteries—the intermingling of spirit and mat-ter, human and divine.

When I was researching a story on witchcraft in Salem, Massachusetts, I interviewed Laurie Cabot, an ordained high priestess descended from Celtic ancestry. She's practiced witch-craft (also known as Wicca) for over forty years, has published several books, and founded the Witches' League for Public Awareness, an antidefamation organization aimed at correct-ing misconceptions about witchcraft. She and her coven were invited to appear on a Phil Donohue show, and *National Geographic* sent a photographer over to the television studio to photograph them in preparation for a story the magazine was doing on "the occult."

For the television audience, the coven ended the interview by connecting their energies and moving chairs and tables across the stage with the power of their minds. After that, the photog-rapher lined them up in two rows for a group shot. When the slides came back, the photographer was dismayed to find blue lines streaking in all directions over the emulsion. He sent the film back to Kodak, who reported that nothing was wrong with the film. When the photographer sent the photograph to Cabot, he asked her if she had any explanation for what all those lines were. When Cabot took me to her office and showed me the

As five-fingered humans, we are given the gift of thought and life into our hands. As five-fingered humans, we are all the same.

—LINDA DEE, OF THE DINE' NATION

framed image, I noticed the lines seemed to connect the bellies, hearts, heads, and hands of the thirteen individuals. "Of course there are lines connecting us," Cabot said. "These are our energy lines. How do you think we could move those tables and chairs around the stage if we hadn't connected our energies?"

This coven had escaped the prison that Einstein talked about. They had no delusions about their oneness, and whether they could see the energy or not was moot. They knew its potential, and they put it to use. Wiccans believe that the earth and all living things share the same life force. According to Cabot, all life is a web, composed of patterns of intelligence, of knowledge, and of divinity. "We are woven into it as sisters and brothers of All."

Kabir, a fifteenth-century Indian poet, used poetry to communicate his feelings about the oneness between human and divine. These lines could only come from someone who understands the unity within the multiplicity:

> *Take a pitcher full of water and set it down on the water—*
> *now it has water inside and water outside.*
> *We mustn't give it a name,*
> *lest silly people start talking again about the body*
> *and the soul.*[4]

The poetry of the mystics comes closer than anything to crystallizing the essence of this oneness, although some religious traditions have gone to great lengths to describe this phenomenon in literal terms. The Catholic teaching of the Mystical Body of Christ refers to a cosmic, sacred connection that bonds one to another. A papal encyclical on the subject speaks of the members as "one in will and affection, united by an invisible bond, linked together in such a way as to help one another. And as in the body when one member suffers, all the other members share its pain, and the healthy members come to the assistance of the ailing.... The individual members do not live for themselves alone, but also help their fellows, and all work in mutual collaboration for the common comfort and for the more perfect building up of the whole Body. So we being many are one body ... and every one members one of another."

We are here to experience and express our intimacy with the Divine and each other through the vehicles of our bodies and their senses. Our physical bodies are the medium through which spirit is made manifest in the world. We awaken every day to an empty canvas and with the tools of our hands, our voices, our hearts and minds, we bring to light that which could not exist without us. We are at once the cocreators and the continuation of creation.

The contemplative artist and visionary Frederick Franck writes in *The Zen of Seeing,* "I know artists whose medium is life itself and who express the inexpressible without brush, pencil, chisel or guitar. They neither paint nor dance. Their medium is Being. Whatever their hand touches has increased life.... They are the artists of being alive."

This is what we're after: to make of our lives a masterpiece, to come to our days as a sculptor to clay, tuned to the voice that guides our hands, open to the spirit that lights our way through the darkness of doubt. Few of us think of ourselves as artists, but it is the process of creation that brings us to life. It is the work of our hands that grounds us in the present, places us in the center of heaven and earth.

Ask any painter when she's painting if she's lost in the past or concerned for the future. Ask any pianist what feelings rise

> We're not hungry for what we're not getting; we're hungry for what we're not giving.
>
> —ANONYMOUS

35

up as his fingers bring to life a concerto or a sonata. Ask a gardener, a masseuse, a writer, a chef, a midwife, a surgeon if, when their hands are engaged in the work of their heart, they feel vulnerable to despair or doubt or defeat. When we are in the throes of the work, when our bodies and all their senses are in alignment with our purpose, there is nothing but the flow of spirit through nature, nothing but the rush of inner moving outward.

A friend of mine, Beth, filled her jeep with rocks from Home Depot in preparation for her weekend task of constructing a stone wall. Late that night, she remembered she was supposed to pick up two people from the airport early the next morning. She panicked at first, realizing there was no room for them or their luggage. Then the anxiety subsided, and a calm resolve took its place. She would get dressed, put on her work gloves, and unload those rocks one by one.

It was dark outside and there was no light to see by, so she just carried the rocks to the place she planned to build the wall. One on top of another, in the pitch black of night, she laid them down as orderly as she could. "It was as if time had stopped," she said. "Hours passed, but I had no sense of it. And though the rocks were big, they never felt heavy." After Beth emptied her Jeep, she went inside and went to bed, knowing it would soon be time to go to the airport.

That morning when she went outside to get in her car, she was stunned at what she saw. Her stone wall glistened in the early morning light, beautifully shaped and brilliantly designed, as if it had been put together by a master of the trade.

Spirit flows through our hands like a current through a stream. It is life-giving, light-filled power that pours out of us in our purest moments of love and compassion. Pierre Teilhard de Chardin writes, "In our hands, the hands of all of us, the world and life—our world, our life—are placed like a host, ready to be charged with divine influence." And yet we hold back. We hold back tenderness, we hold back our power, we doubt our own ability to work miracles, though Jesus himself said, "Any of the works I have done, you can do and more." It is our history that is holding us back—old voices, old ways—while today, this hour, this moment calls to us, "Wake up now! Everything, *everything* is in your hands."

This beautiful poem by Judi Beach offers a stunning tribute to the hands:

The Ways Hands Bless the Self

how they wrap each other in soap,
*   work so well as a team on the towel,*
*   take turns grooming each other*

how they cream each other with lotion

how they clean the whole body
*   slathering the lathered cloth behind ears,*
*   under arms, in folds, between legs*

how they cup the mouth to carry voice farther,
*   cup ears to hear more closely,*
*   make awnings for eyes*

how they scrub the head all over—first
*   with shampoo then just*
*   because the scalp loves it*

how they practice good manners
*   with a handkerchief*

Every perfect action is accompanied by pleasure. By that you can tell that you ought to do it. —ANDRÉ GIDE

how thumbs and fingertips gentle
    hosiery over toes, up calves

how they work the secrets of garter belts,
    bra hooks and tampons

how they press the soft flesh of breasts each month
    looking for what they hope never to find,
    run down the dry riverbeds of stretch marks

how they clip nails, curry hair,
    rein it behind an ear

how they pinch cheeks to coax pink,
    caress feet, massage temple

how they minister to the skin,
    scratch an itch, prick a splinter,
    how they pluck, pop, rub, wipe, wash

how they know the rhythm of the thymus
    and drum it on the sternum

how they offer privacy for tears

how they press together in prayer,
    know mudra, sign of the cross,
      every way of blessing the self.

Two years ago, I was standing in front of my car on the side of the road, videotaping a flock of birds. A van traveling at seventy miles per hour hit my Subaru, and I was thrown into a field, landing underneath my totaled vehicle. When I regained consciousness, I realized that I was pinned under the exhaust system, which was burning through my flesh. While I could move my hands and feet, I could not move my torso, and it appeared to me I was facing my death.

I closed my eyes and prepared for the final merge, the next stage, whatever that might be, and just as I began to say good-bye to life, I heard the voices of two men.

"Oh my God, is anybody there? Is anyone alive?"

From under the wreckage, I cried softly, "I'm here. I'm alive."

"Where are you?"

"Under the car, by the back tire," I said.

"Wait there!" they said. "We'll go get help."

"You *are* the help," I said. "Just lift up the car."

There was total silence. I knew they didn't think they could. I knew my life depended on it. "You can do it. Lift up the car."

And then, in an amazing moment, the car was lifted up and two hands reached down to pull me out. What force came through the arms and hands of these men who thought they were not capable of lifting the car? Why did they think they needed to go for help? Because all our lives we've been told that help is out there or up there. All our lives we've looked outside ourselves for help, when we hold most of the help anyone will ever need right in our hands.

We do not believe in ourselves until someone reveals that deep inside us is valuable, worth listening to, worthy of our trust, sacred to our touch. Once we believe in ourselves we can risk curiosity, wonder, spontaneous delight or any experience that reveals the human spirit. —E. E. CUMMINGS

Child psychologist and educator Joseph Chilton Pearce says that our feelings of limitation are shaped by the trinity of culture, myth, and religion. In the introduction to *The Biology of Transcendence,* he writes: "We actually contain a built-in ability to rise above restriction, incapacity, or limitation, and as a result of this ability, possess a vital adaptive spirit that we have not yet fully accessed. While this ability can lead us to transcendence, paradoxically it can lead also to violence; our longing for transcendence arises from our intuitive sensing of this adaptive potential and our violence arises from our failure to develop it."[5]

This thought is consistent with the words of Jesus in the Gospel of Thomas, "If you bring forth what is within you, what you bring forth will save you. If you do not bring forth what is within you, what you do not bring forth will destroy you."

Our religions and culture have conditioned us toward a deadly passivity that has kept us from bringing forth what is within us, from accessing and expressing that vital spirit within. We have created a life system that has not only outgrown its usefulness, but is actually keeping us from evolving into our next phase of consciousness—the recognition of our own divinity. The violence that is erupting all over this planet is arising out of our failure to create, to shape our lives and our culture with the tools of illumined imagination and enlivened compassion.

While the spirit of humanity is poised on an evolutionary edge, awaiting the hugest transformation in the history of the cosmos, the body is blind to the moment, stuck in time, repeating old patterns over and over. Human beings have created a

The whole secret of salvation hinges on the conversion of word to deed, with and through the whole being. —Henry Miller story of humanity's ineptness. We have conjured up myths and religions and cultures that betray our potential, cause us to fear and hate and kill. We have handed down beliefs and constructed institutions that fail us desperately—rooted as they are in the depleted soil of the past. What we are not bringing forth is destroying us. What we are not creating with these hands of ours is leading us to the edge of destruction, as the forces of darkness grow ever wilder, ever wider.

The question of what to do about the world is the same question as what to do about our individual lives, as the world outside is a projection of the world within. Every thinking person is laboring these days over terrorism. Why is this happening? What can be done? Will we ever be free of it? We're tormented by the heartbreaking violence, the unyielding rigidity of fundamentalism. We realize our weapons are wrong for this battle for consciousness. It's a war of ideas that is being waged, and each of us is a warrior on the battlefield of thought. Each is armed with the force of creative energy, gifted with the power to transform dark into light, fear into love. We are the cocreators of a new way, authors of new myths, carriers of a consciousness of communion and compassion. The light of the world is the torch in our hands.

In the ordinary hours of our daily lives, we are flooded with occasions to be a force for good, to touch another's life in a way that brings joy. "God's being immanent depends on us," says Rabbi Abraham Joshua Heschel. We are the ones who give shape to the invisible one. We are the ones who can disarm the violent with the power of our thoughts, our touch, our gentle

When God said, "My hands are yours," I saw that I could heal any creature in this world.

—RABI'A OF BASRA

41

ways. We are the ones who weave threads of light into all our stories, whose words are a balm to the world's wounds. We are the ones who heal the loneliness, soften the hardness with a touch on the cheek, a hand on the arm. "God does not have hands, we do. Our hands are God's," writes Rabbi Lawrence Kushner.

It was her teacher Annie Sullivan's touch that brought Helen Keller to life. When she wrote about Annie Sullivan, Keller said, "I feel that her being is inseparable from my own, and that the footsteps of my life are in hers. All the best of me belongs to her—there is not a talent, or an aspiration, or a joy in me that has not been awakened by her touch."

Therapeutic touch relaxes the mind, heals the body, and soothes the spirit. Illness creates a disturbance or blockage in our energy field, which extends beyond the skin and can be perceived by a trained practitioner. The healer uses her or his hands to sense the blockage, remove the disturbance, and rebalance our energy to restore health.

Reflexology is a natural healing art based on the principle that there are reflexes in the hands, feet, and ears that correspond to every organ and appendage of the body. Through application of pressure on these reflex points, reflexology relieves tension, improves circulation, and promotes the natural function of the related areas of the body.

In ancient times we stimulated our reflexes naturally by walking barefoot over rocks, stones, and rough ground and by using our hands to climb, build, or work. In today's world, we have lost much of nature's way of maintaining a balanced and

When her fingers were too tired to spell another word, I had for the first time a keen sense of my own deprivation. I took the book in my hands and tried to feel the letters with an intensity of longing that I can never forget.

—HELEN KELLER

42

healthy equilibrium, but there are many touch therapies that help to restore our flow of energy and promote natural health and vitality.

While touching and being touched can lift us up, a lack of touch can be harmful to our well-being. Neurologists have determined that if touch deprivation is severe, structural damage may occur in the dendritic branches of the brain cells. Some suggest that societies that don't touch create aggressive people and cause violent behavior. In *The Power of Mind to Heal,* cellular biologist Joan Borysenko writes: "When we feel cut off from ourselves, isolated from other people, the immune system functions at suboptimal levels." A new field called psycho-neuroimmunology is confirming that our minds and our nervous systems are so interwoven with our immune systems that our emotions, our beliefs, and our imaginings have a tremendous impact on our health.

Studies conducted with babies who display early symptoms of hyperactivity showed that, after thirteen months, of the babies who were regularly held and caressed by their parents, only 12 percent continued to show symptoms. Neuroimaging has shown that stress levels can be reduced in individuals who come into positive physical contact with others.

In an Ohio University study of heart disease, rabbits were fed a toxic, high-cholesterol diet to block their arteries. All the rabbit groups showed consistent results except one group, which displayed 60 percent fewer symptoms. Nothing in the rabbits' physiology could account for their high tolerance of the diet, until it was discovered by accident that the healthier rabbits lived in cages that were at eye level, and the student in charge of feeding them often picked up these rabbits and cuddled and fondled them, holding each one for a few minutes before feeding it. This alone seemed to enable the animals to overcome the toxic diet.

Other experiments similar to this have been conducted and had similar results—human touch has an impact on immune response. Even during surgery, touch has an impact. Doctors have reported that when they grasp a patient's hand at a difficult moment in surgery, they can see the monitor for blood pressure and heartbeat register the calming effect. Perhaps this is why the Samoan verb for "to doctor" is synonymous with "to rub."

The ancient Greek god of healing was Asclepius, son of Apollo, who used his "god hand" and a simple touch to heal the sick and raise the dead. According to the myth, his touch was so potent that eventually Zeus had to get rid of him because everyone was getting better and overpopulation was threatening.

Around 400 BCE in Greece, during Hippocrates' time, hand healers were today's internists who used their palms and fingers to heal. They were called *cheirourgos,* which is the origin of our word *surgeon.* Early touch treatments often consisted of a healer's lifting an illness out of a person and placing it in a tree or an animal, such as a goat. Four centuries later, Jesus laid his hands on people and healed whatever illness besieged them.

Touch healing continued in the early Christian church until the seventeenth century, when Descartes' philosophy on the dualism of mind and body influenced the Catholic Church to turn the "body" over to science and maintain control over the "mind and soul." This was the beginning of the body/mind/spirit split that has kept Western civilization in the dark for centuries, blinding us to the unity in that trinity and to our powers to heal when we are in communion with its essence.

Several healing modalities using the power of energy, touch, and compassion have resurfaced in the past few decades and are being used to induce relaxation, reduce pain, accelerate healing, and alleviate psychosomatic symptoms. While some members of the scientific community remain skeptical of this kind of energetic healing, many studies reveal a positive impact on patients who experience the healing power of touch.

In every sacrament or holy ritual from any tradition, the hands are essential. They baptize with water, confer blessings, elevate gifts brought to the altar, offer communion, call forth the spirit, anoint the dying with holy oil. With our hands, we bless, forgive, nurture, sustain, and offer tenderness to those in need. We come to see that giving is receiving and nothing less.

At a writing workshop I gave once, the participants wrote about trauma in an effort to transform it. For some, the assignment was difficult, bringing up troubling emotions. When the writing was done, I asked the group to form two circles. An inner circle would be composed of those who felt in need of comfort. An outer circle would form around them, and its members would lay their hands on the inner circle, offering love, energy, blessing.

It seemed easy for everyone to decide which circle to be part of, except for one woman who stood on the sidelines with tears in her eyes. When I asked what was the matter, she said, "I want to give people comfort, but I'm afraid if I do that, I won't be able to get any." She hadn't yet learned that there is no distinction between the two. We cannot comfort without being comforted. The very act of extending our hands in the service of another opens us up to receive whatever it is we are offering.

Our hands are a portal for the Divine to be both offered and received simultaneously. We cannot bless another without being blessed ourselves. This is the gift and the mystery of our oneness. It is difficult to articulate, but impossible to avoid. The flow is like that in a tree—while the water comes up from the roots to feed the branches and leaves, the sun's energy filters down through those very leaves and branches to mingle with the water within. One is not more important, more sacred than another. The mother rises to unite with the father, matter rises to merge with spirit. Heaven and earth unite in the creation and service of life. This is the oneness we seek even as we see it all around us—in nature and in our own bodies.

We are the threshold where divine and human meet and give birth to a new and radiant energy, an energy that can transform pain, turn spirit to matter, and repair what has been torn asunder. This is the power we hold in our hands, and it is waiting only for our conscious release, to be poured out in blessings over all we touch.

REFLECTION

Read this passage from Leonard Shlain's *Art and Physics: Parallel Visions in Space, Time, and Light* and see what comes to mind: "Observe from one side of a pane of frosted glass the prints left by the tips of someone's fingers touching the opposite side. A two-dimensional investigator, counting the five separate circles, would conclude that each fingerprint is a separate entity. But we who can appreciate the third dimension of depth know that the five separate fingerprints belong to one unified object in three dimensions: a hand. We also know that the hand is attached to a being that generates mind when time is added to the vectors of space."

EXERCISE

Draw an outline of your hands on a large sheet of paper. Take some time to reflect on what your hands have experienced since your birth. Write these experiences down on the parts of your hands that seem to hold them. If you have learned things through your hands, list what you have learned. Write to your hands, of your hands, for your hands, honoring them with your words in every way you can. If you have colored pencils or pens, color in the energy you feel emanating from them. Create a piece of art called "The Wisdom of My Hands." You may want to work on this over time, but when it is done, frame it and put it on a wall where you'll see it often.

EXERCISE

Sit with both your feet on the ground and place your hands so that your palms are facing each other. Bring your palms as close together as you can without letting them touch, then separate them by a few inches. Slowly bring them back to their original position, then bring them back out a few inches beyond where you stopped before. Return them to their original position, and bring them back out a few inches further apart.

Repeat this movement a few times and see if you begin to feel the energy between your palms. Don't try to make anything happen. Just see if you can allow this energy to surface in a noticeable way. Notice what sensation you feel. Separate your hands again, this time bringing them a couple more inches further out. As you bring them back, stop every few inches and see if you experience any kind of energy field building up. See if you can compress this field, if you can play with it in any way.

Pay attention to what sensations you feel and what it's like to tangibly notice your own energy. Some people have a hard time feeling anything at all, so relax if you don't. It doesn't mean anything is lacking.

EXERCISE

Visit these websites to see how people are using their hands in the service of peace: www.vcn.bc.ca/quilt/ and www.onespiritproject.com/Peace/.

WRITING EXERCISE

Imagine that your hand is a bridge between the conscious and the unconscious. Take out your journal, and after some reflecting, write down a question that has been puzzling you. Accept that an answer to this question will arrive from the deeper parts of you—from your intuition, not your intellect. Place the pen in your nondominant hand, and if nothing comes right away, begin to doodle or draw spirals or your favorite symbol. Keep your hand moving and let the words flow onto the page in response to your question. Enjoy yourself as you give voice to the light from within.

4 No Holding Back

Because everything we do and everything we are is
in jeopardy, and because the peril is immediate and
unremitting, every person is the right person to act
and every moment is the right moment to begin.

—Jonathan Schell

My relationship with my back changed dramatically one day when I was hit by a car, which then landed on top of me and pinned me under its burning exhaust system. I ended up with third-degree burns on my back and hip that required skin transplant surgery.

On the night before this surgery, I engaged in a ritual of thanksgiving for my body that had so narrowly escaped death and now was about to undergo yet another trauma, the harvesting of skin from one side of my back to be grafted onto the other. The bedroom was dark except for the glow of the candles we'd lit, and my partner Annie was at my feet as I started my prayers of gratitude. When I got to the back, she moved to my side and placed her hands on the left side of my back, which was bruised but not burned.

"Thank you, back," I began, shifting my attention up to the most injured part of me as I called to mind all the ways my back had served me in my life. "Thank you for supporting me, for carrying me and my belongings everywhere I've moved in this world. Thank you for helping me carry others who've been too weak to carry themselves. Thank you for carrying me into the majesty of the Himalayas, into the hunger and haunting mysteries of Calcutta, into the numinous quietude of temples and monasteries and cathedrals around the world. Thank you for carrying me into the lives of people who have taught me everything I know about love and kindness and not giving up no matter what. Thank you for bearing the weight of my cameras, my guitars, my tape recorders, so I could bring music to others and bring back home the music and images of people from other places."

My litany went on, but it stayed on the surface, focusing on the back in its most literal, physical sense. It wasn't until after my surgery that I began to get a sense of the *metaphysical* aspects that were crucial to my healing. A dear friend of mine, Diana, who's a physician and healer, came for a healing and brought a collection of stones to place on each of my chakras. I had read enough about chakras to know they are centers for the transmission of vital energy through our bodies—"portals to consciousness," according to C. G. Jung—but I had never explored or worked much with my own.

When Diana saw how deep my burns were, she said there was a serious risk of infection and that I had to focus all my energy on healing. "We have to keep your energy flowing, clear your chakras, and open the passageways so your own energy can get to where it needs to go to heal you," she said. As she laid a stone on my root chakra, she encouraged me to close my eyes and breathe deeply into that sacred, sacral bone, imagining a golden light entering into it from above, energizing it, and passing through it into my legs and feet, grounding me to Mother Earth.

Where I am folded in upon myself, there I am a lie.

—Rainer Maria Rilke

49

She sat on my bed and held my feet. "Feel the energy coming into you from the earth through the soles of your feet, up from the Mother who heals and holds you, nourishes and sustains you. Take this loving energy into your spine and let it merge with the energy coming in from above, from the Great Spirit of the heavens. Let these energies mingle and make their way to the parts of you most in need. Know that as you breathe in and out, these forces from above and below are healing you every moment, as you ask and give thanks."

Diana stopped at each chakra, placed a stone there, and helped me ground myself after a trauma so severe that I felt separate from my own body. She came back nearly every day for weeks, most times in her scrubs after surgery or a long shift in the clinic. And every time, she took her stones, placed them on my chakras, and held my feet to bring me back home into my body. With her guidance and healing touch, I began a relationship with my subtle body that was intimate and vital to my healing.

While science and medicine took care of the physical aspects of my healing, with surgery, x-rays, anesthesia, antibiotics, I was equally responsible for the metaphysical element, the invisible part where spirit and matter converge. I had to visualize wellness, breathe it through my body, befriend every chakra, every vertebra, every muscle, nerve, artery, and new skin cell and love them with all my might. And I believe that it's this level of intimacy, this tender loving communication with our own vital energy, that enables and sustains well-being for all of us.

Anodea Judith, one of the country's foremost experts on the

Order is not pressure which is imposed on society from without, but an equilibrium which is set up from within.

—JOSÉ ORTEGA Y GASSET

therapeutic use of the chakra systems, explains chakras in this way:

> Chakras are spinning vortices of energy, generated from the core of the body at the major nerve ganglia. The word "chakra" literally means wheel or disk, and like a floppy disk, each center contains habitual patterns, or "programming," that enables our life force to interact with various kinds of energy, such as physical, sexual, emotional, mental, or spiritual energies. Metaphorically, chakras are the inner psychic gears that move us along the journey of life. If we want to get up to speed, we need to work our way through the gears.[1]

The activity of the chakras is like a galaxy of planets, each spinning on its axis at points along the spinal cord. Each chakra is designed to supervise and maintain the perfect operations of the bodily systems under its control. This purification is done by spinning in pure or positive vibrations and spinning out impure or negative ones. Our life force nourishes the organs and cells of the body, supporting them in their vital functions.

Every thought and action of ours influences the flow of our life force. It becomes disrupted when we accept, either consciously or unconsciously, negative thoughts or feelings about ourselves. This diminishes the vital function of the organs and cells of the physical body. Our well-being is a matter of mindfulness. We have an internal energy system that will keep our

How you do anything is how you do everything. —ZEN PROVERB

51

bodies in perfect shape, but it is activated and maintained by our thoughts. There is an ongoing dialogue between our mind and our body, and what our bodies look and feel like is a result of this communication.

A healthy chakra spins clockwise and takes in energy. An unhealthy chakra distorts the energy it takes in, and when doing so, it does not nourish the body and spirit in a healthy way. If this unbalanced state persists for long periods of time, both the physical body and the psyche are affected. This leads to disease, or dis-ease, which manifests first in the energy field before manifesting in physical reality.

The distortions become habitual defense mechanisms developed from the specific childhood wounds and traumas we each experience. These images, limiting beliefs, and defense mechanisms become our personalities and govern how we interact with others, thereby shaping the lives we lead. In many different ways, they stifle our life force and distort or abort the creative impulses that well up from our core.

In the Ayurvedic medicine tradition, the chakras represent the interface between the cosmic vibrations of creation and the grosser anatomical systems of the physical body. Ayurvedic medicine has been evolving for the past five thousand years and is based on the Hindu Vedic scriptures, which are the world's oldest documented spiritual writings. It is interesting to note that the seven chakras described so long ago have a basis in anatomy—they correspond to five main nerve ganglia of the spinal column and two areas of the brain, the reptilian and the neocortex.

There is no way to tell people that they are walking around shining like the sun.

—THOMAS MERTON

The chakras of the Ayurvedic system, the meridians of the Chinese acupuncture system, and the sephiroth of the kabbalistic tree of life all describe the subtle energy that links the worlds together. Each uses a unique language to describe the precipitation of the mind of God into energy and physical manifestation. This energy is called *chi* by the Chinese, *ki* by the Japanese, and *prana* by the Hindus. The Kahunas of Hawaii call it *mana,* and Jesus called it *light.* The languages differ, but it is energy they are referring to, and our spinal column is the superhighway for the transmission of this vital force, our kundalini.

The word *kundalini* is one of those buzzwords that create confusion and resistance for a lot of people, but since we're trying to conjure up images and metaphors that help us understand and work with our energy systems, it's important to know where it came from and what it really means. Alain Daniélou writes in *Yoga: The Method of Re-integration:*

> The word Kundalini derived from a Sanskrit word "Kundal" meaning coiled up. It is the primordial energy present at the base of the spine in a triangular bone called the Sacrum. The Latin name "Os Sacrum" suggests that it is a holy or sacred part of the body. The ancient Greeks were aware of this and called it the "Hieron Osteon," noting that it was the last bone to be destroyed when the body is burnt, and also attributed supernatural powers to it. Egyptians also held this bone to be very valuable and considered it the seat of special power.[2]

In the West, sacrum is symbolized by the sign of Aquarius and by the Holy Grail, container of the water of life.

Kundalini, lying dormant in this sacred site, is a great reservoir of creative energy. It is the power of our consciousness, the integrated force of our physiological, mental, emotional, and spiritual bodies. Many Indian mystic traditions refer to it as the divine feminine within, and it is the awakening of this dormant force that leads to spiritual awareness or self-realization. Kundalini, which nourishes the tree of life within us, is coiled up like a serpent and has been called the serpent power. It is described in great detail in the Upanishads. The awareness of the presence of this primordial energy within the human body was considered by the sages and saints to be the highest knowledge.

In the Christian tradition, one might equate this awakening to that of the apostles during the Pentecostal reunion, when they witnessed tongues of fire over each others' heads and experienced a sudden and astonishing ability to understand everything and speak in many languages.

In the Tao Te Ching, the primordial power is described as the mother of all things. Lao-tzu referred to our ability to deal with this energy as the "spirit of the valley." While it cannot be created or destroyed, this energy within us can be directed, deflected, and channeled in the same way that a valley directs, deflects, and channels moving water.

Some say that when the Buddha spoke of the "middle path" as a means to achieving nirvana, he was actually describing the central channel *(sushumna)* through which the kundalini ascends. In her fascinating book *Magic and Mystery in Tibet,* Alexandra David-Neel popularized stories of Tibetan yogis drying icy bedsheets with their naked bodies outside in the middle of winter. One yogi had been seen doing this for two days without pause and had melted the snow to a distance of ten feet around him. Yet his body was at the normal tempera-

The only way forward is in the direction of a common passion, for nothing in the universe can ultimately resist the cumulative ardor of the collective soul.

—TEILHARD DE CHARDIN

ture of 98.6 degrees. The yogis produced this intense heat, called *tummo,* through a combination of intense visualization of deities and concentration on the breath, as the winds *(prana)* were drawn into the lower opening of the *sushumna.* While this is a showy example of the power of kundalini, it is a visual reminder of the power running through us and the potential we have to put it to use.

Our minds have been shaped by Western science and religion, which are rooted in the rational and are wary of the esoteric. As a culture, we have not plumbed the unseen mysteries of the human body, nor have we built bridges to Eastern spirituality, confounded as we are by their plethora of deities and physical disciplines. Like a body half breathing, we've failed to nourish our deeper parts with the medicine and myths of other cultures. But now those worlds are opening up, and borders that once kept us apart are dissolving in the threads of the worldwide web. Finally we are open to the vastness of the whole. Healers around the globe are sharing secrets from the ages, and lives are being saved without scalpels and drugs.

In his book *A Practical Guide to Vibrational Medicine,* physician Richard Gerber writes about a blended worldview of healing that combines the best of ancient and modern viewpoints of the human body and the many new approaches to achieving wellness. The new worldview of healing "sees the body as a complex integrated life-energy system that provides a vehicle for human consciousness as well as a temporary housing for the creative expression of the human soul. In the world of vibrational medicine, illness is thought to be caused not only by

Don't ask yourself what the world needs. Ask yourself what makes you come alive, and then go do that. Because what the world needs are people who have come alive.

—HOWARD THURMAN

germs, chemical toxins, and physical trauma but also by chronic dysfunctional emotional-energy patterns and unhealthy ways of relating to ourselves and other people. The vibrational-medicine approach to healing employs the use of different forms of energy, both electromagnetic and subtle life energy, to bring about healing changes in the body, mind, and spirit of the individual."[3]

While Western religion has not traditionally addressed issues of energy, it is the very underpinning of Eastern religions and philosophies. According to a Hindu myth, the god Shiva created the universe by emanating the sound Om, which was personified as Shakti, the feminine aspect of the Divine. In the saga, the universe was initially a large ocean. The vibrations of Om caused waves on the surface of this ocean, which consisted of the substance "supreme consciousness," personified as Shiva. These waves were the first traces of individualism, and it was through their differentiation that the diversity of forms and matter originated in the universe.

In the course of evolution of the universe, Shakti descends to the lowest form of vibration—physical matter—which is the state associated with the lowest form of consciousness. In the human body, this evolution is reproduced as the descent of Shakti (the inner power) from the top of the head, through the body's energy centers, and down the spine to the base of the abdomen, creating a link between the spiritual realms and life as we know it.

Hindu, Chinese Taoist, and Tibetan Buddhist scriptures refer to an electrical human infrastructure of 72,000 "subtle channels

> The place God calls you to is the place where your deep gladness and the world's deep hunger meet.
>
> —FREDERICK BUECHNER

of vital force." Of these, three are the information superhighways—*ida, pingala,* and *sushumna* in the Hindu tradition—running interwoven around and within the spinal cord. Imagine a caduceus, the symbol that's been used to represent medicine in this culture. It's usually depicted as a winged rod with two serpents intertwined about it. *Sushumna* is the main highway for our life force and is represented by the rod, our backbone. It runs up and down the body within the spine, between the top of the head (crown chakra) and the sacrum (root chakra). This primary current runs between the sun and the earth—*as above, so below.* It is connected to all seven chakras via stemlike channels that extend to the spine and merge with it from the center of the chakra. These stems provide each chakra with its vital energy.

The two serpents, referred to as *ida* and *pingala* in Hinduism, yin and yang in Taoism, and matter and energy in physics, represent the masculine and feminine forces, akin to the positive and negative force of electricity. They crisscross at the very intersections where our chakras are located. Our challenge is not only to activate these centers and release their stored energy but also to keep the dual energy forces of the masculine and feminine in harmonious balance with each other. The wings of the caduceus symbol serve as a visual representation of the astral flight made by experienced yogis who have used the energy to travel at will out of the body onto higher planes.

Though most of us are not interested in astral flights, all of us are invested in living as long and as well as we can. As exotic as some of these explanations appear to be, there are many similarities in the descriptions of psychosomatic unity and structure cropping up in modern-day humanistic psychology and holistic medicine. People who suffer from back problems, and many other physical problems, are finding that mindfulness and energy work are powerful tools for eliminating pain and healing from the inside out.

Conscious breathing is the best means we have of fueling our energy system. Whenever we're stressed, anxious, or fearful, our tendency is to hold our breath,

When we live, love, and have the courage to be, we are engaged in worship, we are expanding our human-ity, we are breaking out of our barriers.

—BISHOP JOHN SHELBY SPONG

All action begins in rest.   —LAO-TZU

which means we're depriving our tissues, cells, and organs of their vital energy. In *Wheels of Light,* healer and teacher Rosalyn Bruyere writes, "Breathing is probably our conscious interface between matter (our body and air) and energy (prana and kundalini). It is the way we accumulate energy. When we breathe, we should feel movement. Ideally, we should feel breath from the hips, expansion in our trunk, and breathing throughout the entire body, even in the feet. We should feel fully alive."[4]

Back pain is a problem for millions of Americans. According to research, low back pain is one of the most frequent problems treated by orthopedic surgeons. Four out of five adults will experience significant low back pain sometime during their life. After the common cold, problems caused by the lower back are the most frequent cause of lost working days in adults under the age of forty-five. If we could retrain our thinking to incorporate awareness of the connections between breathing, energy, and consciousness, we could drastically minimize the potential for pain.

It's been nearly two years since my accident, but I noticed recently that I was still holding remnants of that trauma in my back. It came to my attention when I began this chapter and found myself frozen in front of the computer. I was afraid to go there, afraid of the images it conjured up. I had spent so much energy trying to get past it that I had never processed my way *through* it. I never expressed my terrible sadness at what my back had gone through. I never released the grief of being nearly killed, of having so much of my flesh burned away, of the awful shock it was to my back and spine, of being hit from behind by such an incredible force. I told myself how lucky I was to still be alive and tried to carry on like nothing had happened. But something huge had happened, and it called for my attention and tender love. Energy was locked up somewhere, and I had to find a way to let it go.

I made an appointment with a bioenergetics therapist who was referred by a trusted friend. When I went for the session, I explained to the therapist what had happened and asked for her help in releasing the pain. I showed her my scars, then lay down on the floor in the position I was in under the car. She asked if it would help if she touched my back, and I said yes, that would be fine. Then she asked, "What would you like to say to your back?" I started to talk to my back and my spine, to all my cells and vertebrae, to my new skin and old, crying out in sorrow for the pain and loss. "I'm so sorry this ever happened to you, so sorry for the burning, and for that terrible moment you were struck so fiercely and by surprise." As I returned in my consciousness to the moment of the accident, I thought of the massive impact of the initial hit, the hurtling through space, the crashing of my body on the ground, then the weight of the car landing on top of me, and the burning of my skin under the muffler. I relived every moment, crying my way through as I spoke with deep love to my poor little body.

When the therapist asked, "Are there any sounds associated with these feelings?" I began to moan, then whimper, then wail, and as I let out these sounds I felt an energy coming to life at the base of my spine. It felt dark and massive, but it climbed up my spine and settled in my heart, causing a fear that my heart would explode. "Breathe into your heart," she said, as I grasped at my chest and held on tight. "Breathe, breathe, breathe," she repeated, and as I breathed, the energy moved again, settling now in the middle of my forehead. I grabbed my forehead, felt its pulsing, and tried to breathe and help it along. Within a few moments, the energy traveled upward and suddenly left through the top of my head. And I felt light and

59

calm in its place. The old had left and made room for the new.

Whether our traumas and upsets are physical or emotional, mild or severe, they have a power that needs to be dealt with. If something happens that disturbs our balance, violates our spirits, causes us horror or heartbreak or anger, it impacts our energy in a major way and can obstruct its flow if we don't tend to it consciously, physically, and energetically. Talk therapy is good, but if we keep talking about the same old things without relief, we might be better served by going within, listening to what the body has to say about the matter. In my session with the bioenergetics therapist, I spoke to my back in my language, and she spoke right back to me in hers—a language of sensation that I could feel in every fiber of my being.

We get our power back when we're fully embodied and as aware of our inner world as we are of the outer. Being able to visualize our backbone, to comprehend its amazing gift to us, to know and sense the energy of our own miraculous beings— this is how we stay grounded and full of light. When our root chakra is imbalanced, we're open to fear and insecurity, anger, frustration, depression, lack of grounding, lower back pain, and weight problems.

Eating is a basic first-chakra survival activity. Without food, we do not survive very long. Eating disorders often indicate a root chakra imbalance. Eating is a grounding activity—it helps to bring us down, helps us to feel settled, calm, secure. Excess weight can be an attempt to get rid of high stress, to protect the body, or to replace proper grounding techniques. Eating too little or being chronically underweight can be an attempt to avoid

I assure you that one who comprehends the truth of "nothing to be attained" is already seated in the sanctuary where he will gain his Enlightenment.

—HUANG PO

grounding and physicality because it seems too frightening or confining.

Susan Lark, MD, a distinguished clinician, author, and lecturer, writes in her online newsletter that our body shapes are strongly affected by our patterns of how we allow our life force to flow through our bodies.

> The flow of this energy is deeply affected by your emotions, and chakra imbalances not only contribute to health issues in their associated glands and organs, but even affect where you gain weight. Often, these are the parts of your body where you tend to accumulate excessive amounts of energy or focus your emotions and life experiences too strongly. Because the flow of energy in these chakras is impeded, the body part or parts associated with the chakras will become bloated, swollen and enlarged over time. Conversely, in those areas of your body where you shut off the flow of life energy due to emotional blockages, you end up depleting and de-energizing that part of our body, as well as its chakra and the associated organs and glands. This manifests as constricted or shrunken areas of the body, and often leads to an unbalanced appearance.[5]

One of the symptoms of an approaching nervous breakdown is the belief that one's work is terribly important.

—Bertrand Russell

She suggests that we look at our emotional patterns to see how they are affecting the energy flow through our body. Since the root chakra is the foundation for the whole chakra system, if there is a blockage there, our entire bodies are affected. Referring to this chakra in his book *Bodymind,* Ken Dychtwald writes:

> When a person is tense and tight in this bodymind region, it indicates that he is over concerned with material and survival needs. As a result, he will have difficulty giving and taking in an unrestrained fashion and may try to hoard and possess everything with which he comes in contact. Conversely, when there is vitality and flexibility in this region, it reflects an open, giving, free-flowing way of being in the world.[6]

We are not getting something for nothing. We are getting nothing for everything.

—Lionel Basney

After my session with the therapist, it occurred to me that I probably survived that accident because I was "in the flow" when it occurred. I was videotaping a flock of birds, caught up in the beauty of their choreography, the mystery of their unified movements. I was fully rooted, not only in a physical way, as one must be to film with a steady hand, but rooted in the present. Every particle in my being was focused on the task, in service to capturing that majesty. I was there in the moment, in the very *now* where God hangs out, and I believe it was this that saved my life. When we veer off into the past, we're often wrestling with regrets and resentments, holding on to memories that no longer serve us. When we jump ahead into the future, it's an obstacle course of fears and doubts: *Can I pull this off? Can I ward off those demons?* We have only our strengths in the present moment, only God in our midst when we're standing in the now.

That's the cost of union—we can only feel it if we're fully present, grounded in the moment. And when we are, we're invincible, invulnerable, for the self we become is beyond time and space, is one with the One, more the everlasting whole than the fragile, mortal part. When we're rooted in the present, we know our part in the scheme of things, sense our oneness, feel the flow of spirit up the spine and down, into the heart and out. We feel the grace of awareness, the presence of the other, the calling of the many to whom we are connected.

When the energy from Mother Earth flows into our legs from below, we know we are part of a mighty thing—a natural, organic, living source. Her cycles are our cycles. Her needs are our needs. We are as one with her as we are with the Divine, sharing in her role of yin to its yang, matter to its energy. Within ourselves, we contain the whole. Our backbone is like a lightning rod, grounded in the earth and drawing in the light and power from the heavens. We are each a conductor of divine energy, sending its radiance out through our hands, eyes, hearts, and mouths, and through our auras, which transmit the same energy on invisible waves.

When we are open to this flow, we are a fountain of blessings. We speak with authority, fill a room with our energy, project an aura of confidence and stability. We stand up and proclaim ourselves. Rosalyn Bruyere in *Wheels of Light* writes of a Buddhist teaching about power that says we cannot be pacifists until we have power. To be a force for good, we must rise to the occasion, let go of old notions about humility, and take a stand for justice wherever we can.

So divinely is the world organized that every one of us, in our place and time, is in balance with everything else. —GOETHE

63

Uncovering the truths buried within our bodies grounds us to the earth, focuses our attention, hones our survival skills, and lessens our fear. When we're grounded, survival is not a concern. We know the universe is *for* us, that people enter and leave our lives for the lessons they offer. We know that everything we need comes to us if we don't stop the flow out of fear or greed. When we're grounded, we know that we have more than enough and that generosity of spirit is what sustains the flow.

In some Native American languages, there is no word for loneliness. The people consider all of nature their kin. These original inhabitants were rooted to the earth in the most real way, until the Europeans came and uprooted everything. Some cultures believe that our bones carry stories in them and represent memory. If two people sit back to back and allow their spine bones to touch, they communicate. The other day I read a piece of advice that said if you're stressed, lean your spine against a tree, and the tree's energy will seep into it and soothe you.

Compare this to the messages we get from our culture, which attempt in every way to keep us alienated from ourselves, out of touch with our grandeur and magnitude, as far from our center as possible. It is countercultural, in a way, to be grounded, to stand on our own two feet, to know our worth is priceless and stems from within. From the very beginning, we're taught that looks are what matters and possessions are what's important, and our attention turns outward in pursuit of the meaningless. In an attempt to please, we mind our words, mind our waists, mind our movements, and keep the incredible gift of our own originality from ourselves and the world.

The energy coming out of a large oak can temporarily increase the strength of a human aura, or a person's vitality.

—WILHELM DE BOER

64

When independent religious studies scholar Neil Douglas-Klotz translated the Lord's Prayer from its original Aramaic, he discovered a whole different meaning for the phrase "lead us not into temptation." Translated from the original, it says "don't let surface things delude us, but free us from what holds us back."[7] It's a great mantra to repeat when we're trying to get grounded and in touch with our backbone. To be free from whatever holds us back—this is the key to a vital life. This is the means to opening our channels, freeing our energy, and building a life that's authentically ours.

REFLECTION

Lie down on your bed and begin to breathe deeply from your belly. Focus your attention on your back. Visualize your spinal column as a tunnel through which energy travels, communicating important information throughout your body. This tunnel may be clogged with emotional debris and energetic blockages, but you can clear it out with the power of your imagination and the flow of your breath. Beginning with your first chakra, imagine a healing vortex of light spinning away and clearing out this tunnel that is your spine. Visualize this radiant light working its way slowly up your spine, swirling around every vertebra, and opening every chakra and meridian it comes in contact with. Your spine has twenty-six vertebrae. See if you can hold your attention on one at a time as you continue to breathe and let your energy rise from vertebra to vertebra.

EXERCISE

Take your shoes off so you can feel the floor under you. Stand upright with your feet shoulder-width apart, toes slightly in. Press into your feet as if you were trying to push the floorboards apart between your feet. As you push down into your feet, you will feel a solidity come into your legs. Inhale deeply and bend your knees, letting your belly relax. Now exhale and push into your feet slowly, pushing as you did before and allowing your legs to slowly straighten. Do not let them straighten all the way, but bend them again and inhale as you go down into your legs. Push again against the floor as you exhale, pushing your energy downward through your body.

Keep your legs slightly bent, keep breathing, and move slowly. You should start to feel a slow vibration in your legs as you push against the floor. This vibration is the charge of energy moving through your legs and into your first chakra. It can be used to push out blocks, to increase your sense of contact with your body, or to make you feel more awake and refreshed.

Exercise

Any activity that makes you more aware of your body will strengthen your root chakra. Incorporate some fun physical activity into each day. It could be gardening, yoga, dance, biking, walking, working with clay, sports, chi gong, or tai chi. The important thing is that you enjoy it and look forward to doing it.

Writing Exercise

I call this exercise "Lay Your Burdens Down." An Algonquin elder once said that the key to happiness is in giving each task the necessary time to complete it fully. In today's hectic world, many of us are racing from one task to another, not giving any of them the time they deserve. As a result we're stressed, strained, and rarely satisfied with ourselves. Take some time now to make a *not*-to-do list, and let go of things that you honestly do not have time to do, do not like to do, and can commit right now to doing no more.

Sexuality and the Sacred 5

> There was a time when you were not a slave. Remember
> that. You walked alone, full of laughter, you bathed
> bare-bellied.... You say there are no words to describe
> this time, you say it does not exist. But remember. Make
> an effort to remember. Or, failing that, invent.
> —**Monique Wittig,** *Les Guérillères*

In the first prayer I ever uttered, I asked God to change me into a boy. I must have been four years old. I prayed that prayer over and over, on my knees, in my bed, on my tricycle. I'd never seen a penis, so that wasn't what I wanted. It was the special thing that boys had that made them better than girls. Whatever *that* was. I couldn't define it. I just knew, at that early age, that being a girl was second-rate, and I didn't want to settle for it if there was any way I could change it.

I couldn't, of course, and then came puberty, when my mom informed me that I had to start being careful in the presence of boys. In the most elusive allusion to sexuality, she let me know that whatever happened, I was the responsible one. "They can't control themselves," she warned me. That was it for my sex education.

On to eighth grade at St. Anthony of Padua, when, during Lent, we took the last thirty minutes on Friday to read pamphlets on holy subjects. Sister Anna Christine lined up about thirty pamphlets on the blackboard chalk trays, and we'd all race for the ones that had anything to do with sex to make up for our lack of home-schooling on the subject. One day I grabbed one called "Honoring the Sixth and

Ninth Commandments," a code for purity. I remember a section on masturbation that warned against it for many reasons, one directed to girls specifically. It turns out we weren't supposed to masturbate because it would be dangerous or wrong for us to get used to having an orgasm without a male in the picture. It might lead us to think we didn't need them. God forbid we should give priority to pleasing ourselves.

During my two years in the convent, the issue of sex never came up. Later, after I had left, I was raped one night and I blamed myself, with my mom's words ringing in my ears. "How did it get like this?" I wondered. How did men get to be in charge of everything when they couldn't even control themselves? Why did I hate myself for being raped? Why was sexuality presented as something impure and sinful? Why would God give us these bodies if he didn't want us to enjoy them?

When I took a closer look at my culture, my religion, and the history of civilization, the answers started to come into focus. *It wasn't always like this.* And we must reckon with the shadow and shape of our past, for all of it lingers still in our very cells. In the words of the Jesuit mystic and paleontologist Teilhard de Chardin, "In each of us, through matter, the whole history of the world is in part reflected.... Everything that the body has admitted and has begun to transform must be transfigured by the soul in its turn."

In my workshops, when women express what they were told about their bodies, what they were told about being women, about their roles as wives, about the value of their feelings, their words become a virtual litany of sorrows. We must face this,

When the feminine is sacred, the body is not left out.

—CAROL FLINDERS

68

acknowledge the darkness, understand the history of it, mourn it, and let it go, so we can proceed unencumbered to fashion lives that are of the light. We must get beyond our fears, and to get beyond our fears, we must know where they came from.

There was a time when a female deity was credited with creating the world, when a woman's body was perceived as an immanent and transcendent symbol of the power to give life and love, when sexuality was revered as a sacred act that led to intimacy with the Divine. Religious art celebrating the sacredness of women's bodies goes back thirty-five thousand years, when sex was integral to the cosmic order and erotic rites were rituals of alignment for the life-giving female and male forces. A woman's body was viewed then as an attribute of the Goddess herself. In our ancestors' view of the world, everything was spiritual and imbued with the sacred. Matter and *mater*, earth and mother, were revered as one and the same. The word *goddess* was used in written records from the Bronze Age, and ruins in every ancient culture contain statue fragments of female deities.

Having been raised a Roman Catholic, I found the concept of the "sacred feminine" to be an alien one. But one day I visited a Unity Church, and the minister led the congregation in a guided meditation where we imagined ourselves in the arms of God. Music was playing; a soft wind was blowing through the open windows. She asked us to imagine God's warmth and light, God's forgiveness, God's gentle mercy entering into our hearts and our whole beings: "Feel the tenderness and strength of God supporting you ... Feel God's light entering into you,

My me is God.

—CATHERINE OF GENOA

illuminating your very essence … Feel God's breath on you … Feel the safety of being in her arms." At that moment, my whole body trembled. The minister said "her." She called God "her."

This was a minister in a Christian church, not some pagan at a solstice ritual. A rush of exhilaration surged through me. It was the first time in my life I'd imagined God as a woman, and I felt closer to God in that moment than ever before. It was suddenly believable that I was made in the image of God. I didn't have to try to fit into a pattern that wasn't right. This was a perfect fit. And on that day I walked out of some kind of prison.

The ancients felt a deep affinity with the moon, and in their languages words for spirit, soul, wisdom, and time always related to the moon. Names for the Great Goddess usually have their roots in words for womb or vulva. The original power was always the woman's, and this power, or energy, increased at menstruation. In Dakotan, *wakan* means "spiritual," "wonderful," and "menstrual." Female blood was a sacred element in the agricultural rituals of Neolithic peoples, and a symbol of the psychic-physical bonding of humans to their mothers and the Great Mother.

But at the onset of patriarchal power, when the sky gods upstaged the earth gods and goddesses, menstrual blood became taboo, and sex and the sacred were torn asunder. Around the year 200 CE the church fathers proclaimed that children conceived during menstruation were born impaired. By the thirteenth century, Albert the Great and Thomas Aquinas claimed it was a mortal sin to have intercourse during menstruation. By the sixteenth century, theologians brought it down to the level of a venial sin, though some sects classified it as mortal only for the partner who demanded it. Women's bodies had become men's business, and the sanctity of our cycles was publicly debased.

Pope Gregory saw menstruation as the result of sin and praised women who abstained from the Eucharist during this time. For centuries women had to undergo a special purification after giving birth, before they were allowed to reenter a church. What was viewed as sacramental in the time of the divine feminine became sordid and suspect under the patriarchs. The very innermost regions of women's lives, the holiest and most sacred aspect of their femininity, was taken from their control as women became more and more the property of others.

Despite the clarity of Jesus's message, "Whoever divorces his wife and marries another woman commits adultery" (Matthew 19:9), early followers interpreted it differently for men and for women. For the man, only intercourse with someone else's wife was adultery; but for the wife, intercourse with anyone but her husband was adultery. Adultery was a kind of crime against property, and since an unmarried woman was not yet anyone's property, it was not adulterous to sleep with her.

Archaeologist Marija Gimbutas was involved with excavations in southeastern Europe and the Mediterranean from the 1960s to the 1980s, which revealed the existence of a prehistoric goddess-oriented culture. In speaking about the goddess culture before it was penetrated by the Indo-Europeans, she calls it "matristic," because the word *matriarchal* suggests dominance, comparable to patriarchy. The society she explored was a balanced society, not one in which powerful women usurped everything that was masculine.

> Men were in their rightful position, they were doing
> their own work, they had their duties and they
> also had their own power. This is reflected in their

If the women of the world were comfortable, this would be a comfortable world.

—SAMUEL ZAN

71

symbols where you find not only goddesses but also gods. The Goddesses were creatrixes, they are creating from themselves. As far back as 35,000 BCE from symbols and sculptures, we can see that the parts of the female body were creative parts. The vulva is one of the earliest symbols engraved, and it is symbolically related to the seed and to growth. It was a different view from ours and had nothing to do with pornography.[1]

The question arises, then, if this was such a perfect culture, why or how was it preempted by a violent, male-dominated culture? Cultural historian Elinor Gadon says, "When we look back across the historical time of patriarchy ... there seems to be some terrible inevitability, a relentless desire to crush the female essence, human and divine. The question of why is among the most puzzling of our time."[2]

Gimbutas's research led her to believe that it was a matter of might over right. The invaders who migrated from southern Russia had horses and weapons, while in prehistoric Europe, there were only hunting weapons. The old, matristic culture clashed with the invaders, who brought their new ways and ideas. Patriarchy won, and its proponents had to make the people afraid of the Goddess, so they would abandon her. By the fifteenth and sixteenth centuries, she had become a satan, a monster, said Gimbutas.

Reverence for women, for their fertility and creativity, was lost. There went our connection to nature, our honoring of the body, our sacred, sexual rites of passage. There went the exquisite male-female balance that seemed to prevail during those times. In a recent interview, writer Tom Robbins said: "The Goddess, in her many guises and manifestations, was the most dominant, holy figure on earth for thousands of years and yet she has been so successfully eradicated that certainly the majority of American women have simply no idea that she ever existed, let alone had the power that she had."[3]

Cultural anthropologist Ruby Rohrlich-Leavitt reminds us that when the patron of the scribes changed from goddess to god, only male scribes were employed in the temples and palaces, and history began to be written from an androcentric viewpoint.

The new monotheistic religion was founded on the precept that a masculine deity created life without any female participation. The first commandment announced the disappearance of the Goddess and forbade the worship of anyone but Yahweh. God was male, and the male was God. By 389 CE, the Roman emperor Theodosius had issued an edict forbidding worship of any deity but Father and Son. Bible stories had been appropriated from Mesopotamian culture, including the Flood, the Garden of Eden, and the Tower of Babel. Same stories, new god. The people of Greece were still praying to the earth goddess Demeter, so the church named her St. Demetra—then later changed it to St. Demetrius.

While it was precisely women's sexual power that was venerated and sanctified in the old religion, this power was demonized and denounced under the new patriarchy. The church proclaimed women a constant danger to men and issued edict after edict to protect men from women. In the second century, St. Clement of Alexandria wrote: "Every woman should be filled with shame by the thought that she is a woman." By the end of the century, women's participation in worship was explicitly condemned, and groups led by women were branded heretical. By the year 200 CE, most Christian communities endorsed the opinion expressed by Paul in a letter to Timothy, "Let a woman learn in silence with all submissiveness. I permit no woman to teach or have authority over men: she is to keep silent."

The sixth-century Christian philosopher Boethius wrote in *The Consolation of Philosophy,* "Woman is a temple built upon a sewer." Bishops at the sixth-century Council of Macon voted as to whether women had souls, and in the tenth century, Odo of Cluny declared, "To embrace a woman is to embrace a sack of manure." While Lutherans at Wittenberg debated whether women were really human beings at all, Orthodox Christians held women responsible for all sin, using Ecclesiasticus 25:24 as their guide: "Sin began with a woman, and thanks to her, we all must die."

A religious war against women took the form of witch hunts, which were well-organized campaigns initiated, financed, and executed by church and state throughout the thirteenth through sixteenth centuries. The church-blessed inquisitor's manual for the hunting of witches, the *Malleus Maleficarum,* vilified women as the carnal source of all evil, proclaiming that "all witchcraft comes from carnal lust, which in women is insatiable." Church-educated male physicians were in competition with traditional wise women who were burned at the stake for the crime of healing. Since women were supposed to have pain in childbirth, the officials reasoned, it was wrong for these healers to help ease the pain. Despite her reputation for Christian piety, my own ancestor, Rebecca Nurse, was hanged for being a witch in Salem, Massachusetts, at the age of seventy-one.

Linking sex with sinfulness and domination, church leaders in the Middle Ages sanctioned sex only if performed in the male above–female below position. The church official who wrote Codex Latinus Monacensis 22233 asserted that for a wife to depart from the prescribed position was as serious a sin as murder. Communion was refused to those who had sex for pleasure. Archbishop Stephen Langdon wrote that "woman must always be available to her husband, lest he seek sex elsewhere, even at risk of her own life." The wife must allow herself to be killed through complications of pregnancy and birth rather than tempt her husband to sin.

This is our sexual inheritance. This and many centuries more of this. The memories of the burning times are in our cells. But so are the earlier memories of our freedom, of our full-bodied

All knowledge is rooted in our sensuality.

—BEVERLY HARRISON

74

sensuality, of the time before, when life and love, sex and passion, nature and God were revered as one. If we contain the horror, we must also contain the honor. While the masculine God has ruled for the past seven thousand years, it is the Goddess who held the attention of our ancestors for all the years before. If we wanted to give them equal time, we'd hold to a masculine image of God for centuries to come, but I think we're too smart for that.

We can see from history the havoc that has been wreaked by our dualistic thinking. It is not either/or that we need, it is the balance of both. As evolving creatures, we learn from our mistakes, and it is clear the time has come for the sacred feminine to be reinstated. It is time for the two to become the one, time for the merging of heaven and earth, mortal and divine. Neither males nor females can know themselves until they find the other in their own true nature, nor can we as humans know our God until we feel God's presence in our breath and blood.

Morris Berman writes in *Coming to Our Senses* that the body and the soul were seen as antagonistically related and that the dichotomy between "tame" and "wild" became official in the thirteenth and fourteenth centuries. The psyche became disconnected from the body, and all feelings of aliveness were thereafter based on the adrenaline rush that comes from engaging in conflict.

To break the mental patterns that have dominated human life for millennia takes diligence, forgiveness, and vision. As Matthew 10:36 reminds us, "Our enemies live under our own roof." They have outposts in our heads, and our spiritual work is to rout them out. Women and men alike have been victims of

> Our first duty is not to hate ourselves.
> —SWAMI VIVEKANANDA

> The body is the corporeal ground of our intelligence.
> —ADRIENNE RICH

75

a system that has maintained control over our hearts and minds for thousands of years. To heal ourselves, we need to reclaim our bodies as expressions of God and vehicles of divine life, love, and pleasure.

Sue Monk Kidd says this so poignantly in her *Dance of the Dissident Daughter:*

> The spirituality we've inherited from patriarchy is laced with a denial of the natural. Patriarchal spirituality becomes a flight from earth, flesh, temporality and the present. Sacred feminine consciousness seizes us by the shoulders, looks in our eyes, and tells us with a passion and simplicity: *If you don't get anything else, get this. This is your life, right now, on this changing earth, in this impermanent body, among these excruciatingly ordinary things. This is it. You will not find it anywhere else.*[4]

The paths of the Infinite Garden must be traversed by the body, the heart and the mind as one.

—Essene Gospel of Peace

In *Ecotherapy: Healing Ourselves, Healing the Earth,* Howard Clinebell writes, "Scholars have shown that the self-esteem and spiritual empowerment of many women is enhanced when they are encouraged to use female images of the divine, such as spirit, goddess, Sophia…. Reclaiming the so-called 'feminine side' of divinity and of themselves can open some men and women to a deeper experience of God."[5] Our challenge is to construct a spirituality that fits us and feeds us, to develop a spiritual life so alive and compelling it informs every one of our words and deeds, and to become so steeped in the presence of

God that we do not confuse any event or person as something other than a sacred unfolding.

The goal is not to replace a male god with a female version. The goal is to restore balance, knowing that the true one contains the two. The question is never, what sex is God? The question is, how can we image God in a way that fosters our sense of oneness with the Divine? How can we become the authors of our own divine experience, designers of the landscape in which we find the holy in ourselves and each other? How can we conjure up a faith that frees us to experience, *as part of its expression,* the ecstasy our bodies are built for? How in the world do we reclaim our eroticism, surrender to its holy joyfulness, lose ourselves, once and for all, in the ecstatic union of divine and mortal? We can only do this when we abandon our notions of separateness, see our bodies as the bridge between heaven and earth, and feel the breath of God on the westerly winds. As the great Sufi master Hafiz says:

To change our realities we have to change our myths. —RIANE EISLER

> *Now is the time to know*
> *That all that you do is sacred.*
>
> *Now, why not consider*
> *A lasting truce with yourself and God.*
>
> *Now is the time to understand*
> *That all your ideas of right and wrong*
> *Were just a child's training wheels*
> *To be laid aside.*
> *When you can finally live with veracity*
> *And love.*

Hafiz is a divine envoy
Whom the Beloved
Has written a holy message upon.

My dear, please tell me,
Why do you still
Throw sticks at your heart
And God?

What is it in that sweet voice inside
That incites you to fear?

Now is the time for the world to know
That every thought and action is sacred.

This is the time
For you to deeply compute the impossibility
That there is anything
But grace.

Now is the season to know
That everything you do
Is sacred.[6]

We are poised on the outer rim of evolution. We are "the axis and leading shoot" of it, as Teilhard de Chardin said. Our own bodies are the vehicle for the next stride forward. We are inches from the face of God, and yet our gaze is turned backward, upward. It seems impossible to think of the radiance of God shining within, shining ahead of each step we take. There is nothing in sight that is not sacred; nothing in our midst and nothing within that is not of the beloved. Though we've been cast for eons in supporting roles, it is our time to shine like the stars we are and take a leading role in the unfolding progress of life on earth. We can no longer abide teachings that perpetuate the myth of separation between ourselves and God, ourselves and each other, for it is this kind of thinking that ruptures our relationships and keeps us from the greatest intimacies of our lives. We and God are the river and the flow. We are the sound of God's breath, the cells in God's body, and where we move, God moves. In my own love song to the Divine, I say it like this:

Like the all in the oneness,
Like the branch and the vine
Like the call and the answer
Like the drink and the wine

Like the earth and the heavens
Like the forest and trees
Like the gate and the pathway
Like the hawk and the breeze

Like the iris and petals
Like the jewel and the mine
Like the known and the knowing
Like the laugh and the line

What then was the commencement of the whole matter? Existence that multiplied itself for the sheer delight of being and plunged into numberless trillions of forms so that it might find itself innumerably.

—SRI AUROBINDO

Like moonlight and darkness
Like nowhere and near
Like the oak and the acorn
Like pain and the tear

Like the quest and the seeker
Like rain and the flower
Like the sea and the islands
Like time and the hour

Like union and yearning
Like the vision and view
Like waves and the water
So I am to you.

So I am to you, Love, and you are to me
We dwell in each other, like salt in the sea.[7]

When I first read Teilhard de Chardin's *The Divine Milieu,* I was a novice in a religious order, preparing for vows. All heaven broke loose when I read his words about the divinization of matter and the role of human consciousness in the sanctification of human endeavor. I began to understand that we are not here to deny ourselves pleasure, to transcend life in the hope of finding God on the other side of it, but to immerse ourselves wholeheartedly in the miracle and mystery of being, to find God in the very essence and heart of matter. The incarnation is an ongoing event, occurring minute by minute with the birth of every child.

My disconnect between spirit and matter dissolved as I sat there in the chapel, dressed in black, shrouded in silence, with Teilhard's book in my hands, preparing to become a bride of Christ. His words helped me see and feel the Divine coursing through my cells, streaming through every living thing on earth. "The divine assails us, penetrates us and moulds us. We imagined it as distant and inaccessible, whereas in fact we live steeped in its burning layers." His theory of a noosphere delighted me as I visualized this great envelope of consciousness around the planet, knowing my own thoughts were part of it.

Noosphere comes from the Greek word for psyche, soul, mind, and according to Teilhard, we are creating, with our consciousness, a new sphere above the biosphere wherein the final convergence or fulfillment of life will occur. It is the mysterious pleroma to which St. Paul referred, the consummation of the world in which "the substantial one and the created may fuse without confusion in a whole which, without adding anything essential to God, will nevertheless be a sort of triumph and generalisation of being."

Teilhard wrote that "the march of Humanity develops indubitably in the direction of a conquest of Matter put to the service of the Mind.... Thought might artificially perfect the thinking instrument itself; life might rebound forward under the collective effect of its Reflection."[8] While I agree that we are indeed marching forward, I would like to advance the argument one step further, adding some yin to his yang.

It is not a conquest, but a *consecration* of matter that is called for if we are to protect the earth and its creatures from destruction. Teilhard himself said we have reached the point where we must choose between suicide and adoration, and while he focuses on the mind, I see the heart as the fulcrum or pivotal

> Spirituality arises out of our nature—it's native to us.
>
> **—SUE MONK KIDD**

81

point of transformation. Thought might perfect the thinking instrument, but feeling—love—can transform it. Ideas are dependent on our sensuality, and feeling is the basic ingredient that mediates our connection to the world. As the Christian ethicist Beverly Harrison writes, "All power, including intellectual power, is rooted in feeling. If feeling is damaged or cut off, our power to image the world and to act in it is destroyed."

Perhaps beyond Teilhard's thinking layer is a feeling layer, beyond the noosphere an even greater *erosphere,* animated and charged with our desire for union with all life, divine and human, and charged as well with God's desire for union with us. Perhaps desire is the key, the root of our longing, the foothold from which we make our ascent to oneness. Eros, the Greek god of love and desire, was said to be responsible for the embraces of Uranus (heaven or sky) and Gaia (earth), and from their union were born many offspring. Eros has been defined as an intermediary between the gods and humans, an unlimited desire, an active force of creativity. Maybe it's time to develop a spirituality of passion, where we place *eros* (feeling) on the altar next to *noos* or *logos* (thought). Maybe the epiphany of consciousness we're awaiting will arrive when we make that shift from head to heart, when we entertain the possibility that our sexuality, our craving for union and pleasure, is not only *from* God but *for* God and *about* God. What might happen in our personal lives if we approached lovemaking as an act of prayer, a sacrament of union? What if we thought of our bedrooms as temples, where every act of love was an honoring of the Divine in each other, a gesture of conscious gratitude and

Love sets the world on fire through the intimacy of sex and the compassion of justice.

—DIARMUID
O'MURCHU

self-giving, a symbol of our ability to transcend mortal boundaries and plunge headlong into the immortal beloved?

If it feels blasphemous, it's only because we have centuries of
conditioning limiting our thoughts, shackling us to an image of
humanity that dishonors our magnitude. But we can't wait for
institutions to change, for permission to be granted to become
embodied, to embrace the divinity of our own beings. As the
brilliant philosopher Beatrice Bruteau writes, "We cannot wait
for the world to turn, for times to change that we might change
with them, for the revolution to come and carry us around in
its new course. We are the future. We are the revolution."

And the revolution is a revolution of consciousness, a depar-
ture from dualism and an advance toward synthesis. It is a
valuing of the whole, an honoring of the complementarity, the
life-producing potential that arises when the feminine and
masculine merge, when *eros* and *noos* embrace. It is not one or
the other, but the marriage of these two that will lead to the creation of a new world—a world that, conceived in passion, will
birth compassion and deliver us from the false boundaries that
have kept us separate. Thought has brought us to where we
are, but only feeling will move us forward. Only feeling will
bring us to our knees in adoration. It is the yeast, the leavening,
without which the bread of life cannot rise.

I saw a film recently that showed the actual process of conception. It was not a simple matter of a sperm penetrating an
egg, as we've all been taught. The ovum itself has tiny, delicate
follicles (with the beautiful name of *corona radiata*) around its
entire rim that reach out and draw the sperm in. It is a dance of

> An evolution
> conscious of itself
> could also direct itself.
> —TEILHARD DE CHARDIN

83

desire, the female beckoning the male, the sperm responding to the touch of the ovum, the merging and dissolution of the two into one. Aleister Crowley, in *Eight Lectures on Yoga,* defines desire as the "need of every unit to extend its experience by combining with its opposite." It is desire, not thought, that sparks new life. And we will not raise ourselves up from this ghetto of global insanity until we honor our feelings as we honor our thoughts and technologies, until we *extend our experience* by uniting with, not warring against, our perceived opposites.

The world will change as we change, heart by heart, mind by mind. It will come to peace as *we* come to peace—with our passions, our sexuality, our beautiful, sacred bodies—and detach ourselves from any people or organizations that don't support a full-bodied faithfulness to our own true nature. In *Quantum Theology,* Diarmuid O'Murchu reminds us that in the passion of human loving, the passionate God manifests the divine eros—in stark contrast to the *detached* God of later theistic culture. He invites us to reclaim the creativity of our eros, the fire of energizing love, and "outgrow the mechanization of sex which patriarchy imposed on our world and which has dominated both our attitudes and behaviors" for millennia.[9]

Embodiment is a sacred act, a movement toward God. When we surrender to the ecstasy our bodies can feel, we're rooted in the present, in the very *now* where the beloved dwells. When we're fully embodied, we're aware of our senses, tuned in to the physical, open to rapture and the release of all tension. Despite what we were told, there is nothing wrong with pleasure for the sake of pleasure. It's God's gift to us, and we ought

> God's ecstasy creates the world, and the world's ecstasy realizes God.
>
> —BEATRICE BRUTEAU

not kick the gift horse in the mouth. Climb back into your body and remember the feel of sexual energy racing through your being from head to toe. Remember the bliss of union, the sounds of delight, the tears and trembling in the face of oneness. God *is* that rapture. The Persian poet Rumi says: "Listen to the moan of a dog for its master. That whining *is* the connection. This longing you express *is* the return message." Our bodies are the receivers of God's transmissions, and every part is there for a holy purpose.

As we stand on the cutting edge of a new way, waving goodbye to the old, we must give attention to the habit of fragmented thinking that allows us to see ourselves as separate and forsake our connectedness and responsibility to each other. A mentality that leads to the burning of women at the stake is as horrifying as a mentality that leads to two million young women a year undergoing female genital mutilation—removal of the clitoris and labia—to reduce their desire for sex before marriage, or to thousands of young souls losing their lives in wars around the world. Today's tragedies are a manifestation of our collective thoughts, as our personal lives are manifestations of our personal thoughts.

If you thought you'd fail, you probably did. If you thought you were unworthy, you probably allowed people to take advantage of you. If you thought you were a sinner, you probably opened yourself to accusation and blame. Any thoughts we entertain that perpetuate a notion of "us and them" are dangerous thoughts that lead to destruction. If we think of ourselves as divine instruments, we will invite for ourselves and others only blessings, only praise. To honor our sacredness is the first step we can take as torchbearers for a new way.

The other day I was riding in a taxi from a small town in upstate New York to the Albany airport. I was exhausted from an intense week at a writing conference with three hundred women, and all I wanted to do was close my eyes and enjoy some silence. The driver started complaining about a new taxi company that had just come into town. "They're thieves," she said. "They overcharge, they don't even put your bags in the trunk. They're just here to try and put us out of business. We all hate 'em and hope they go belly-up."

My heart was sick at the sound of her words, but I was too exhausted to respond. The more she talked, the angrier she got, and I had a deep, uneasy feeling in my gut that it's this kind of energy that is fueling the war we're in. The consciousness of our world leaders is informed and fed by the consciousness of all of us. Whatever happens on the bottom rises to the top. I've wished since then that I'd roused enough energy to engage her, ask her some questions that might have redirected her thoughts.

One way we can contribute to peace in this world is to be accountable for our thoughts and words, refusing to generate energy that is not of the light. It's easy to get angry at politicians, at the patriarchy, at systems of abuse that have kept women and the poor and people of color down for so many centuries. It's easy, but it doesn't help. What helps is for us to be alchemists, transforming the lead of the past into the gold of a new creation. A poem, a song, a play, or a dance can fuel another's imagination, calm another's storm. As artists and activists, we have a huge opportunity now to put our faith into action, into creations that reflect and inspire the very thing we're looking for.

What's at stake here is life itself, and if we don't begin to find God in the bodies we see in the mirror, if we don't reel our God in from the heavens and honor God's holy presence in the flesh and bones in our own neighborhoods, we're betraying ourselves and the Divine. We have sexual organs to keep God coming into this world, for it is only through our bodies that God

The past cannot prevail against the power of the Now.

—ECKHART TOLLE

86

can be seen. We have been gifted with an exquisite and extraordinary capacity for sexual pleasure, and nothing is an accident. This potential for eroticism, this aptitude for mind-blowing bliss, this ability to let loose a creativity-stimulating flood of endorphins—this may be the force that jump-starts our dimmed and dulled imaginations. Perhaps if we'd leave our cubicles, come home early, and cuddle up with our lovers (or ourselves) for a wild foray into ecstasy, the lights would come on, new neurons would fire, and we'd remember everything—our purpose, our passions, and the right way home.

It's about love, the heart, feeling, living. Everyone's saying it—the mystics, the artists, the visionaries and lovers of life—and in the most beautiful ways. Rumi says, "Let yourself be silently drawn by the stronger pull of what you really love." Mary Oliver says, "You only have to let the soft animal of your body love what it loves." Meister Eckhart tells us, "God expects but one thing of you: that you should come out of yourself and let God be God in you."

William Blake says, "Arise and drink your bliss for everything that lives is holy." Teilhard wrote that "nothing here below is profane for those who know how to see." Joseph Campbell said that "the task of the true hero is to shatter the established order and create the new community." God said to Isaiah, "I'm sick of your sacrifices. Learn to do good, search for justice, help the oppressed." What more do we need? What are we waiting for? Sacrifices are out. Service and justice-seeking are in. Learn to do good. Practice on yourself. We can only love others as well as we love ourselves.

Consecrated human love becomes Holy Communion. Human divine lovemaking becomes the place where Christ is known and felt and seen and tasted, again and again.

—ANDREW HARVEY

Audre Lorde reminds us that the erotic is the nurturer and nursemaid of all our deepest knowledge. In *Sister Outsider* she writes:

> Once we begin to feel deeply all the aspects of our lives, we begin to demand from ourselves and from our life-pursuits that they feel in accordance with that joy which we know ourselves to be capable of. As we begin to recognize our deepest feelings, we begin to give up, of necessity, being satisfied with suffering and self-negation, and with the numbness which so often seems like their only alternative in our society. Our acts against oppression become integral with self, motivated and empowered from within.[10]

Our bodies know this. They speak to us in longings, in desires, in joyful cries and whispers. And they will lead us home, if only we listen.

REFLECTION

What was communicated to you, as an adolescent, about your body and sexuality? Has it contributed to a life of wholeness? Is there a difference in what you learned and what you are passing on about sexuality? Is your spirituality informed by your sexuality in any way? How?

WRITING EXERCISE

For many of us, it's hard to even know if we're embodied, and this exercise helps us get in touch. To do it, lie on your bed and place your hands on each chakra, as you make your way up the body. Beginning with the root chakra at the base of the spine, proceed to the genitals (second chakra), the solar plexus or stomach (third chakra), the heart (fourth chakra), and so on. At each chakra, close your eyes, feel the energy through your hands, and imagine, if your body were the earth, what might be occurring in this chakra. Two examples below, from my journals, show what I felt at two different periods in my life.

Example from 2002:

If my body were the earth, I'd feel:
an earthquake in my root chakra
a drought in my second chakra
a volcano in my solar plexus
a heat wave in my heart chakra
melting glaciers in my throat chakra
a cloudy sunrise over my third eye
a sinkhole opening up in my crown chakra.

Example from 2004:

If my body were the earth, I'd feel:
an oak tree rooting in my first chakra,
a misty summer morning in my second chakra
a wheatfield growing in my solar plexus
a rainforest storm in my heart chakra
a geyser erupting in my throat chakra
an aurora borealis in my third eye
a desert sunrise in my crown chakra.

6 The Hourglass Dress

The body is a sacred garment. It is your first and last garment. It is what you enter life in, and what you depart with, and it should be treated with honor.

—Martha Graham

I learned at an early age that my body was a temple of the Holy Spirit. That thrilled me. It meant that God really did live inside me. In preparation for our first Holy Communion, Sister Grace even gave us an image to flesh out the concept: "Think of it like a flame burning inside you. Your body is like a container for the flame of God." That made it easy to love myself. That, and the commandment to love others as I love myself. It seemed that my most important duty as a Christian was to honor myself as a temple of God and love myself in practice for loving others.

I was athletic and muscular as a child. And I was never thin, which didn't bother me because I wasn't striving to be. I was striving to have fun, to be good, to do well in school. Then I hit the teen years, and everything changed. The body became the main focus. Spirituality flew out the door when puberty hit, and there was no one around to bridge the gap between sex and the sacred. No one talked to us *then* about our bodies being sacred temples. Our looks were what mattered, and with the arrival of fashion model Twiggy, thinness was in.

I managed to find myself a boyfriend, but he thought I was too fat and called me Horse in front of his friends—a fate I felt I deserved for weighing 125 pounds.

Suddenly it became harder for me to love myself, and as I began to judge my body, so did I start to judge others. And so did I forget, for many years, that my beautiful body was home to the Divine.

It seems to happen almost by default that our spiritual lives are threatened by a culture that obsesses on the body and overlooks the spirit. There are plenty of voices criticizing our weight, our wrinkles, the size of our bellies, but who is calling us to honor these bodies as sacred garments and as temples of God? Is it the poets we must turn to instead of the priests, the mystics instead of the makeover artists? Catherine of Siena helps us remember with her beautiful poem translated by Daniel Ladinsky:

> *What is it*
> *you want to change?*
> *Your hair, your face, your body?*
> *Why?*
> *For God is*
> *in love with all those things*
> *and He might weep*
> *when they are gone.*[1]

As we try to undo the damage we've sustained as individuals in a culture obsessed with unnatural thinness, it helps to step back a bit and see things from a different vantage point. This fable, in all its simplicity, helps us see the underpinnings of a social phenomenon that affects all of us, one way or another.

The mind and the body are famous for holding the heart ransom.

—CATHERINE OF SIENA

91

The Hourglass Dress: A Fable

Once upon a time, in a land not far from here, there was a king who
had a dream. In this dream, he saw the image of a woman in an hourglass dress, so tiny at the waist he could wrap his hands around her and
his fingers would touch. "I must find this woman whose waist I can
span with both my hands, for that is the sign of the truest beauty," the
king proclaimed when he awoke. "Fetch the dressmaker to make this
dress, and I will offer jewels and riches and a place in my palace to any
woman who can wear the dress."

Word went out throughout the land that the king was seeking
women with an hourglass shape to live in his palace and surround him
with beauty. From the north and south and east and west, thousands
and thousands of women flocked to the palace, eager to please the king
and to share in the riches that he was offering. But alas, not one could
fit in the dress.

For they were hardy women who had worked in the fields, tended
the animals, given birth to children, raised families, and eaten enough
to be strong and healthy. Each was beautiful in her own way, but none
had a waist tiny enough to fit in the hourglass dress. The king was
growing frustrated with the search for the perfect woman, so he
ordered the dressmakers in all the lands to make nothing but these
hourglass dresses.

"We must teach them early, before it's too late," said the king in his
frantic effort to gain control. He ordered dolls with hourglass figures
for all the young girls so they would learn about beauty and tend to
their shapes from an early age. Before long people everywhere thought
of beauty as an hourglass shape. They said good things about women

who had it and bad things about women who didn't. To avoid being shamed by being too large, many women began to starve themselves. They became weaker and weaker in body and spirit and spent most of their time minding their shape so they could fit into the king's special dress.

Men tried to help the women achieve this hourglass shape, for now they only wanted women who looked like this. They made undergarments that pushed women's flesh from one place to another. Women laced themselves into stiff corsets that were shaped like the dress, but it was hard to breathe and move about. They bought expensive potions that falsely promised to dull their appetites. And doctors operated on one after another, removing ribs, making some parts bigger and some parts smaller. For the sake of this "beauty" dreamed up by the king, women sacrificed greatly and taught their daughters to do the same. Some even died.

And back at the palace, women were still coming from miles around. Millions and millions tried on the dress, and millions and millions didn't fit. They left the palace feeling bad and sad that they were not the right shape and not beautiful at all. In the end, after all the millions failed to squeeze into the dress, only thirteen women accomplished this feat. And these thirteen moved into the palace, where the king showered them with jewels and gifts and paraded them for all to admire.

Days turned into months, and each day was much like the last. They started to feel bored and were always hungry. And they worked very hard to keep their hourglass shapes, running up and down the palace steps to work off the small bit of food that they ate. One day as they were eating their tiny portions of carrots and celery and lettuce leaves with nothing on them, one of the thirteen spoke out, "I'm sick of this! What's so great about this hourglass shape if it's all I ever get to think about?

"The king says that only those who fit the dress are beautiful, but when I look about at the other women, I find beauty there no matter what their size. I find beauty in their strength, in every curve and muscle, in their tender eyes and loving hands. I find beauty in the sound of their voices, in their laughter and tears, in the ways they move and the things they say. I even see beauty in the wrinkles in their faces. Where did this notion of beauty come from anyway—from one king's dream? No, beauty is bigger than that. Beauty is what you see when someone is real."

"Hmmm ...," muttered the others, nodding their heads. "She's right."

"Before the king's dream, we all thought we were beautiful just as we were," said one.

"We were happier then, too. And we ate what we wanted. And we were strong," said another.

"And free," another added.

"And we had fun, and danced and played. We had real things to talk about and real things to do."

"But we didn't have these jewels, or the king's attention, or these fine clothes," whispered someone.

"True," said another, "but has it made you happy to put your whole mind on the shape of your waist and eat nothing but morsels and run upstairs and downstairs hour after hour?"

"I guess not."

The more they talked, the more they learned from each other's feelings. No one had been happy starving herself. Each had longed for the days when she could eat what she wanted and not be judged for the size of her waist. And each lived in fear of outgrowing the dress and being cast shamefully out of the palace.

Their talking made them feel brave and less alone. The more they talked, the stronger they felt, and the more they longed for the life they had had. One day they decided to be true to themselves and to leave the palace and this life of struggle.

"No!" shouted the king when they revealed their plan. "After all I've done for you, you cannot leave me! It is only your beauty that feeds my soul."

"If it's real beauty you hunger for," they said, "then look again at the people around you with eyes that go deeper than flesh and form. Look at their faces, the spark in their eyes, the joy in their movement, the kindness and love they share with each other—*that,* my king, is *real* beauty."

And so it was that the thirteen women left the palace, returning to their homes, far and wide. They remembered the power of sharing their feelings and gathered together with circles of people in every village, sharing what they knew about *real* beauty and passing the word to all around that *a waist is a terrible thing to mind.*

Despite the lack of mass media, the king in the fable was pretty effective in conjuring up an unattainable standard for beauty and encouraging women to strive for it, at least until they returned to their senses. But now, thanks to a $40 billion-a-year diet industry, a $20 billion cosmetics industry, and a constant barrage of ads that foster self-hatred and insecurity, staying true to our senses is a Himalayan challenge.

The goal is to be healthy, to consume consciously, to exercise enough to keep energy flowing through our bodies, and to honor our bodies as the sacred vessels that they are. If we're living with that kind of mindfulness, our bodies will be the sizes they ought to be. University of Colorado law professor Paul Campos, author of *The Obesity Myth,* claims that dieting is responsible for making people fat by triggering a "starvation response" in the body, which, when dieting stops, starts storing "emergency" fat in increasing amounts, a pattern repeated after each failed diet. Dieting alters our metabolism, so that when we return to normal eating habits after dieting, we gain weight because our body has learned to operate on fewer calories. It's a no-win situation.

Campos contends that diet promoters, drug companies, and weight-loss surgeons have whipped up an irrational panic over weight. Makeover shows advocating plastic surgery are the latest television hit, and bookshelves overflow with the latest best-selling diets. In the 1980s, newspaper articles on obesity ran at about sixty a year; last year there were more than seven thousand. Ninety percent of girls between three and eleven years have a Barbie doll as their standard of beauty. Her dimensions are the human equivalent of 38-18-28. In real life, you'd have to have plastic surgery and several ribs removed to achieve these measurements, and then you'd hardly be able to walk. A few facts compiled by the Council on Size and Weight Discrimination show the impact of our cultural obsession with unnatural thinness. It reads like a litany of sorrows because it *is* that.

> Dieting has become the Western world's answer to Chinese foot-binding: institutionalized torture of women's bodies.
>
> —Tom Sanders

- Seventy-five percent of American women are dissatisfied with their appearance, and 50 percent are on a diet at any one time.

- Young girls are more afraid of becoming fat than they are of nuclear war, cancer, or losing their parents.

- Forty-two percent of first-, second-, and third-grade girls want to lose weight. Forty-six percent of nine- to-eleven-year-olds said they were sometimes or very often on diets.

- Forty-five percent of boys and girls in grades three through six want to be thinner. Thirty-seven percent have already dieted; 7 percent score in the eating disorder range on a test of children's eating habits.

- Seventy percent of normal-weight girls in high school feel fat and are on a diet.

- Over half the females studied between ages eighteen and twenty-five would prefer to be run over by a truck than to be fat, and two-thirds would choose to be mean or stupid rather than fat.

- A survey of college students found that they would prefer to marry a blind person—or even an embezzler, drug user, or shoplifter—than someone who is fat.

- Since 1998, the number of stomach-shrinking surgeries has quadrupled to one hundred thousand annually.

- Up to 35 percent of normal dieters will progress to pathological dieting, and of those, 20 to 25 percent will progress to partial or full-blown eating disorders. The death rate for eating disorders is 5 to 20 percent.

We are products of our culture and these statistics are evidence of our vulnerability to manipulation. People are having these feelings because they are encouraged to feel this way by the images they see and the things they hear, in the media, in their families, and among their friends. Our self-esteem is an amalgam of what we hear and see in our outside world and what we hear and see in our inside world. One of the main ways we can help ourselves and our loved ones is by being conscious of what we say about our bodies. What comes *out of* our mouths is just as important as what goes *into* our mouths.

Many years ago I was having lunch with a friend who weighs over three hundred pounds. I made a disparaging comment about some part of my body being too fat, and she responded with a ten-minute consciousness-raising session on the impact of those words. "Do you know what it feels like to be a fat woman trying to love myself, and having to listen to you, who's so much smaller than me, talk about how you can't stand yourself being so fat? Can you see how that translates to me—that if you hate yourself for being fat, then you must really hate me because I'm a lot fatter than you?"

Ever since then, I've noticed how it feels to be around women, especially women thinner than I am, who speak about their bodies with disgust. These words hurt us, and not just ourselves but everyone around us. It's like shooting off bullets. We have to stop colluding in conversations about our bodies that are less than loving. Every cell responds to our thoughts, feelings, and words about our bodies, and we hurt ourselves terribly when we say hateful or mean things about our bodies. We can't have joyful, passionate, spiritual lives if we don't begin with self-love, self-respect. If we come out of the gate hating what we see in the mirror, we don't have a chance.

> God and I have become like two giant fat people living in a tiny boat. We keep bumping into each other and laughing.
>
> —Hafiz

I found it interesting in Buddhist countries like Nepal and Thailand, where monks are everywhere, that even though the monks all eat just a small amount every day—some only what they get in their begging bowls—some monks are thin as rails and others round as Buddhas. Our bodies have a mind of their own and a shape of their own, and if we're living consciously, if we're treating our bodies as sacred garments, they'll be the perfect size. The question is not, *what do I need to lose?* (in terms of weight) because every time we lose something, a part of us wants to go and find it, which is why diets never work for long. The question is, *what do I hunger for and how can I find it?* Or *what am I protecting myself from and what do I need to feel safe, fulfilled, satisfied?*

We need to be conscious of what images and words we are taking in and putting out. If we are aware of what the media is attempting to do, we won't become its victims. We need to be watchdogs at our own thresholds. That means that we look at every magazine and every ad with a new eye, homing in to see exactly how it's trying to make us feel—in effect, immunizing ourselves against its poison.

Lisa Sarasohn, author of *The Woman's Belly Book,* decided to do some research one day in the lingerie department of a local department store. She studied the tags hanging on the girdles and read what they said about the benefits these items were supposed to deliver. She writes on her website (www.loveyourbelly.com): "I noticed that the promotions for these undergarments read like an FBI directive for suppressing foreign insurgents: 'Achieve firm control … obtain total control … eliminate undesirable elements.' Here it is, the evidence: the girdle is an instrument of social control, a device to contain and restrict the expression of women's natural power."

That's the kind of astuteness we're looking for. If we're pit bulls at the gate, the four to six hundred ads we're exposed to each day won't hurt us, won't make us feel insecure, won't have us spending money on products designed to change us because we don't need to change. Words may seem innocuous, but if we let them sink into us unconsciously, they can affect how we feel about ourselves.

I recently heard a plastic surgeon talking on television about how easy it was to do stomach surgery. "You just take a handful of flesh out and pull the remaining skin down like a window shade, re-creating the navel. The scars won't go away, but they'll fade in time. A family comes back together because the woman is no longer ashamed of her deformity," he said. If we're not paying attention to the words and images we let into our bodies, then we're open to contemptible messages like this one. Whether we're aware of it or not, the messages seep in and stay there for a long time. That's why you know exactly what brands are being advertised when you hear, "Plop, plop, fizz, fizz, oh what a relief it is," or "Let your fingers do the walking," or "Just do it." We assimilated them unconsciously, decades ago.

If reality is imagination times vividness, and we're exposed to a constant repetition of vivid images of unnaturally thin women held up as "supermodels," we are going to feel something is wrong with us if we don't fit into the prescribed pattern. And if we want to change those feelings, we have to change the inner pictures and words we say to ourselves.

I had a set of note cards published once with images of women from around the world. One was a Hawaiian woman, beautifully abundant and goddesslike, whom I photographed during an ancient hula festival on Oahu. These note cards made their way around the country, and years later I received a letter

To honor and energize our bellies is to engage in a sacred act—one which is either culturally subversive or restorative, depending upon your point of view.

—LISA SARASOHN

from a woman in Wisconsin who wrote: "Dear Jan, I've always been fat and I've always hated my body. But someone just sent me your card of Mapuana dancing and I cried when I saw it. She is beautiful, even though she's fat, and for the first time in my life, I think I can be beautiful, too. I've put the card on my altar and every day I'm thankful that you took this picture. It reminds me to love myself every day, no matter what size I am."

This is the kind of transformation we're talking about. It's a fundamental change in our thinking. She couldn't imagine the possibility of fat being beautiful until she saw an image of a beautiful, majestic dancer who also had a big body. These images are rare in our culture, where we're inundated with photos of thin blue-eyed blondes. And that's not going to change unless we make our feelings known. It doesn't take much effort to speak out, and it often leads to positive changes.

Some time ago I shopped in a store called Pretty and Plump, and when I wrote out my check, I said to the cashier, "This name is really terrible. It makes me want to hide when I walk in here. Why don't you change it?" She had no power, of course, and the next time I went in, I said to the cashier, another woman, "I like this store, but I'm going to have to boycott it until they change the name. I find it really offensive, and I'm not going to shop here anymore."

I didn't go past the store for a few weeks after that, but when I did, I laughed out loud as I drove by. The old Pretty and Plump sign was gone, replaced by a new one, Real Sizes. I'll never know if it was due to my little boycott, but I like to think it was. I have a friend who always goes to the manager when she's in a store

An old woman is never old when it comes to the dance she knows.

—IBO PROVERB

101

that doesn't carry cool clothes in sizes over 12. She's very friendly and just informs the manager that she'd like to spend her money in that store, but until they start carrying fashionable clothes that fit her, she won't be doing that. Stores often add a few sizes to the lines they carry after she's let them know it matters to someone.

Just saying how we feel is an empowering act, and it encourages others to do the same. We may not be able to change the culture we live in, but we can change our attitudes about ourselves and resist the devaluing projections that come our way. We do this by reclaiming our bodies, reframing our notions about weight and age and wrinkles, and remembering that we are temples of the Holy Spirit.

Just think of your belly for a moment. It is the center of your body, the center of your electromagnetic field, your center of gravity. It is the home of your solar plexus chakra, the *seat of your soul,* the site of your soul power.[2] It's the center of your creativity, your energetic base camp. It's the place where the energy of your emotions is transmuted into your passion for life. You know there's a lot of energy there because it's where you experience "knots in your stomach" when you're conflicted or hurt, "butterflies" when you're excited, "gut instincts" when you're assessing situations.

The solar plexus is one of the key power chakras. The ability to stand up for ourselves and be self-reliant comes from this chakra. Our compassion to care for ourselves and others lies here, as well as our personal honor. Ambition, willingness to take risks, our ability to handle a crisis, generosity, and our ethics are the strengths that develop here. How can we not *love*

Women are not forgiven for aging. Robert Redford's lines of distinction are my old-age wrinkles.

—JANE FONDA

these bellies when they are the containers of such traits? We have a precious vase full of the most unique treasures in the world, and every day millions of us wake up wanting to smash it. Nothing good can come from hatred. Our bellies will only transform when we transform our relationship to them.

Mantak Chia, founder of The Healing Tao, a system designed to harmonize mind, body, and spirit through breath-work, exercises, and meditation, refers to the solar plexus as the main storage battery for *chi,* our energetic life force. Taoist yoga often represents the lower abdomen as a fiery cauldron, which "cooks up" the energy needed to open and liberate the rest of the body. The fire in our belly is the spark that ignites the desire rising up from our second chakra and transforms it into action. Also, because it is our first connection (in the womb) with the external world and continues beyond the cutting of the umbilical cord, our solar plexus represents the strongest connecting link to other people on the feeling level, according to meditation teacher Genevieve Paulson. It is here that *chi* energy is absorbed, transformed, balanced, and distributed from both the macrocosm (heaven and earth *chi*) and the microcosm (the other centers and organs within our body).

We experience our deepest emotions and truest intuitions in our bellies. This is the area of self-image, self-confidence, self-respect. If this chakra becomes blocked, through negative beliefs, self-doubt, or lack of movement or self-expression, the flow of energy through our whole being gets clogged, wreaking havoc on our health, our emotions, our creativity. Elinor Gadon writes in *The Once and Future Goddess,* "I suggest that

I do not believe that new stories will find their way into texts if they do not begin in oral exchange among women in groups hearing and talking to one another.

—CAROLYN HEILBRUN

103

women's wombs are their power centers, not just symbolically but in physical fact. When we say we act from our guts, from our deepest instincts, this is what we are speaking of. The power of our womb has been stolen from us."[3]

To reclaim our power, we have to confront and change the emotional patterning that is recorded in our subconscious. These records must be emotionally confronted over and over again, and this involves more than an intellectual understanding of the problem. It calls for diligent emotional commitment, spiritual discipline, dedication and willingness to give up the old patterns, and *guts*. Literally. It's the solar plexus that keeps the brain supplied with energy, and that two-way dialogue is essential.

The French philosopher and spiritual teacher Omraam Mikhaël Aïvanhov likens the solar plexus to a projector and the brain to a screen that manifests, expresses, and publishes whatever the plexus feeds to it. The pictures projected onto the screen of the brain come from the plexus. "So when you want to meditate or to undertake any intense intellectual activity, don't rush into it or try to concentrate suddenly, without preparation, otherwise your brain will just seize up and you won't accomplish anything worthwhile," he writes in *Man's Subtle Bodies and Centres.* "Begin by concentrating on your solar plexus and then, when you feel that you have reached a state of peace and inner warmth, you can begin to work because your brain will be sustained and nourished by the energies flowing from your plexus."[4]

Our abdominal center, which the Japanese call *hara,* is home to our first three chakras, which deal with grounding, physical embodiment, basic needs and drives, and directed action. Our legs, extending the *hara* in connection with the earth, establish our rootedness and enable mobility. Further, the *hara* is perceived as our life source and spiritual umbilicus. As Lisa Sarasohn writes in *The Woman's Belly Book,* one who cultivates *hara*—through meditation, movement, massage, or martial arts—"unites with the nourishing, creative, regenerative flow of the universal life force."[5] These are not self-indulgent practices. They are acts of faith, of love. They are the body's ways of praying.

In his book *Hara: The Vital Center of Man,* Karlfried Graf Dürckheim writes that along with the development of *hara* comes security, confidence, courage, creativity, serenity, authenticity, sense of purpose, sense of kinship and connection, boundless energy, and stronger immunity from disease. He believes that by leaving behind the chest out–belly in posture and attitude of the West and adopting the belly-centered posture and attitude of *hara,* individuals can live a calm, grounded, and more balanced life. In Dürckheim's words, one who develops *hara* experiences a power that "is not a power one has but a power in which one stands."[6]

Western science has made some discoveries that align with this belly-centered philosophy, bridging the physical and the metaphysical. It turns out that our abdominal area carries the largest mass of nerve ganglia and has been called our second brain. Professor Wolfgang Prinz of the Max Planck Institute for Psychological Research in Munich recently wrote about this in *Geo,* a German science magazine.

Prinz said that the digestive tract is made up of a knot of about one hundred billion brain nerve cells, more than are found in the spinal cord. The article suggests the cells may save information on physical reactions to mental processes and give out signals to influence later decisions. It may also be involved in emotional reactions to events. He said: "People often follow their gut reactions without even knowing why, and it's only later that they come up with the logical reason for acting the way they did. But we now believe that there is a lot more to gut feelings than was previously believed." Professor Prinz thinks

> As activists, we must develop a mindset of anticipation. We must no longer surf the wave. We must become the wind that creates the wave.
>
> —DAZZLE RIVERA

the stomach network may be the source for unconscious decisions, which the main brain later claims as conscious decisions of its own.

Tuning in to our tummies may be the solution we've been looking for. If we can activate our belly brains and cultivate our *hara,* merge our yin with our yang, and focus as much on the interior as the exterior, we may end up realizing we are perfect *just the way we are.* Though perhaps, another paradox might accompany this insight.

Barry Kapke, bodywork therapist and founder of Insight Bodywork, writes that it is common to experience a deep joy and at the same time a profound sadness when we shift from the mind-centered experience to one where we start to feel our bodies and our wholeness. "It is the recognition of our 'split,' the realization of how far away we have been from our bodies. In the Persian language, this ennui of recognition is called *durie,* 'homesickness.' In the *hara,* we come home to our unity. Cultivation of the *hara* develops the depth to include and integrate both the mastery of the masculine and the mystery of the feminine in the embodied 'now.'"[7]

If the cultivation of your *hara* sounds a little too exotic for you, rest assured that you can achieve this same level of wholeness by dedicating yourself to a regular practice of bodywork (massage, shiatsu, acupressure, reiki), physical exercise (walking, swimming, dancing, tai chi), and a spiritual practice where your focus is on your breath and inner body. This is the bare-bones minimum requirement, in my opinion. The outside world is simply deranged, in terms of the body, and if we don't set up our own rituals of self-love, we become susceptible to its self-hating rant.

I just learned a new word from the Internet. The word is *pro-ana.* That's short for pro-anorexia. It turns out there are about four hundred self-styled "pro-ana" websites currently online, where girls and women at every stage of the disease go to chat with fellow sufferers and get the latest tips on losing weight and hiding their bingeing habits. There's no mention of seeking treatment, but there are tricks for maintaining a state of starvation, "trigger" galleries of emaciated women, competitions for weight loss, and pages of what is referred to as "thinspiration," quotes like "nothing tastes as good as thin feels." Searching the term *pro-ana* results in over twenty thousand hits.

According to the National Eating Disorders Association, five to ten million girls and women, and one million boys and men, suffer from eating disorders in the United States, and between 5 and 20 percent will die from it. In 90 percent of women, the disease begins between the ages of eleven and twenty-two. For the most part, they're still in our care at the onset. This gives us another reason to be mindful of how we speak about and care for our bodies. Our young ones are looking to us for how it's done. If you want a child who grows up to be a self-loving temple of God, the best thing you can do is model that behavior. We have no control over our children's choices after they reach a certain age, but our influence in their early years is significant.

This wonderful poem by Myra Shapiro tells a twofold story and gives a sense of how closely we're being watched by the young ones.

> Think of all the beauty still left around you and be happy.
>
> —ANNE FRANK

The Corset

The corset of my Tante Annie
held her to the symmetry
of her youth—an immigrant
sent south to help her uncle
tend his store. (I want to shelter her—
the broken English, the strangeness
of a Jew, of a body at fourteen.)
She was alone. Four boys ganged her.
For one year she had to stay in an asylum.

> *No one told. North, she met her husband*
> *whose artistic, fluent ways enabled her*
> *to ripple like a fountain. But not so fast—*
>
> *first she grew fat, so that each morning,*
> *bone by bone, a corset laced the chaos*
> *to its parts: full breasts, slim waist,*
> *round hips: a figure eight to match my age*
> *those summer nights I shared her room*
> *and saw the miracle, how, stay by stay,*
> *lace by lace, she loosened the reined flesh*
> *and sent it tumbling—ahhh a machaiah!*
> *fold by fold, sigh by sigh, the drench of it*
> *so delicious I told everyone*
> *when I was grown I wanted fat*
> *like hers, vast and operatic.*[8]

For Tante Annie, fat was probably her protection against further invasions, a sure way to keep people out. That's why a lot of us hold on to our fat, unconsciously. And that's why mindfulness is important to well-being. It helps us understand the choices we make and helps us make different ones when the time comes.

The important thing, in the long run, is to love ourselves *as we are,* so we can love others with abundance and grace and honor the Holy One who dwells within.

REFLECTION

See if you can give yourself ten minutes every day for this soothing meditation from the belly.

1. Choose a piece of music that you find relaxing and find a quiet place to sit where you won't be disturbed for twenty to thirty minutes.

2. Sit comfortably, on the floor or in a chair. Find a comfortable upright position and keep your back straight. Your hands should be placed comfortably in your lap.

3. Begin your meditation with a deep cleansing breath and close your eyes as you exhale. With your eyes closed, focus on your breathing. Slowly, take in five long, deep breaths through your nose, filling your abdomen with each inhalation. Notice your belly rising as it fills up like a balloon. Then just as slowly, exhale though your mouth, allowing your belly and lungs to release the air.

4. As you exhale, imagine the events of the day being carried out through your mouth on a gray cloud. Release your worries and begin to relax your entire body and mind.

5. Keep breathing in and out, letting your tensions out as you exhale. Feel the tension in your muscles begin to subside.

6. Now, with each inhale, imagine a divine white light collecting inside your body around the solar plexus, the network of nerves in the abdominal cavity behind the stomach and just below the place where your rib cage meets. With each breath you take in, this light grows stronger, more vibrant and soon begins to increase in size. Within a minute or two, the light encompasses the entire midsection of your body.

7. Now, begin by pushing the lower portion of the light down toward your toes slowly. Imagine the white light pushing all the stress and tension out

of your muscles one at a time. Imagine this stressful energy like a gray cloud being pushed down your lower extremities and out your toes. Use the same technique to push the light from the solar plexus up your back, neck, and head, pushing the stress out the top of your head. When your stress is gone, take a few minutes to feel the white light swirling about in your belly. Keep feeling your belly rise and fall as you breathe, and thank it for being the source of your power and your creativity.

EXERCISE

If you don't already do an hour or more of walking, tai chi, chi gong, or some other meditative physical exercise weekly, begin now.

EXERCISE

Say a short prayer of thanksgiving, light a candle, or observe a moment of silence before you eat. Thank the food for bringing you health and happiness.

EXERCISE

Throw a dinner party for a group of women friends, or host a potluck brunch. Let them know the theme is going to be "Loving Our Bodies." Write the following questions on pieces of paper and have each woman draw one, one at a time, and give her answer. Feel free to make up your own questions.

- How do you define beauty? Is your definition big enough to include you?
- What are the most common things you say to yourself about your body? Where did they come from?
- If you could change something about your body, what would you change? How do you think this would change your life?
- How do you feel when a woman smaller than you starts talking about how fat she is? Do you ever say anything about it?
- Who in your life has made you feel most beautiful? How?
- Do you ever think of your body as a sacred vessel?
- If someone asked your mother, your sister, or your daughter if you loved your body, how might each of them respond? Why?
- What are your favorite ways to treat yourself? How often do you do this?

WRITING EXERCISE

Write a love letter to your belly. Ask forgiveness for the mean things you've thought and said about it. Make commitments for the new ways you will treat it.

7 The Heart of the Matter

This is not my body, it is the temple of God;
this is not my heart, it is the altar of God.
—**Hazrat Inayat Khan**

Our heart is the place where the winds from above meet the fires from below, causing a combustion of original grace. From the very beginning, it is the heart that leads. When the mother's heart sends a "spark" to certain cells in the fetus, they, in turn, start a rhythmic beating and eventually become the heart muscle. The pulsing creates an electrical field with north and south poles, much like the polar field surrounding the earth. These poles provide an "orientation" to the other cells, which now know to differentiate according to their distance and direction from the pulsing heart. One group of cells becomes fingers, another becomes toes, and on it goes. From heart to heart, life itself is passed along.

Our heart energy precedes us as we navigate through life, extending beyond us as an aura potent enough to affect those in our path. Producing 2.5 watts of electrical energy at each pulsation, at an amplitude sixty times greater than that of brain waves, the heart creates an electromagnetic field that radiates twelve to fifteen feet beyond our body itself. The magnetic component of the heart's field, which is around five thousand times stronger than that produced by the brain, is not impeded by tissues and can be measured several feet away from the body.

Research from the Institute of HeartMath (IHM) in Boulder Creek, California, shows that our heart's field changes distinctly as we experience different emotions, and it is registered by the brains of people around us. On their website is an informal experiment with a boy and his dog, Mabel, demonstrating how one heart field can calm another heart down. IHM researchers monitored the heart rhythms of both the dog and the boy, then had Mabel enter a room by herself. Her heart rhythms were jagged and erratic. Then Josh entered the room and greeted Mabel, petting her and emotionally bonding with her. At this point Mabel's heart rhythms made a significant shift, synchronizing with Josh's heart rhythms and staying close to his rhythms throughout their visit. When Josh got up and left the room, Mabel's heart rhythms clearly shifted again, becoming very spiked and jagged. Although the experiment was not a formal study, it appears that Josh's calm heart field connected with Mabel's heart, helping her to feel secure and relaxed.[1]

That we have an effect on others is a matter of fact; the *kind* of effect we have on others is a matter of consciousness. We can radiate blessings and light or negativity and darkness. Every occasion we have to be with people is an occasion to bless or blame. It is in our best interests to be mindful of our energy as we scatter it about, because, as *A Course in Miracles* reminds us, the cost of giving is receiving. Hence, its wise counsel:

> When you meet anyone, remember it is a holy encounter. As you see him, you will see yourself. As you treat him, you will treat yourself. As you think of him, you will think of yourself. Never forget this, for in him you will find yourself or lose

We are tied together in a single garment of destiny, caught in an inescapable network of mutuality, and whatever affects one directly affects all indirectly.

—MARTIN LUTHER KING JR.

yourself.... The voice you hear in him is but your own. What does he ask you for? He is asking what will come to you. The answer that I give my brother is what I am asking for. And what I learn of him is what I learn about myself. We make no gains he does not make with us and we fall back if he does not advance.[2]

When I was young, my mother assigned me a task from her chair at the sewing machine where she regularly handed out morsels of wisdom. "Whenever you pass by someone on the street, always look them in the eye, give them a big smile, and say hello." Being shy and new to a big city, this seemed to me a frightening burden. "Oh, Mom, do I *have* to?" I asked pleadingly, trying to get off this hook of responsibility. "You never know," she said, "that person could be having a bad day and your smile could make a big difference." I was never sure then if that was the case, but I did it anyway, honoring her wishes, and now it's a habit I'm grateful for. Now, when I smile and say hello, I know I am offering a gift that simply goes unseen.

Recent magnetic images of actual heart energy show the energy arcing out from and curving back to the heart, forming a kind of doughnut-shaped torus. This is the electromagnetic field that carries our energy outward as it brings in the whole spectrum of radio and light waves that our brain/body uses in its conception and perception of the world. As our heart is the center of this torus, so is our earth the center of such a torus, and so is our solar system, with the sun at its center as our heart is at our center.

Ecstasy, I think, is a soul's response to the waves holiness makes as it nears.

—DOV BAER

In his book *The Biology of Transcendence,* scholar and teacher Joseph Chilton Pearce presents the exciting probability that our hearts are electromagnetically enmeshed with the energy of the universe, which leads to a whole new meaning of "we are the world." With every beat of our heart, the heavens may be coursing through us.

> We seem to live in a nested hierarchy of energy systems that extend possibly from the minuscule atom to human to planet, solar system, and ultimately, galaxy. Because electromagnetic torus fields are holographic, it is probable that the sum total of our universe might be present within the frequency spectrum of any single torus. One implication of this is that each of us centered within our heart torus is as much the center of the universe as any other creature or point, with equal access to all that exists.[3]

If so, we can access the universe through our hearts. We can feel our oneness with the earth as Meister Eckhart did when he wrote: "If I put my cheek against the earth's body, I feel the pulse of God." With open hearts, we can "see the world in a grain of sand," as William Blake did. We can open up to the signals coming into our hearts through the fields in which they are nested, and respond to the future that is calling us forward. We can feel the beloved like a fire within, as Rumi did, writing:

> *The heart is your student*
> *For love is the only way we learn*
> *Night has no choice but to grab the feet of daylight.*
> *It's as if I see your face everywhere I turn.*
> *It's as if Love's radiant oil never stops searching*
> *For a lamp in which to burn.*[4]

If we open the gates of our heart—risking everything, loving bravely, forgiving extravagantly—we can transform our lives, walk into each day knowing we are already loved, already healed, already part of the breathtaking whole. We can feel the warmth of love's oil burning and cast its light from deep within. If we refused for a day to be numbed and defensive, to don our armor, to be silent and withholding, and we released what we could of our love for life, heaven itself would come pouring out with balm for our wounds and wine for our chalice.

When our hearts are closed, we feel lonely and alone, weak and in danger, fearful and faithless. We wait for love to find us. We wait for God to help us. We wait for life to knock on our door with the world in its hands, when all the while it's in our hearts and in the hearts of everyone we see. We are like the apostle Philip, who says to Jesus, "I do see you, but I want to see God." And Jesus responds, "Whoever sees anything at all is looking into the eyes of the Only One Who Is."

As much as God is in the temples, the churches, the mosques, God is in our hearts, awaiting birth through our gestures, our touches, our passionate embraces, our howls of delight, and our pregnant silences. We are the created ones who give birth to the Creator as the Creator gives birth to us. The story is ongoing, the myth still unfolding, the creation still occurring, every day, in us and through us. We are the means by which God's being expands in the universe, as we learn from Meister Eckhart's poem, translated by Daniel Ladinsky in *Love Poems from God*:

Listen to your life. See it for the fathomless mystery it is. In the boredom and pain of it, no less than in the excitement and gladness: touch, taste, smell your way to the holy and hidden heart of it, because in the last analysis all moments are key moments, and life itself is graced.

—FREDERICK BUECHNER

Expands His Being

All beings
are words of God,
His music, His
art.

Sacred books we are, for the infinite camps
in our
souls.

Every act reveals God and expands His Being.
I know that may be hard
to comprehend.

All creatures are doing their best
to help God in His birth
of Himself.

Enough talk for the night.
He is laboring in me;
I need to be silent
for a while,

worlds are forming
in my heart.[5]

Here we have the mystics speaking of birthing the Divine, of worlds being formed in our hearts, as science posits the wondrous probability of our heart's energy field being one with the heart of the universe. All heaven is breaking loose, and we are beginning to see the underlying unity implicit in all creation. *As above, so below. As in heaven, so on earth.*

And yes, as Meister Eckhart suggests, it *is* hard to comprehend because our thinking has been shaped by the cultures and religions of our time, which have fostered notions of difference and separation. Dualistic thinking, focused in the intellect, separates divine from human, spirit from matter, me from you. Unity consciousness, centered in the heart, brings these together. The commandment is not to love your neighbor as you love yourself, but to love your neighbor *as* yourself. To find yourself *in* the other, and the other *in* you.

We are evolving toward this consciousness, but it is a challenging trek, entrenched as we are in old ways of thinking. As Joseph Chilton Pearce says, "That we are shaped by a culture we create makes it difficult to see that our culture is what must be transcended, which means we must rise above our notions and techniques of survival itself, if we are to survive."

I can imagine that people looking back on our world from a hundred years in the future will be horrified that we allowed forty thousand children a day to die from hunger when there was plenty of food to go around and that we poisoned our rivers, destroyed our forests, and considered war a viable option. I can imagine them with furrowed brow, poring over documents of our devastating history, trying to understand the suicide of children, the stoning of women, the obesity of one nation and the starvation of another. Why we spent more on

> Everything we need to know about life can be found in the fathom-long body.
>
> —BUDDHA

smart bombs than smart children. Why we killed people to show people that killing people is wrong. Why so many billions of dollars were spent on drugs, plastic surgeries, prisons, and weapons, when just a few of those billions could have met the basic needs of every person on the planet. We are all involved in one of the greatest mysteries on earth: Why don't we care for each other?

We've created a high-tech civilization with a Stone Age mentality, expanding exponentially in the technical world while the heart goes unattended, the spirit unexpressed. For the past two millennia, we have experienced the masculinization of God, while the feminine aspect has been not only dispensed with but disguised and denigrated. God has been presented to us as a male from masculine authorities all the way down the line. Religion has been wrapped in the literal and the linear, at the expense of mystery and depth, and only now, when the whole system is in chaos and on the verge of collapse, are we collectively understanding the gravity of this oversight.

When the Nobel Prize–winning chemist Ilya Prigogine spoke about systems evolving, he said that as long as a system is stable, you can't change it, but as it moves toward disequilibrium and falls into chaos, the slightest bit of coherent energy can bring it into a new structure. Referring to this in a recent radio interview, Joseph Chilton Pearce said, "We are islands of coherent energy which bring about the organized, entrained energy for a new situation."

We are evolving into beings who understand the necessity of wholeness and the urgency of balance. To reach our spiritual

There never was a more holy age than ours, and never a less.

—ANNIE DILLARD

maturity, as individuals and as a human family, we must root ourselves as deeply in the heart as the mind, becoming as fluent in feelings as we are in facts. Our lives stem from our faith, and if this faith is not informed by affection, if it lacks the power of emotion, the force of passion, it is a barren field of brain waves.

It makes sense that we're undergoing a crisis in health care. We're a society who is sick at heart, looking everywhere but within for cures and antidotes. Whether we read the newspapers, listen to the news, or not, our hearts are taking in the energy of the world, and it is bringing us to our knees.

We can change things, but we have to see it in our imaginations first. We have to imagine a world that works, see it in our minds and feel the joy of a world at peace. Individually and collectively, in order to bring it about, we have to fasten our minds to the possibility of a heart-driven world. If we don't see it first, feel it first, we haven't the means to manifest it. We draw reality toward us by imagining what we want as vividly as we can, then speaking that reality into the world and feeling as if it has already happened. The power that transforms it from probability to actuality is the power of our passion as we imagine it. The more we feel it in our cells, our flesh, in the marrow of our bones, the more we assist its birth in the world.

Just imagine for a moment how would it feel if all the churches agreed that since we've honored a male God for thousands of years, and since God has no gender anyway, for the next few thousand years they'll offer an image of God as mother? How might that change things? How might it change things if instead of looking back at how our forefathers did things, we looked forward at the future we want to dwell in and created systems and institutions from that perspective? How would it feel if every parish or congregation, every community, every town and city had a less-privileged counterpart that they cared for, traveled to, interacted with, learned from? How would it feel if our universities and corporations worked together to create and execute an ethics of ecology based on reverence for the earth and restoration of what's been ravaged?

"Nice idea, but it'll never work," you're probably thinking, because our conditioning has us strapped into a straitjacket of denial to restrain us from outbursts of love and desire. But this is the time for outbursts. This is the time to think big, to transform our rage and outrage into courage, so we can *lead with the heart.* The other night I was at a dinner party with a lawyer and a corporate executive, both of whom are retired and quite affluent. I mentioned Matthew Fox's statement about humanity outlawing war as it once outlawed slavery. "In order to bring it about, we need to be able to think it, and speak of it, and feel it in our bodies," I said. "That's the first step. Can you imagine it?" I asked them.

"Impossible," they both said, within seconds. "It's human nature to be at war. You can't change that with your mind, or with your feelings." And so it will continue, until more of us can imagine it, speak of it, and embody a new way for humans to act in the face of conflict. It will come, for that's our destiny as conscious, evolving beings. If we don't destroy ourselves beforehand, we will eventually self-divinize and look back at this time as just another barbaric episode in the long process of becoming one.

Thousands of people around the globe are already tuned in to this potential and are engaged in the heart work to facilitate it. Research in intuition has revealed that the body's perceptual apparatus is continuously scanning the future. IHM researchers state, "We have found compelling electrophysiological evidence that shows, under controlled experimental conditions, that both the brain and the heart process information about the

> Humanity has outgrown its ancient policies and must bestow the new dispensation out of the hunger of its own heart.
>
> —MANLY P. HALL

emotionality of a stimulus *before* this stimulus is presented to research participants." They are currently developing a theory based on holographic principles explaining how intuitive perception accesses a field of energy into which information about "future" events is spectrally enfolded.

It is not so far-fetched a thought, after all, to imagine creating from the future, pulling down into our concrete present a reality that we select from a variety of virtual possibilities. Pir Vilayat Inayat Khan reminds us in his book *Awakening* that "an electron can exist only if circumstances are created that favor its appearance; before that, it exists only in a virtual state. If we don't create a place for the Divine in the here and now of our daily lives, the Divine will continue to exist in a state of virtuality, or potentiality."[6]

Jesus repeatedly said, "Not I, but the Father within me does these things."[7] And we know from our Bible scholars that in the original Aramaic, the word that was translated as "father" refers to the creative spirit, the vital force within. Jesus was acknowledging himself not as the doer, but as the vehicle of the doing. *We are the light bulbs, not the lights.* If you have ever done anything creative in your life, added something original to the cosmic canvas, then you know what it means to have the force flowing through you. As I write these words, I wonder at the flow of it, and even more so at the source of it. I labor, not to think, but to stay true to my feelings, to offer from my heart a synthesis of all that is stored there. I will never have anything as concrete as an answer, but I trust that the energy beneath these words will inspire others to penetrate more deeply into the mystery and add what evolves from that journey to the mix.

This is how we contribute consciously to evolution—by paying attention and sharing what we learn. In his book *The Great Work,* cultural historian and visionary ecologist Thomas Berry writes: "We must consciously will the further stages of evolutionary process. Our responsibility is to be present to the Earth in its next sequence of transformations. While we were unknowingly carried through the evolutionary process in former centuries, the time has come when we must in some sense guide and energize the process ourselves."[8]

When we trust our instincts, act from our heart, create with compassion, and offer our creations as gifts to the world, we can rest assured that we're doing our part. It's not up for grabs whether we're right or wrong, for there's no such thing in the land of the heart. As physicist Niels Bohr writes, "Opposite a true statement is a falsehood; but opposite a profound truth may be another profound truth." The world of experience is far beyond the world of dualism.

When I speak of birthing the Creator, I am not offering up an image for judgment. If I say it in public, it is not an opportunity for someone to stand up and say, "Oh no we don't!" It's an opportunity for someone to imagine a different point of view. That's why I'm so busy creating and trying to find an outlet for what gets born. It's all from the heart. It's how I love, how I share my joy, how I know who I am. It's what brings me to life and lets me know every day that I'm part of the ever-spiraling flow of creation. I'm part of evolution, and what I do matters. That's what we want, isn't it? That's what we're crying for—lives that matter.

But to make a difference we have to make some waves. We have to say things, do things, think things, and share what comes up. The spirit within seeks expression in the world without, and we are its voice, its instrument. In the very heart of our own matter is the one that calls out to be heard, the love that yearns to be shared. This is our life force, our vitality, transcending boundaries, merging inner and outer, human and

> The throbbing vein
> will take you further
> than any thinking.
>
> —RUMI

123

divine, thought and matter in an endless cycle. It is through our feelings and senses that we perceive this force, and through our feelings and senses that we share it with others. In our creative works, this force gets carried from soul to soul, heart to heart. We pass on God in the gift of our creations. This is the rapture and mystery of the whole endeavor.

In his book *Bodymind,* psychologist Ken Dychtwald elaborates on this process:

> The emotions that begin in the gut will continue on through the bodymind in an attempt to express and release themselves. If uninterrupted, they will pass through the chest where they will be transformed by the qualities of this area. It is here that raw and naked feelings get "dressed up," so to speak, as they prepare themselves for presentation to the world at large. In the chest, the emotions become amplified by the force and drive of the lungs, animated with the passion and liveliness of the heart, and encouraged onward by the expressive elements of the arms and face.[9]

As we go about creating our lives, our words and actions transform into the world we belong to, the world we are shaping. As the food we eat becomes our bodies, so do our expressions become the world. We are living in a country that was once just a thought in the imaginations of a few men. We go to work in buildings that were conceived in thought; we listen to

Once open to the heart, we recognize the universe as benevolent and our personal self to be the center of that benevolence. The moment we place that center outside ourselves, we have betrayed and denied our heart.

—JOSEPH CHILTON
PEARCE

124

music, watch movies, read books that are concrete manifestations of someone's feelings and passions. And these creations touch our hearts, change our minds, move us to action. Energy becomes matter, matter becomes energy, and our hearts are the crucible where the transformation occurs. It is where the creator and created give rise to each other.

In their book *SQ: Spiritual Intelligence, the Ultimate Intelligence,* Danah Zohar and Ian Marshall suggest that the deep psychic energy source of the artistic personality is associated with the heart chakra. The first three chakras are concerned with survival and life in the ordinary world—establishing our roots, achieving intimacy and parenting children, acquiring personal knowledge and power. "But with the energy of the heart chakra we make the transition to a concern with higher things.... The heart chakra is where thought and feelings meet, where we experience an openness to others and to new things, an expanding sense of beauty and a deep idealism."[10] Our heart is the transitional point where our physical essence connects with the cosmos.

Our heart chakra is related to the element air and is accessible through the breath. The Hindus call the breath *prana,* which means "first unit." They believe it contains the essence of all vitality, since it is the point where the spiritual and physical worlds come together. To access this vitality, we need only breathe deeply and release the tensions we feel in our bodies.

Shallow breathing keeps our heart from being fully opened. If we are anxious or stressed, we tend to hold our breath, tighten ourselves against tendencies to release our pain, nervousness, or

I, O Arjuna, am the Self, seated in the heart of all beings.
—**BHAGAVAD GITA**

125

anger. Holding our tension in is like building a suit of armor around our heart. It may keep out some pain, but it also keeps out joy and comfort. And it severs our heart from its connection to the mind and the senses. Blocked at the center, we become divided. Our sense of love and connection with others diminishes, and the fire within us smolders.

I once visited a friend who was teaching a music course at a university in Washington, D.C. She had a guest in the class, an Argentinian musicologist who had been studying with some medicine women in the Andes. The musicologist asked for a volunteer to participate in an exercise, and a young man offered to lie down on the carpet as she held a pendulum over each of his chakras. The pendulum swung in wide circles over his first three chakras and his sixth and crown, but remained at a standstill over his heart and throat. They were emitting no vibrations whatsoever. She asked him to breathe deeply, then she held his feet and sang a chant over him.

She asked five others of us to sit at his head and by his arms and legs. Then she gave us a tone to sing, instructing us to sing it through clenched teeth so it would reverberate in our own bodies first. We did this for a few minutes, then she retested his chakras with the pendulum. At this point, the pendulum arced in circles over all his chakras, indicating that his energy was now flowing freely.

When the exercise was over, the young man said that his girlfriend had just left him and he was full of sorrow and anxiety. His heart was breaking, and he had no words to express his grief, so his heart and throat centers closed down. The woman told him to start breathing consciously, and that with the power of his breath, his inner spirit, he could revitalize his own energy system. "You can breathe your way back to health," she said. "Just stop a few times during the day, close your eyes, and breathe love into your heart and your whole being. Your breath will open your centers and the flow of spirit will heal you."

At the Institute of HeartMath, three hundred people were trained to focus on love and appreciation when they began to feel angry or frustrated. After one month, when tested for changes in the body, they found that the antiaging hormone DHEA had increased 100 percent and the stress hormone cortisol had decreased 23 percent. In fifteen control groups, there was no change in the hormones. Studies have revealed clear changes in the patterns of activity of the autonomic nervous system, immune system, hormonal system, brain, and heart when we experience emotions such as appreciation, love, care, and compassion. We know the tools for healing ourselves, and we know from research that if all is well within, if our hearts are open and joyful, then this is communicated electromagnetically to everyone in our midst. We are like walking radios, transmitting the most beautiful music of all time.

Teilhard de Chardin writes in *The Heart of Matter* that "man has no value save for that part of himself which passes into the universe." Our value is in the invisible realm, and our task is to communicate our spiritual essence, to pass on the substance of our deepest love. "It is no longer a matter of simply seeing God and allowing oneself to be enveloped and penetrated by God— we have to do more: we have to disclose God (or even in one sense of the word, *complete* God) ever more fully."

Through the consecration of our lives, the sanctification of our endeavors, the divinization of matter, Teilhard believed we would access the divine milieu and experience ourselves as bearers of the purest of love. He writes that "Some day, after we have mastered the winds, the waves, the tides and gravity, we shall harness the energies of love. Then, for the second time, man will have discovered fire."[11] I believe we have discovered

Every time we walk down the street, we are preceded by hosts of angels singing, "Make way, Make way, Make way for the image of God."

—HASIDIC SAYING

this fire, and it lives within the heart of each one of us, waiting to be released as burning love in the world.

REFLECTION

Use this simple meditation often to create and nurture compassion in your life. This can be practiced in just a few minutes, so try to incorporate it as a part of your daily life.

Sit in a comfortable position on the floor or in a chair, with the back flat, your head upright, shoulders relaxed, and chest open. Rest the hands in the lap or on the knees. Close your eyes, deepen the breath, and release any thoughts from the mind. Gently repeat the following softly out loud or in your mind:

> *May I be safe from all danger*
> *May I be held in the arms of God*
> *May I be strong in spirit and body*
> *May I be true to my heart and soul.*

Repeat the phrases again, changing "May I" to "May you" while you think of a specific person, a group of people, or the whole planet.

Finish with a few slow, deep breaths, feeling compassion, love, and kindness flowing through your body. Take a moment or two before moving on with the rest of your day.

EXERCISE

Take a moment to imagine the place in your body where you experience feelings of tenderness. Place your hand there. Imagine the place where you feel most fully the indwelling of the Divine. Place your hand there. Imagine where you feel your deepest joy and put your hand there. And now, your deepest sorrow.

Move your hand to the place where your body's wisdom resides. Now to where you feel your center is. And now to the place that seems a threshold through which passes the power of your love. And now to the entry place where you receive the powerful love of others. If your hand has moved at all, give thanks to all the places it moved to.

EXERCISE

Spend time outdoors in clean air, especially near mountains or beaches. Learn a breathing meditation. Do yoga postures that open the chest. Shake your hands and arms frequently. Hug people.

WRITING EXERCISE

Read Judi Beach's poem below and feel your own heart for a few minutes, as you ponder what it's gone through in the course of your life. Light a candle, put on a piece of music, and give yourself ten minutes of uninterrupted time to write freely, finishing this line, "My heart isn't breaking, it's …"

The Heart Doesn't Break

The heart doesn't break. It's muscle,
after all, though it can be strained
or pulled, or even bruised. It hurts
when it learns a new exercise

but grows stronger with practice:
the aerobics of patience, the yoga
of kindness, the deep-need bends,
and all stretches toward compassion.
It aches, too, when it first hugs itself,
astonished at its own strength. Think
Gibran: Your pain is the breaking
of the shell of your understanding.

But the heart doesn't break—it takes care
of itself. It knows how to love, how
to find grace in a gesture, and if
you keep your head from steering
the wheel of the heart, you can learn
self-forgiveness, an act which cleanses
the blood, so every reach of the body fed
by that blood is healed.

Don't believe the heart breaks.
You take its pain like an insult
you try to rise above or like a blemish
you try to hide, even from yourself,
in the basement of your intestines
or the attic of a migraine. It wrings itself
of wrong action, squeezes auricle
and ventricle of each poor decision
lodged in the heart of the matter.

Because the heart doesn't break,
it may skip a beat trying to keep up
or bring tears to wash your eyes.
Funny thing, tears.
They flush the eyes, the ducts,
the sinuses, but mostly
cleanse the heart. Your tears
are not flaws like leaks in a new roof,
but the overflow of a heart-pump
so it doesn't drown in sorrow,
so it swims in a joyful tide.

Praise your tears. Praise the heart
that is moved to release them.
Praise the pain of letting go,
but let go. Let your tears slake
the thirst of the new-sprouting seed
of your understanding.

8 Praising Our Own Geography

I see my two whole breasts
drooping on my dimpled abdomen,
and I love them. I love
the way they resemble inverted mountains
with their worn peaks pointing
toward the center of the earth. My round belly
folds against itself like an ancient anticline.
My bones are buried down there somewhere,
invisible, but strong as bedrock.
If the age of my body was the age
of the planet, I would be venerable,
and so I venerate myself.
My stretch marks are my story
stratified and every line holds a piece of time
as precisely as an index fossil.
All this skin fits me suddenly,
and I understand
what Eve knew before the bite
of shame and self-absorption:
This is what it means to be well made

and wonderful. I praise
my own geography at last.
       **—Sandy Supowit, "One Morning in
             the Bathroom Mirror"[1]**

People have adored breasts since the beginning of time. More than twenty-five thousand years ago, our ancestors were creating sculptures of full-breasted, multibreasted goddesses that honored the Great Mother they revered. Because she bled in rhythm with the moon, mysteriously produced offspring, created milk from nothing, and had a vast capacity for giving and receiving pleasure, woman's body was imaged as a sacred vessel by our Paleolithic and Neolithic ancestors.

In *Sacred Pleasure,* Riane Eisler reminds us that "it was *precisely* women's sexual power that was venerated and sanctified in the old religion." Until Christianity came along to suppress the traditions that associated sexuality with the spiritual and the divine, people *celebrated* the body. To them, all life was imbued with the sacred, and the body of woman was an attribute of the Great Goddess herself.

But we've come a long way, baby, and now, with the rise of Christianity and other world religions, spirituality and nature have been torn asunder. The Roman Catholic Church encouraged people to disassociate from their natural bodies and to make every effort to control and mortify the flesh. Instead of honoring the body as a holy temple of the Divine, they dishonored it, called it evil, dirty, and sinful, and began a reign of terror against the body, against womanhood, against expressions

> The past and future veil God from our sight; burn up both of them with fire. **—RUMI**

of sexuality that has damaged us more deeply than any war or epidemic in history. The erotic rites that were once a means of coming closer to the Great Mother were reclassified as carnal wrongdoings, sinful exhibitions of the weakness of the flesh. The great pendulous, nurturing breasts once associated with the Great Goddess have been appropriated as possessions of men, and after five thousand years of male-dominated civilization, breasts are valued now not for their life-giving capacity but as commodities and erotic playthings for men.

For us to reclaim the sacredness of our own bodies, to experience the mystical ecstasy of divine energy flowing through us, into and out of us, we need to detach for a moment from what we've been taught is true and reconnect with what we actually *know* is true through our own lived experience. Poets from East and West urge us to do this.

Walt Whitman writes, in the preface to *Leaves of Grass:*

> Re-examine all you have been told in school or
> church or any book, and dismiss whatever insults
> your own soul; and your very flesh shall be a great
> poem, and have the richest fluency, not only in
> words, but in the silent lines of its lips and face and
> between the lashes of your eyes, and in every
> motion and joint of your body.

Rumi, the Persian poet, writes, "Stop learning. Start knowing." Kabir, the Indian poet, writes, "If you have not lived through it, it is not the truth." In other words, *embody your life,*

Things are not as they seem. Nor are they otherwise.

—**Lankavatara Sutra**

I found god in myself and I loved her. I loved her fiercely.

—**Ntozake Shange**

134

arrive at the truth from your own experience, do not take your cues from the ones who rule but from your own inner feeling and knowing.

Most of us have been taught to image our bodies from a male perspective, and struggle to conform not to our own desires, but to what is considered desirable by the culture at the time. Over the centuries, we have been reshaping our bodies according to external dictates, resulting in feelings of inadequacy and self-hatred when we fail to sculpt ourselves into unnatural shapes.

We even risk our health to fashion ourselves according to the desires of others. Cosmetic surgery to augment the breasts increases every year and doubles every five years, according to Sarah Grogan in her book *Body Image*. First carried out in Japan in the 1950s, breast augmentation surgery using silicone implants became common in the United States in the 1960s, despite serious problems with rejection by the body's immune system. Today, more women prefer saline implants, which cause less damage if they leak.

Recently at a workshop, a woman apologized for hurting me when she hugged me. "It's these implants," she confessed. "They're hard as rocks. I've hated them ever since I got them." When I asked why she got them, she said it was her father's idea. "When I was fifteen, he leaned over and whispered in my ear on Christmas morning, 'Honey, maybe next year we can get you some new breasts for Christmas.' And that's just what he did. It costs $5,000 to undo it, and now I don't have the money," she said.

The body communicates information about the state of your life force in a predictable progression of increasing value, starting with intuition and moving through urge, discomfort, pain, chronic pain and disease. —ILA SARLEY

Our personal wounds and the World Wound are not separate.

—JOAN HALIFAX

135

Why is it that, despite serious health risks, over one million women in the United States have been coerced by a myriad of forces to alter the size and shape of their God-given breasts? What fear or desire lies beneath these decisions? Where do the messages come from that lead to them?

And why is it that breastfeeding, one of the miracles of the human body, is not embraced by every new mother? How did it happen that something so natural, so sacred, so healthy as breastfeeding could be upstaged by an industry profiting from man-made formula? If anything is a sacrament, breastfeeding is. "Take and eat of this, this is my body, this is my blood." It doesn't get more real, more grace-filled, more concretely sacramental than that, and yet who is there to pronounce its sacredness, if not those of us who sense the holy in that act of love, that deep well of nurturance?

We know the miracle of these bodies. We know that in these breasts, in these wombs, in these hearts and hands and hollows of ours, divine mysteries are occurring constantly. Why then do we accept another version of the Divine? Why do we continue to act as if our bodies are something other than holy? If we're going to transform our relationship to our bodies and reclaim the sacredness of our natural beings, we must wrestle with these questions.

Susan Brownmiller, in *Femininity,* explores the paradox for women of having breasts that on the one hand are private and hidden from view and on the other, exposed constantly as commodities for public consumption and entertainment:

The garden within is the sacred sanctuary where we connect with the Goddess, the deep Feminine, the underground source of female empowerment and expression.

—VICKI NOBLE

Woman's body is both the immanent and transcendent symbol of the power to give life, love, and pleasure.

—RIANE EISLER

136

No other part of the anatomy has such semi-public, intensely private status, and no other part of the body has such vaguely defined custodial rights. One learns to be selectively generous with breasts—this is the girl child's lesson—and through the breast iconography she sees all around her, she comes to understand that breasts belong to everybody, but especially to men. It is they who invent and refine their myths, who discuss breasts publicly, who criticize their failings as they extol their wonders, and who claim to have more need and intimate knowledge of them than a woman herself.[2]

How many times have we heard the expression "Anything more than a handful (or mouthful) is wasted?" Wasted on what? For whom? These are *our* breasts, *our* chalices of holy milk, *our* sources of erotic pleasure. They do not belong to others, they do not warrant judgment of any kind from any person, for they are part of *our* sacred beings.

Our souls entered into these bodies to accomplish their divine mission. One is nothing without the other. The Divine, being invisible, needs our bodies to become manifest in the world. As our breasts are containers of life-giving milk, our bodies are containers of life-giving spirit. They are sacred, and in order for us to connect with the Divine, to access its power, to experience its bliss, we have to humbly accept that. And we have to abandon, once and for all, the erroneous, small-minded, sacrilegious notion that the body is evil and keeps us separate from the Divine.

We are earth's organs and limbs; we are syllables God utters from his mouth.

—ANNIE DILLARD

The body is our connection to the Divine. It was made for pleasure, made for bliss. We have our five senses (and more yet to uncover) to taste, touch, see, hear, and smell the elegance of God in every thing we encounter. Our bodies and breasts are meant to be enjoyed, meant to feed and nourish and nurture in every way they can. Can we rejoice in their erotic power, their nurturing power? Can we honor them as sites of pleasure, sources of life?

How life-altering it might be for young girls if we honored their breast-budding with ceremony and ritual, celebrating the first signs of womanhood, witnessing in words and song, with poetry and pomp, the amazing marvel of these human bodies. How empowering to guide our young ones into womanhood with reverence and rejoicing, instead of the haunting silence that is the norm. What a gift it would be for us—as mothers, sisters, aunts, grandmothers—to create a sacred tradition of welcoming our young family members into a sisterhood of support and honor.

We know it's time to turn the tides. We've known for a long time that something is wrong about how this culture deals with the female body, particularly our breasts. We know it is dishonorable, if not sacrilegious. We know it hurts us on many levels. We know it leads to imbalances that are destructive and despicable, and for the most part, we feel powerless to change it.

But we can change ourselves and our attitudes, which in turn will change everything around us. We can begin to love ourselves, to stop colluding in negativity, to thank the Creator for the gift of our breasts and the pleasure they've given to us and to others.

The familiar life horizon has been outgrown; the old concepts, ideals, and emotional patterns no longer fit; the time for the passing of a threshold is at hand.

—Joseph Campbell

The accumulated darkness of the ages is dispelled at once by bringing light in, not by trying to chase the darkness out.

—Sri Aurobindo

A young friend wrote to me recently, "As a teenager, I learned of the women of one African tribe who would greet each other by cupping their own breasts with one or both hands. As adolescents, my friends and I adopted this gesture in jest, but it stuck. For us, two hands cupping both breasts meant it was a 'good day,' one hand cupping the same-sided breast was a general greeting, and when we would cup the opposite breast with one hand, it came to mean we needed 'carrying' that day—an extra hug, or note … even a shoulder to cry on."

For most of us, this would be an unimaginable act, but how powerful for these girls to have taken it on, to communicate so boldly and tenderly through the cupping of their breasts. They were not silenced by the culture; they were not ashamed of their young bodies; they were who they were, doing what they wanted, bound by no rules but their own. Liberated, like the poet Emily Dickinson, who wrote in 1862:

> *I'm ceded—I've stopped being Theirs—*
> *The name They dropped upon my face*
> *With water, in the country church*
> *I'm finished using, now.*

It is time for us to cede—to stop being theirs, and start being our own. Time for us to celebrate our bodies exactly as they are, to love our flesh that houses spirit. To look in the mirror and see in that image the luscious, loving beauty of the Great Mother herself. This is what it means to be well made and wonderful. May we praise our own geography at last.

God is the force within us experienced as our love for life.

—JOSEPH CHILTON
PEARCE

139

Before launching into this project, I had a "Divining the Body" dinner party. I invited twelve friends to come and engage in a conversation about our bodies. We talked into the wee hours, and by the end, I knew which body parts would become chapters of this book. After that session, Pene Bourk wrote this piece on the breasts, and I'm thrilled to include it here.

Breastuses

Penelope Bourk

In antiquity, Isis searched the breadth of Egypt, the length of the Nile, for the severed parts of her husband Osiris after his battle with the serpent Apophis. The phallus was all she found—the last remnant of her consort's earthly divinity.

When a woman loses her connection to her body, when a girl dissociates from her flesh and bones, who searches with her for what has been lost? How does she learn to gather up, to reassemble, to reinhabit the severed parts? To restore to her body her divinity? Breasts, for instance—or "breastuses" as my four brothers, their friends, and my father called them, my mother remaining entirely silent on the subject.

The statue of Artemis at Ephesus was a wonder of the ancient world. As "Potnia Theron," Queen of Wild Things, Artemis nursed the cosmos. Rows and rows of pendant breasts, clustered like grapes, hung from her chest, from neck to waist. The breasts of Artemis fostered the divine in the human, as well as in other creatures.

Yet for many women today, the breast has become a vestigial organ with respect to divinity, a mere appendix. Cancer has exacted many of our breasts. Among women who have retained their physical breasts, many have lost their connection to these fleshy wonders.

I began disowning my breasts long before carrying them had carved grooves in my shoulders. It began when my father told my mother it was time, and I had to shed my snuggy undershirt for a stiff cotton brassiere, which left the small of my back cold and bare. I remember the trip with my mother to the department store. She and I had never been the mother-daughter pair that loved shopping together, but this trip was even more brusque than usual. When we reached "Foundations," my mother handed me over awkwardly to an old woman in a black dress with a measuring tape around her neck, who looked at me, then at my mother, sternly over her spectacles, and said to my mother, rather meanly, I thought, "About time." I left strapped into a C cup, the old woman muttering in a sinister cackle, "You aren't done yet, dearie. You'll be back."

As I think about it now, it is almost archetypal, the old crone, the mother, and the maiden. It could have been an Artemisian celebration, full of wisdom and delight. But my mother had grown up without a mother, had no words for what we were doing, and no inkling of ceremony. When the brassiere hooked closed, constricting my chest, when I stood up (the old woman had instructed me to "fall into it"), and my little pools projected out suddenly like warheads in front of me, only then did my loss hit me. Womanhood would be an armed prison.

Embodiment means we no longer say, I had this experience; we say, I am this experience.

—SUE MONK KIDD

141

My experience with boys only exacerbated the severance. My first boyfriend, when my parents weren't home, would plead to sit on the couch and "just touch." For an hour, he would try to fondle my little prisoners. After a few months, when he'd figured out how to undo the four-hook bra with one hand, the boneless blobs plopped down on my chest. I was mortified.

What puzzles me now is why I didn't simply say no and walk away. Instead I stayed. My breasts might as well have been dead dough. He could knead the dough balls forever and they would not rise—for my breasts were already a ruin. I'd abandoned them or rather they'd been expropriated the previous year. They were no longer mine. Nor were they the only parts of myself I abandoned.

I remember one day as a fifteen-year-old, witnessing in silence what seemed to me a horror. A year after her partial mastectomy, never spoken about as other than a woman's problem, my mother gave birth to her fifth child. My mother, always frugal, was determined to nurse, which she did, always alone, in the dark, perched on the edge of the big bed in her room. One day she asked me to bring the diapers up and fold them on the bed beside her. For the first time, I saw her struggling to insert the nipple of her misshapen breast into the baby's mouth. I saw the vicious, sickle-shaped scar, an inch wide, six inches long, a deep burgundy—darker than the nipple that hung from the remainder of her breast. I gasped. My mother was hurt, I suppose, by my shock. She gave up nursing not long after that. There may have been no relationship between my gasp and her weaning the baby to the bottle, but whenever I passed my brother, lying in his crib alone with the bottle propped, I mourned.

High school continued the nightmare. Boys would push pencils through my sweaters, as if at a target. In Home Economics, we had to make a dress. The fashion was for snug shirtwaists, and the teacher measured me for the pattern. "That can't be right," she muttered. "You may have to add a gusset under the arm." I was mortified. I didn't add a gusset. I wore my new dress to a party, lifted my arm to dance, and the underarm area of the dress ripped right up to my shoulder.

I could have amputated the breasts right then and there for shame. When I came home in tears, my mother said, "Gusset it, and get yourself on a diet." I shredded the dress, but the self-disgust was harder to shed. And my breasts kept growing regardless, hanging from my chest like twin missiles pointed at the whole world.

It was nursing my own child that finally reconciled me to my actual breasts. My firstborn's birth was so traumatic that he slept through his entire time at the hospital. My husband and I brought the two-day-old infant home without my ever having nursed. We were alone there, with no doula, no mother of the new mother, no mother-in-law, just me with my horror and detachment from the breast, and my husband, an only child, who'd never held a baby in his life, let alone witnessed a woman nursing. When the infant finally woke, he was starving. But he was not a natural nurser. He would not take the areola of the breast in his mouth and latch on. Rather he took only the little nub of a nipple and gummed it. Imagine his shock and mine when the milk let down, the double-D breasts opening like a full-on shower nozzle, milk

I finally realized that being grateful to my body was key to giving more love to myself.

—OPRAH WINFREY

143

flowing not only from the nipple but squirting from pore-like openings all around the areola, into his eyes, his nose, as well as through the nipple like a river into his tiny mouth. Our poor son almost drowned!

It was later that evening, when the feeling of the milk letting down had become familiar, when the baby learned to take more of the breast into his rosebud mouth, when we'd found an old rocking chair, that my son and I could relax, knowing hungry and drowning were not necessarily one and the same. Only then did I feel the breast reconnect to me.

Nursing was my opening to a body that had been sealed off from me, like a body in a cave, its mouth covered by an immovable stone. From that subtle thread of connection to my interior, joining breast to navel to uterus to vagina, spread a renewed capacity to inhabit myself and to re-sexualize in the best sense, to feel.

Our lovers, male and female, and our infants can help us in the reconstruction of the divine body. Yet it is we women who must gather up our lost parts. It is we women who must offer the sanctity of the body back to ourselves, to one another, and to the people we love, who love us. As the word became flesh, so the flesh becomes spirit, which becomes again, through writing, shared words of understanding and works of love. What if it is not necessary to lose the divine body, as many of us have, or to struggle alone so long to repair it? Would that it were the indomitable, the natural, the outspoken and championed birthright of all, universally, to affirm the body—to affirm our bodies—as our spiritual inheritance, the legacy to humans from the Divine.

REFLECTION

After your bath or shower, pull a chair up in front of a full-length mirror, keep the lights low, light a few candles, sit down, and look at yourself. Imagine that your soul took on this very body in order to help it do its work in the world. Imagine that the invisible Divine is using your body to be made visible in the world, and it is the perfect shape to hold its radiant energy.

Starting with your face, rub lotion over all your body, thanking each part one at a time for all the ways it has served you and helped you share the Divine with the world.

EXERCISE

Invite a circle of women whom you know and trust to a celebration. Let them know it is a ritual to honor the Great Mother and the sacredness of the breasts. Have each woman bring her favorite comfort food for sharing and something that she created for the altar (a photograph, a poem, a recipe, an afghan).

Assemble these items in advance: one white taper and candle holder and one small chunk of sculpting clay for each person (Fimo, Sculpey, or Premo are all available in local crafts stores); one large white candle for the altar; altar cloth and items for the altar that represent earth, air, fire, and water; and portable player and music CDs or audiotapes such as *Returning* by Jennifer Berezan, *The Yearning* by Tim Wheater and Michael Hoppé, or *From the Goddess/O Great Spirit* by On Wings of Song and Robert Gass (available from www.ladyslipper.org).

Create a space that will allow you to sit in a circle, or go to a place in nature where you can form a circle and have some privacy.

Set up your altar and place in the center a large white candle representing the Great Mother. Have a white candle available for each woman present. Put on some music and take three to five minutes to give everyone a chance to close their eyes, breathe deeply, and get fully in their bodies.

After a few minutes, with the music playing softly, guide them in this meditation:

> Remember back to the time when your breasts started budding and feel again how that felt. Remember how old you were, if you were comfortable or not with this new development, if anyone talked to you about this. (Pause for a few moments and allow time for these memories to surface.) Remember how things changed for you as you grew into your new womanhood, how you felt about looking in the mirror, how you talked with your friends about this new happening, how you started relating to boys differently. (Pause for reflection.)
>
> Remember what it felt like to touch yourself when you bathed, and what it felt like to have your breasts touched by another. Remember the joys or the sorrows that came with these experiences. Remember the conflicts that arose, the struggles you had within yourself because of what you had been taught about how to behave, what was right and wrong. (Pause for reflection.)
>
> Remember the times when you felt most free with your body, when you rejoiced in the pleasures it could give and receive. Remember the sweet, tender touching with a loved one. Remember the kisses, the fondling, the joy of giving yourself and another the sensual pleasures of your physical being. Remember the miracle of being touched, being loved, being a gift to another, and receiving the gift of another's body. (Pause for reflection.)
>
> Remember that your soul entered into this body to do its work in the world, to become a manifestation of the Divine on this earth. Remember that the Great Mother is coming through you at all times,

entering you with every breath, surging through your body with every pulse, feeding your spirit with her own abundant breasts, sustaining you every day with food, air, water, pleasure, love—always there for you, always there in you, always there by you. Always, always there.

Imagine yourself at the breast of the Great Mother, in her arms, on her lap, safe, nourished, comforted and know you are made in her image—*your* breasts the source of comfort and nourishment, *your* breasts the source of pleasure and joy, *your* breasts the merging of heaven and earth, mother and child, divine and human.

You are a sacred vessel, a chalice filled with divine energy. Your breasts are symbols of eternal nurturing, of the never-ending flow of love from the Mother to you, from you to the world, from this world back to the source. Your breasts are holy. Your breasts contain the Milky Way. Your breasts are beautiful, blessed, and full of grace. So be it and blessed be. (Pause a moment.) Take a few moments to give thanks for your breasts, for your entire body, and then open your eyes when you are ready.

Once the women have all opened their eyes, ask who would like to share a story with the group. It could be a story about what images came to mind during the meditation, a story from her past that relates to her breasts, or a story about the item she brought to the altar. Before each woman speaks, have her light her own candle from the source, the Great Mother candle.

After everyone has shared a story, close the circle and enjoy eating all the comfort food that everyone brought.

WRITING EXERCISE

The poet Ruth Krauss once wrote a marvelous poem about the breast, and writing teacher June Gould invited her class to create their own breast poems in the style of Krauss. Read the following poem by Toni Farkas, and then write your own version in a similar style. Start each line with "This breast" and complete it with any statement that comes to mind. Feel free to have fun with this!

After Ruth Krauss

This breast—suck up to it!
This breast quivers on contact
This breast floats slowly across the China Sea dipping its hand in the blue-grey water
This breast is compost, grapefruit peels and rotting meat
This breast suckles wolves and fills the marble basin of the Fontana di Trevi with its pearly liquid
This breast was the envy of Marilyn Monroe's breast
This breast is strip-mines, diamonds and off-shore oil rigs
It is questions, peaches and the slums outside Rio
This breast is your mother's face before she was born
This breast speaks Swahili
This breast can shade caravans in the Sahara, fill the sails of ships rounding Cape Horn and do triple pirouettes
This breast is hungry and wants a soft-serve ice-cream cone
This breast holds warriors in its arms and licks their wounds with its speckled tongue
This breast drops down flat when not in use and can be folded in thirds like puff pastry
This breast is a bullet and the wrinkled clutching of a newborn baby
This breast points its nipple at a star, then another, then another until all are lit in the sparkling net of black sky.

Claiming Our Voice

Of all that God has shown me
I can speak just the smallest word,
Not more than a honey bee
Takes on his foot
From an overspilling jar.
—Mechtilde of Magdeburg

When my mother was living in upstate New York, she invited several friends over for a Christmas party. Since there was a fireplace in her newly rented apartment, she gathered lots of newspapers, put in some kindling, topped that off with some seasoned logs, and lit the fire just as the first guests began to arrive.

There was a great flurry of welcoming, shaking off snowboots, putting on slippers, hanging hats and coats on the coat rack. Lots of hugging, oohing, and aahing over the tree and carrying plates of food and fudge into the kitchen. Nobody noticed that the house was filling up with smoke until they all started coughing. By that time, the smoke was so thick they could hardly see each other. It was then my mother realized she had never opened the flue.

Our throats are like the flue. When we don't open them up, speak our truths, blurt out our feelings as they arise, the fire within turns to smoke. The throat chakra is our will center. It is known in Hinduism as the *visuddha,* which means "purification." It is the place where the wisdom and feelings of our heart and lower chakras synthesize with the energies from above to be released as something new into the world. Its healthfulness is related to how honestly we express ourselves. If we lie, or refuse to speak authentically, we constrict its energy, violating the body and the spirit. If we express our truths fearlessly, open the flue fully, we increase the flow of energy throughout our entire being.

When Tibetans talk about the human being, they talk about the body, the voice, and the mind. The location for body is in the head; for voice, in the throat; and for mind, in the heart. Our voice—the intermediary between the subtle realm of mind and the physical realm of body—bridges the immaterial and material. It is the voice that translates spirit into matter and matter into spirit.

Most liturgies are sung or chanted, whether in the Eastern or Western traditions. The mantras of Hinduism are sacred sounds conserved in the ancient languages. There are special sounds for certain illnesses, different mantras to bring one into a state of clarity or emptiness. The mystics of Islam, the Sufis, combine mantric chanting with rhythmic movements of the body, bringing themselves into states of transcendental ecstasy. In the Roman Catholic tradition, we were always told by the nuns that "singing was praying twice." In the convent, a kind of entrainment or spiritual resonance occurred when the whole community chanted psalms and intoned prayers together. Changing from speaking to singing or chanting transforms *unity* from a concept to an experience. Healing happens in the presence of this kind of sound-making. We become *sound* in body and spirit.

Our heart's desire is to be heard and understood, to transmit and receive the truth as we perceive it. We speak our choices

To be properly expressed, a thing must proceed from within, moved by its form.

—MEISTER ECKHART

150

with our voices, and every choice we make—to speak or not to speak—has a consequence on an energetic level. When I worked in corporate environments, I remember sitting in business meetings, wanting to say something, but failing to speak out of fear of what others would think, fear that what I had to say wasn't smart enough or worth the time and attention of others. I'd hold back and by the end of the meeting I'd be exhausted. I'd have a headache. I'd be angry and negative and disenchanted.

When I think of it now, I see that it was my own inauthenticity that caused the distress in my body and emotions. I had closed the flue and suffocated my own fire. And not only that, I had deprived the others of my good energy and insights, a piece of truth that might have sparked a new idea.

For whatever reason, many of us have this fear of expressing. We have endless conversations with ourselves about why we shouldn't say what we're feeling or thinking. *It might hurt someone's feelings. I'm being selfish. If I don't have something good to say, I shouldn't say anything at all. Everyone else knows more than me, so I'll let them talk.* And oddly enough, we believe these excuses are worth our silence. Someone has convinced us of the validity of not talking. Somewhere along the line, we've picked up the belief that it is virtuous to be silent, when the exact opposite is often true.

It is virtuous to let our energy and words flow out of us. It is virtuous to speak our feelings, to be true to ourselves and others. It is virtuous to speak out for justice, for peace, for those who have no voice. There comes a time when silence is betrayal, and that time is upon us. Our world is in a mess because we

This hour in history needs a dedicated circle of transformed nonconformists.

—MARTIN LUTHER KING JR.

151

have not spoken our truths. Our health is suffering because we do not speak. It is our speaking that heals us, that leads us from the murky waters of wondering into the clarity of awareness. We can only know ourselves through the process of self-revelation, and that is the reason we are here.

When I was making my peace pilgrimage around the world, the whole question of speaking versus nonspeaking came to light when I was visiting a Catholic-Buddhist monastery in Japan. It was a small retreat farm that had been hand-built by Father Oshida, a Dominican priest who left the comforts of urban life behind to create an environment for simple living, communal sharing, physical labor, and meditation.

Ten people lived in this community, and they gathered in the chapel every morning before dawn for Lauds and meditation. We sat in a circle around the altar, which was merely a cloth on the floor in the center of the room with a chalice, candle, plate, and water bowl on it. After Mass and breakfast, everyone worked silently in the fields during the day. At five o'clock, we stopped for Vespers, more meditation, dinner, and an evening talk by Father Oshida. At night, I immersed myself in Buddhist literature, trying to get an understanding of this spiritual tradition.

After a few days, I was in a quandary. While my Western Christian roots inspired this pilgrimage with its "go and teach all nations" mandate, the Buddhist way seemed to be more about silence and meditation. I wondered if I should give up the whole idea of making this pilgrimage and just go home, sit quietly in meditation, and be at peace knowing that all things were unfolding perfectly.

One night during his spiritual teaching, Father Oshida asked me if I had any questions. I told him about my confusion and the emotional reverberations I was feeling as I tried to reconcile Christianity and Buddhism in my heart. "Here I am out here trying to make a difference in the world, but being here makes me feel like I should just go home and try to make a difference in myself. What am I supposed to *do*? What would Buddha or Jesus do?" I blurted out, with tears in my eyes.

"The point is not to convert the world, but to convert our souls to God," said Father Oshida. "You don't have to ask what Jesus or Buddha would do. You are an incarnation of the same force. Experience this. Go beyond what you have learned and live from your heart. Follow that call and you will have the answers to all your questions." That night, on my little cot in my simple cell, it occurred to me that I didn't have to choose between Christianity and Buddhism. I needed to synthesize them, incorporate both into my practice, so I would be a whole that contained the two—silence *and* speaking, meditation *and* action. My pilgrimage then became an act of living prayer. It wasn't about changing the world or changing myself. It was about experiencing myself as an incarnation of a great force and being as true to my heart as I could be.

The Indian mystic Ramana Maharshi says that "our own self-realization is the greatest service we can render the world." We have been led to believe that service is about doing for others, but service that matters comes from our essence, and that essence must be uttered out of us. We find ourselves in the expression of our selves, in our engagement with others. It's who we are that touches people, even more than what we do. In order to be of use, then, we need to show up, be present emotionally, share what we have in the process of sharing who we are.

Audre Lorde wrote in *Sinister Wisdom*:

> We have been socialized to respect fear more than
> our own needs for language and definition, and
> while we wait in silence for the final luxury of

Prayer ones the soul to God.

—JULIAN OF NORWICH

Power is the ability to take one's place in whatever discourse is essential to action and the right to have one's part matter.

—CAROLYN HEILBRUN

fearlessness, the weight of that silence will choke us.... The transformation of silence into language and action is an act of self-revelation and that always seems fraught with danger. We fear the very visibility without which we also cannot truly live ... and that visibility which makes us most vulnerable is that which is also the source of our greatest strength.[1]

The final luxury of fearlessness never comes. There is always a consequence to our revelations. We speak. Others react. If we live in fear of what others think about us, we will be frozen in place, unloved and unlovable, for what can others grab on to, what can they be attracted to, if we do not send our spirits out? If we do not speak out now in defense of our Mother Earth, in defense of nonviolence, in defense of the hundreds of animal and plant species becoming extinct, what will be left for those to come? In his book *Risking,* David Viscott writes: "If you have no anxiety, the risk you face is probably not worthy of you. Only risks you have outgrown don't frighten you."

It is a risky business to live out loud. It takes courage to plunge into our depths in search of our own light and healing power, for most of us have learned to look outside ourselves for this. In *The Courage to Heal,* psychologist Ely Fuller is quoted as saying, "If you enter into healing, be prepared to lose everything. Healing is a ravaging force to which nothing seems sacred or inviolate. As my original pain releases itself in healing, it rips to shreds the structures and foundations I built

> We are not to fear the strangeness we feel. The future enters into us long before it happens.
>
> —RAINER MARIA RILKE

154

in weakness and ignorance. I am experiencing the bizarre miracle of reincarnating, more lucidly than at birth, in the same lifetime."

The healing of my own spiritual misperceptions involved tremendous anxiety and the ripping away of structures that I felt my whole life depended upon. When I was a young postulant in a religious community taking my first theology class, a Jesuit priest stood in front of the room and asked each of us what we believed about God. One by one we recited our beliefs, recalling sentences from the Baltimore Catechism about who God was, why He made us, what He wanted from us. The priest challenged those beliefs one by one, tore them apart, belittled them as nothing more than memorized statements, reflections of someone else's authority.

"What do *you* believe?" he shouted. "I don't want to hear what you've memorized. I want to hear what you feel. Who *is* this God of yours?" His words were a hammer, shattering our naïve images of God. I started to cry, wondering how he could do this. How could he stand there and destroy God when we'd just given our whole lives over to God, left behind everything to *be with* God? It was a moment of devastating loss, incomprehensible sadness. I felt as if everything I believed in, everything on which I had based my life, was no longer true. The silence in the room was deafening; the void I felt, terrifying. We sat there, thirty of us, for what seemed an eternity, reckoning with the obliteration of God as we had known him.

Finally the priest broke the silence. "You must come to know what is true about God from your own experience," he said.

You choose the fact you like best; yet none of them are false, and it is all one story.

—URSULA LE GUIN

155

"Arrive at a faith that is deeper than your learning, one that is rooted in your ultimate concern and rises up from the nature of who you are." He said that we needed to let go of *beliefs* and conjure up a faith of commitment, one that rises up from within ourselves, from a deep awareness of our own godliness. For the first time, I understood the biblical paradox about losing our lives in order to find them.

It was no longer sufficient to repeat what others had been telling me all along about God. It was time to look deep within to discover what I believed from my own lived experience. It was time to speak for myself, *from* my self, about the most profound mystery of all. And for this, I was ill-prepared, having learned since childhood *what* to think, but not *how* to think.

It took the whole semester to find my voice in the midst of all the other voices in my head, and it was a painful and painstaking process. I was so afraid of being wrong. How could I possibly trust my own feelings in the matter? How could I dare stand up and share my faith, my ultimate concerns and commitments, without the certainty of a catechism behind me? In time, my knees stopped shaking, my voice stopped trembling, and I grew accustomed to the power and grace of speaking my truth.

And while there was a consequence to that practice—I was eventually dismissed from that order—I realize today that it was the greatest gift I was ever offered. Not only did I learn to look within for the answers I sought, I found God in myself and have never since needed to look any further.

There are no enlightened people. There is only enlightened activity.

—SUZUKI ROSHI

156

Letting go of old voices and notions of authority is a process we all engage in as we move toward the inner light. On his deathbed, Buddha said: "Do not accept what you hear by report, do not accept tradition. Do not accept a statement because it is found in our books, nor because it is in accord with your beliefs, nor because it is the saying of your teacher. Be lamps unto yourselves." And as writer Colin Wilson once remarked, "Turning on the light is easy if you know where the switch is."

In my workshops around the country, we do a ritual that helps us find that switch. Participants are invited to make a list of all the inherited negative voices in their heads, things they've been told about themselves since they were young that have kept them from believing in themselves and actualizing their potential. Within a few minutes, they create lists of dozens of harsh voices from the past. "You're so ugly, you'll never get a man." "What makes you think anyone is interested in what you have to say?" "You don't have a creative bone in your body." "You'll never amount to anything, you're so stupid." And on and on.

Once the lists are completed, we put a candle in the middle of the room, turn down the lights, and form a circle. Then one by one, we read our litanies of sorrow. As each one reads her list, sometimes crying her way through it, the others bear witness. Many nod their heads, as if to say, yes, I've heard that one, too. Often there are gasps at the bewildering cruelty, astonishment at the harshness of words uttered so carelessly to the young and vulnerable.

Once the litany is completed, every woman makes her way around the circle to get a hug from the others. A sigh of relief fills the room. We have let it out. We have released the demons, exorcised the voices that have held us back, taking the first step in the long journey back to ourselves. Now we are ready to claim the voice that is truly our own. Simone de Beauvoir wrote that "it is in the recognition of the genuine conditions of our lives that we gain strength to act and our motivation for change." Telling our stories is the road to recognition; it is the pathway into ourselves and the bridge across our own barriers.

In order to break down and transcend the old voices, we must acknowledge them, bring them into the light of day. When we share these voices in a group with others, we see how many of them we have in common. We understand that the problem is not internal, but external—caused by a culture that is invested more in our silence than in our self-actualization, more in our buying than our being.

In *Voice Lessons: On Becoming a (Woman) Writer,* Nancy Mairs writes, "Our stories utter one another.... If I do my job, the books I write vanish before your eyes. I invite you into the house of my past, and *the threshold you cross leads you into your own.*" This is what happens when we share our stories. They not only help us clarify and understand the particularities of our lives, they help others enter more fully into the experience of their lives. When we acknowledge our vulnerabilities, our victories and failures, our fears and wildest dreams, we give others permission to do the same. In our speaking is our freedom, our future—for our lives grow from the seeds of our stories. As we speak, so does life unfold.

It is hardly possible to read the newspapers, listen to the news, open ourselves to information about the environment, about the world's children and the legacy we're leaving them without our hearts breaking open. The violence of it all feels so out of control that we're tempted into silence. Asking the same questions, facing the same imbalanced, outmoded power structures, we feel impotent, listless, agitated. *What can I possibly do?* is a question that haunts us.

Security is mostly a superstition. It does not exist in nature, nor do the children of humans as a whole experience it. Avoiding danger is not safer in the long run than outright exposure. Life is either a daring adventure or nothing.

—HELEN KELLER

We are more isolated now than ever before, hardly aware of our neighbors' names, much less their passions or politics. And the spiritual influence of the East has quieted us, altered us. The "go and teach all nations" mandate is giving way to a "be still and see that all is well" mode, and in many ways that is good. We do not need to evangelize, but we do need to actualize—our potential, our ability to take a stand against violence and wrongdoing. We need to activate our faith, to breathe its essence into the world, to serve as architects and artists of a global transformation. We are the originators of a new living faith, creators of new sacred texts, rewriting the narrative of our time.

And how do we transform the old, give birth to the new? We speak out. We do one thing. We come together in circles. We say what is true for us, how we feel about things. We listen to each other's voices, and in the process of sharing, a sense of heartfulness rises up, neurons in the brain cavort in delight, and a higher consciousness surfaces that holds the answers for the future.

A great intelligence is arising. We can feel it in the air. We can hear it and see it in the voices of our children. And we can help it along by being conscious, by watching the workings of our mind and canceling out thoughts that do not serve us. We can help it along by embodying our faith, feeling our feelings, tuning in to our heart's desire.

Scientific research at the Institute of HeartMath has proven that we have the power to affect our own DNA. Feelings of

Each time I begin work on a new piece of writing,... I confront within myself extreme dread that the subjectivity that I have fought so hard to claim will not assert itself. Paralyzed by the fear that I will not be able to name or speak words that fully articulate my experience or the collective reality of struggling black people, I am tempted to be silent. —**BELL HOOKS** love, gratitude, and appreciation cause our DNA strands to relax and unwind. When this happens, we can access more codes, achieve higher levels of creativity and consciousness. Emotions like anger, fear, and frustration cause these strands to tighten up and switch off certain codes. When we allow ourselves to dwell in these emotional territories, we diminish our own potential to think creatively and access the full spectrum of our imagination.

We create our reality by choosing it with our feelings. Emotions are the evolution of consciousness through our bodies. As we express them, we feed, heal, and cleanse the body. As we learn to feel our feelings, define ourselves from the inside out, we learn the art of creating ourselves. In listening to our own and each other's stories, we begin to see where we've been inhibited, how our choices have been compromised, our creativity stifled. We begin to see the ways we are bound by tradition, nudged into our "appropriate roles" by industries that provoke our insecurities to get us shopping for antidotes.

Writer and suffragist Florida Scott-Maxwell says, "You need only claim the events of your life to make yourself yours. When you truly possess all you have been and done, which may take some time, you are fierce with reality." How do we possess what we have been and done? How do we claim the events of our lives? We *examine* our lives, mine them for the wisdom gained through experience, and find ways to share the nuggets of that wisdom. It's not being a know-it-all. It's not acting as if

i keep hearing

tree talk

water words

and i keep knowing

what they mean.

—LUCILLE CLIFTON

160

we have all the answers. It's simply a matter of sharing our feelings, our insights, our new thoughts and questions about the life we're engaged in. That's where our meaning comes from. It's the source of the intimacy we hunger for. It is the way we live in communion instead of isolation.

Opening our throat flues causes a great internal combustion, energizing us for the huge and wonderful lives we came here to live. A great power is released when we open this channel, letting the spirit from above fan the fire below. It is the place where mind and heart mingle, where new life is created and uttered into the world. It is a birthplace of healing, for ourselves and others, for our planet and its creatures—a place of lullabies and poems, of psalms and songs. May we find the voices unique to us and sound them bravely into this world of need.

REFLECTION

In the Islamic tradition, people are encouraged to let their words pass through "the three gates" before speaking: *Is it true? Is it kind? Is it necessary?* If it doesn't pass this test, it ought not be spoken. What are your feelings about this teaching? Would it be difficult for you to follow?

EXERCISE

Spend a day paying close attention to everything that comes out of your mouth. Listen carefully to your words and notice if you are saying things you would not want to come true. Practice speaking as if your life were a materialization of your words. Do this as often as you can.

Exercise

Get a book of poetry out of the library, or go buy a book of poems by Mary Oliver, Billy Collins, Rumi, Hafiz, or Kabir. Read one poem a day out loud before you get out of bed. Notice how this makes you feel.

Writing Exercise

Read the following poem from Sandy Supowit's book, *Halves of Necessity.* When you are finished, write a poem of your own that includes the lines:

"These days I hear …" (What kinds of things are you hearing these days? What are people talking about?)

"My body has become …" (Your body is always responding to the words it's exposed to. What has your body become in response to the words/sounds/voices it has taken in?)

"I try to stop myself from …" (You may have an inner voice that is trying to keep you safe, healthy, conscious of your choices. Is it guiding you to refrain from anything?)

Glossolalia

> Though I speak with the tongues of men and of angels, and have not charity, I am become as sounding brass, or a tinkling cymbal.
> **—1 Corinthians 13:1**

These days I hear
you wear a Jesus bracelet,
talk to saints, talk to angels.
I hear you still read
the Bible every night
as if it were a battlefield
and you the Christian soldier
marching through.
Your body, always excess
baggage, has become a bent
burden that bends you now
in perpetual prayer
even when you stand up straight.
On my knees, you used to say,
I am closer to heaven,
another case, I think,
of not being careful
what you wish for.
I try to stop myself
from preaching,
try to keep from quoting
your scripture about faith
without works, about being swift
to hear and slow to speak,
but here I am, rambling
on along with you,
each of us speaking
in a different tongue,
not one word of it holy.

Let's Hear It for the Ears

> You are the conch who having heard the ocean all your
> life tucks forever that perpetual motion in your calcium ear.
>
> **—Judi Beach**

One year, on the way to a writer's conference in upstate New York, I was having dinner with friends in a small Italian restaurant. Just as we were finishing, three men walked in with guns. They ordered us into the kitchen and told us to lie on the floor with our eyes shut. They instructed the men to take out their wallets and put them by their sides. Then they told the women to take off all their jewelry and put it by their purses. When everyone had done this, they came around and took everyone's money and jewelry as we lay there frozen, in fear for our lives.

Once they had collected our belongings, one of them took the owner into the office while the others guarded us to be sure no one moved or looked up. I remember a moment when I had an image of all of us from above, as if I was looking down from the ceiling. I didn't feel fear or panic, but I remember a huge tear falling from my right eye as I looked on this scene feeling a terrible sorrow that as a human race we'd come to this. I didn't realize then that I had left my body, but when I got to the conference the next day, it was clear that a part of me was missing. I felt disassociated, remote, numb. In the midst of that trauma, it seemed my soul had left, and I had to do something to get it back.

One of the presenters at the conference was a longtime friend and teacher who had worked with shamans in several cultures around the world. Eleanor took me to a bench on the grassy quad of the college campus and told me to relax and close my eyes. As I did, she began to circle round me, chanting the same sounds over and over—heya heya aya aya, heya heya aya aya—shaking a rattle as she went. She circled and circled, chanting and rattling, and I lost myself in the ancient sounds, transported to another place and time.

At one point, she placed the rattle in my hand, and with eyes still closed, I continued the rattling as she circled and chanted. My body rocked with the beat of our sounds until they came to an end, culminating in silence. I don't know how much real time had passed, but I felt I had journeyed beyond all barriers of time and space, mesmerized by the sound of rattle and chant.

When I opened my eyes and looked at the rattle, I was astonished. Though it had felt in my hands like an ancient, earthy instrument, like a healing gourd filled with seeds, it was in fact a plastic rattle, bright yellow and orange, bought for a child at Toys 'R' Us. Like a cosmic jolt, the sight of that rattle hurtled me back to the present moment, back from the land of soul, back from the timeless place to the park bench, the green grass, the singing birds, where the two of us laughed till we cried. And in the journey back, so came my soul.

Sound is the primordial substance of the universe. Every creation story begins with sound. Every sacred text names sound as the source, the heart of all existence. In the beginning was the word, then came light. The ancient alchemical formula for creation is "sound plus intention." The word *universe* means "one song." It's no wonder we're in love with music. It's where we came from. It's what we are.

> The body is held together by sound—the presence of disease indicates that some sounds have gone out of tune.
>
> —DEEPAK CHOPRA

165

Before Einstein clarified that matter and energy were two different forms of the same thing, the German philosopher Goethe had referred to sacred architecture as frozen music, giving us a metaphor to understand the mystery of our own bodies. Einstein said it like this: "We may therefore regard matter as being constituted by the regions of Space in which the field is extremely intense.... There is no place in this new kind of physics both for the field and matter, for the field is the only reality." We are the field, only intensely so. We are slowed-down sound and light waves, a walking bundle of frequencies, tuned to the music of the cosmos. We are souls dressed up in sacred, biochemical garments, and our bodies are the instruments through which our souls play their music.

When we're in tune with the heavens, in service to our soul's mission, we feel an inner harmony. We're in balance, resonating to the vibrations of the earth as an embryo resonates to the heartbeat of the mother. Our sound, then, the sound of our life, is a beautiful tone with a majestic timbre, a perfect pitch, and the vibrations emanating from us are crystal-clear waves of energy. As soloists, we're virtuosos, music to the ears of everyone around.

When we're out of balance, what happens inside and around us is dissonance and discord. The beautiful melody we are meant to be becomes the scrape of fingernails on a chalkboard. It's not an attitude adjustment we need, it's an energy adjustment, a frequency change, and we can use sound to correct ourselves and rebalance our energy. Intuitively, we all know this. Every time we choose which CD we're going to listen to, our

> The sky and its stars make music in you.
>
> —DENDERAH TEMPLE
> WALL INSCRIPTION,
> EGYPT

decision is based on energy. We know the power of music, and we apply it accordingly. Our bodies know what they need, and if we need to calm down, we don't go for hip hop. Nor would we play John Philip Sousa at a wake or Bach at a prom. When Eleanor came to help me through the trauma of the robbery, she knew the healing power of rattles and chants, and that's what she brought to heal me.

Deepak Chopra tells us that atoms, cells, and tissues are bound together by invisible threads made of faint vibrations, referred to as "primordial sound" in Ayurveda, the traditional medicine of India. These tiny vibrations hold our DNA together and are the strongest force in nature. Trauma, illness, or accidents can alter our DNA sequences, and in that case, Chopra writes, "Ayurveda tells us to apply a specifically chosen primordial sound, like a mold or template slipped over the disturbed sounds pushing them back into line, not physically, but by repairing the sequence of sound at the heart of every cell."[1] Painful emotions that get locked in our body as a result of trauma can be released in many cases by certain sounds that bring them back to their original resonance.

Jonathan Goldman, director of the Sound Healers Association and author of *Healing Sounds,* writes about the power of sound to rearrange molecular structure, change the rhythm of our brain waves, and alter our heartbeat and respiration. "Everything in the universe is in a state of vibration, including every part of our body. When we are in a state of health, all the parts are vibrating in harmony. If one part begins to vibrate at a different rate, this is what we know as disease.

> Cells can be changed, activated and stimulated by sound and music because every cell within the body is pulsing a signal, is giving a sound. And that sound is life itself. Without that sound there is no life.
>
> —SIR PETER GUY MANNERS, MD

167

One of the basic ways of healing the physical body with sound is to project the correct resonant frequency of the organ, or whatever is out of harmony, back into the body."[2]

Transformational use of sound goes back to our ancient roots. It is considered the oldest form of healing, and it played a predominant role in the early teachings of the Greeks, Chinese, East Indians, Tibetans, Egyptians, North American Indians, Mayans, and Aztecs. Knowledge of sound was a highly refined science based on the understanding of vibration as the primary causative form of the universe. All the ancient mystery schools taught their students the use of sound as a creative and healing force. By the time Egypt built the pyramids and sphinxes, there were organized choruses of twelve thousand voices and orchestras of six hundred pieces. Some historians and sound specialists believe it was through their use of directed and controlled sound that much of the heaviest labor was accomplished on the pyramids.

David Lubman, an acoustical engineer, believes that the Maya may have built their pyramids to create specific sound effects. He found that if you clap your hands in front of the 1,100-year-old Temple of Kukulcan, in the ancient Mayan city of Chichen Itza, the pyramid answers in the voice of the sacred quetzal bird. "I have heard echoes in my life, but this was really strange," says Lubman in a *National Geographic* article. A handclap at the base of Kukulcan's staircase generates what Lubman calls a "chirped echo"—a *chir-roop* sound that first ascends and then falls, like the cry of the native quetzal.

I have heard that the body listens to rhythms the mind can't even hear. The wind and the sunset are like a dog whistle to the bones, but the mind is deaf to their high, clear missive.

—JOHN LEE

The elusive quetzal, also known as the *kuk,* inhabits the cloud forests of Central America, and its iridescent feathers were among the most precious commodities in Mesoamerica. To the Maya and Aztecs, the quetzal's emerald green tail feathers were more valuable than gold.

At Kukulcan, Lubman made recordings of the echo and compared them with recordings of the quetzal from Cornell University's ornithology lab. "They matched perfectly. I was stunned," Lubman says. "The Temple of Kukulcan chirps like a kuk." Lubman envisions Mayan priests facing a crowd at Kukulcan and clapping. The pyramid would then "answer" in the voice of the quetzal, a messenger of the Gods.[3]

Looking upward, astronomer Johannes Kepler attempted to find common rules between music and movement in the solar system and to explain the harmony of the world. He saw the planets moving around the sun "to a single cosmic rhythm," according to Frank Wilczek and Betsy Devine in *Longing for the Harmonies.* Kepler's ideas were rooted in Pythagoras's theory that the universe is built upon number and that the workings of the world are governed by relations of harmony. Both men believed that music is associated with the motion of the planets and both used the phrase *music of the spheres* to describe the interaction. In *Harmonices Mundi,* published in 1619, Kepler derived his theory of musical harmony and then his cosmology of the heavens and the earth, allotting musical intervals and musical motion to the planets. Recently, scientists using advanced mathematical principles based on the orbital velocities of the planets have equated different sounds with

We are the stars which sing—we sing with your light.

—ALGONQUIAN TRADITIONAL SONG

different planets, and amazingly enough, they seem to be harmonically related, according to Jonathan Goldman.

Ani Williams, harpist, singer, and sound healer, who has been studying the relationship between the sound of the planets and the human voice, theorizes that our individual vocal patterns at the time of birth mirror the planetary and star patterns. She also found correlations between human physical and emotional health and the patterns of sound frequencies of the voice. "Not only is the human voice a mirror of the person's current condition, it's also a mirror of the Cosmic print at the moment of birth. For instance, if Saturn is in the east, Pluto is off to the west, and the Sun is overhead at the moment of someone's birth, you can take all those positions, and the positions of the rest of the planets at birth, ascribe tones to them, and map the frequency patterns—and this map will mirror the individual's voice tone."[4]

Researchers who have been working with this have devised digital tuners to measure these frequencies and realign them. If stress or emotional upsets have caused the blockage or disappearance of certain "tones" in the body-mind symphony, these frequencies can be played back to the body and wholeness can be restored.

The NASA recordings of the sounds of the planets, which you can hear online, demonstrate the awesomely beautiful "songs" of our solar system.[5] Listening to the rings of Uranus is like being inside five-thousand-mile wide Tibetan bowls and bells. Jupiter sounds like a precious metal gong that is being rubbed around the edge with a wooden stick. The voice of the earth sounds like dolphins, birds, and a celestial choir. A televi-

Song is the intelligence of the universe.
—Yaqui Indian saying

If you love it enough, anything will talk to you.
—George Washington Carver

170

sion special in Japan touted the effectiveness of these earth sounds in alleviating sleep disorders in children.

The great dancer Isadora Duncan wrote in her book, *My Life,* that awakening to the power of sound was the first step in the dance. "It would seem as if it were a very difficult thing to explain in words, but when I stood before my class of even the smallest and poorest children and said: 'Listen to the music with your soul. Now, while listening, do you not feel an inner self awakening deep within you—that it is by its strength that your head is lifted, that your arms are raised, that you are walking slowly toward the light?' they understood. This awakening is the first step in the dance, as I conceive it."[6]

Listening is active, not passive. It is a gesture of surrender and engagement that involves our whole being and can carry us from chaos to calm in moments. Just yesterday I was in the midst of an emotional upset that had me in tears. I left my house to drive to the store and when I started the car, James Twyman's CD *Emissary of Light* began to play. When I heard him singing the *Prayer of St. Francis,* my sorrow subsided and I calmed down immediately. When I started to sing along, a feeling of joy and peace rose up and washed away every trace of turmoil.

In *Heaven's Face Thinly Veiled,* Sarah Anderson includes an excerpt from a letter that nineteenth-century novelist Geraldine Jewsbury wrote to her friend Jane Welsh Carlyle describing the power of music: "I had an advent the other night. I went to hear the 'Creation,' the very grandest thing in the shape of music I can conceive. It seemed to take one into a

I don't just write music to esthetically satisfy somebody. The reason I write music is that I feel it's a vehicle or channel which leads to your true self, your essence.

—GEORGE RUSSELL

171

new world of sound, it broke one up altogether, and called one out of oneself, possessed one like a new spirit. It was music that had nothing to do with passion or emotion, but when it was over one felt as if one had been banished to a realm of common things, without sunshine, and nothing but an east wind. I have been miserable ever since, as I used to be, when a child, after a great pleasure."[7]

Alfred Tomatis was a French physician who for nearly fifty years explored the functions of the human ear and the importance of listening. He believed that there are two kinds of sound: sounds that tire and fatigue us, and sounds that energize us. In his research, he discovered that high-frequency harmonics, such as those found in Gregorian chants, have therapeutic potential and the capacity to charge the central nervous system and the cortex of the brain.

His theory was confirmed when he was called upon for help by the leaders of a Benedictine monastery in southern France. Shortly after Vatican II, the monks had become depressed and fatigued for no apparent reason. After finding seventy of the ninety monks slumped in their cells weary and forlorn, Tomatis reached his conclusion—the problem was not psychological or physiological, it was audiological. The new abbot had eliminated the six to eight hours of chanting that the monks had been doing as a daily ritual, and without the therapeutic and energizing effect of their chanting, they could not maintain their rigorous schedule of prayer and work. While an outsider might have found the chanting exhausting, the monks were nourished by its sound. It lowered their blood pressure, slowed down their

Both music and scientific research are nourished by the same source of longing, and they complement one another in the release they offer.

—ALBERT EINSTEIN

172

breathing, and boosted their moods and productivity. Dr. Tomatis recommended that the monks return to chanting, and within six months, they were back to their happy, healthy selves.

In his book *The Mozart Effect,* teacher and music visionary Don Campbell refers to the rise in popularity of Gregorian chant as one of the greatest unanticipated events in our time, right up there with the fall of the Soviet Empire and the tumbling of the Berlin Wall. More than four million copies of the CD *Chant* by the Benedictine Monks of Santo Domingo de Silos in Spain have been sold, and it reached the top of *Billboard*'s classical *and* pop music charts in Europe and the United States. Writes Campbell, "I believe that the resurgence of Gregorian chant and other sacred music signals that the modern psyche is ready for recharging through the generative power of sound."[8]

Campbell tells the story of Willis Conover, who hosted *The Voice of America Jazz Hour* from 1955, treating an estimated thirty million listeners behind the Iron Curtain to a nightly program of jazz and other rhythmic music banned by the authorities. In 1996, the *New York Times* eulogized him as "the man who fought the Cold War with cool music ... and who proved more effective than a fleet of B-29s. No wonder. Six nights a week he would take the A-train straight into the Communist heartland."

According to Dee Coulter, who specializes in the relationship between musical patterning and neurological development and who wrote *The Brain's Timetable for Developing*

The voice is a barometer of the soul.

—HAZRAT INAYAT KHAN

173

> The new religion will be one of Invocation and Evocation, of bringing together great spiritual energies and then stepping them down for the benefiting and the stimulation of the masses. The work of the new religion will be the distribution of spiritual energy.
>
> —ALICE A. BAILEY

Musical Skills, jazz can lift the listener into theta consciousness, the highly creative brain-wave state associated with artistic and spiritual insight. Because jazz moves into chaos and from chaos creates order, she recommends it for optimal creativity and for dealing with complex issues that do not lend themselves to simple, linear solutions. Imagine what might result if the folks in the White House war room exposed themselves to Miles Davis, Diana Krall, or Louis Armstrong before deliberating.

The idea of using music as a force for good was brought to life in a novel crowd-control experiment in Leicester, England, a few years ago. According to an article in June 2001 in the *Guardian,* bars and clubs began to play, at closing time, music from popular British children's television programs, including *Magic Roundabout, Mr. Benn,* and Looney Tunes cartoons. The idea was to lull patrons by the associated nostalgia into avoiding violent drunken brawls. Perhaps if bars or stadiums in the United States played Kermit the Frog's "Rainbow Connection" or Disney's "When You Wish Upon a Star" at closing time or after a game, patrons would depart with the same sense of joy and well-being that these songs were written to inspire.

Don Campbell offers some compelling examples of how music enhances vitality and creativity not only in humans, but in plants and animals as well. It's been proven that cows serenaded with Mozart give more milk, that plants grow best in the early morning when birds are singing, that playing Baroque music to Asian immigrants enhances their ability to learn English, that "Musical Udon" made with tapes of Vivaldi's

Four Seasons and the chirping of birds in the background is popular among noodle-buyers in Tokyo, and that the density of yeast used for brewing Japanese rice wine increases by a factor of ten when exposed to the music of Mozart.

The Secret Life of Plants by Peter Tompkins and Christopher Bird is full of stories of flowers, plants, and entire fields of corn whose growth has been stimulated by the sound of music. When T. C. Singh, a botanist from Madras, India, had an assistant play an Indian devotional song known as a raga to his mimosas, he noticed after two weeks that the number of stomata in the experimental plants was 66 percent higher, the epidermal walls were thicker, and the palisade cells were longer and broader than in the control plants, sometimes by as much as 50 percent. After being exposed to another *raja* for five weeks, played twenty-five minutes a day on a seven-stringed lutelike instrument, his balsam plants shot ahead of their unserenaded neighbors and produced an average of 72 percent more leaves than the control plants and had grown 20 percent higher. At about the same time, a Canadian engineer in Ontario broadcast the violin sonatas of Johann Sebastian Bach to a test plot of wheat and produced a crop not only 66 percent greater than average, but with larger and heavier seeds.

Some remarkable research has come from the Japanese scientist Masaru Emoto, whose book *Messages from Water* illustrates the impact of sound, prayer, and words on water molecules.[9] Dr. Emoto freezes different samples of water and exposes them to different stimuli before photographing the water crystals. In one photograph, he shows water that has

If we wish to heal the natural world that we are in imminent danger of destroying, we are going to have to listen in radical humility to its voices, attend faithfully to its rhythms, and enact quickly what they tell us.

—ANDREW HARVEY

175

been exposed to heavy metal music. The pattern is chaotic and disorganized. An image of the same water exposed to Bach shows crystals that look like a perfect snowflake with beautiful geometric designs. Images of a polluted pond over which Tibetan monks prayed and chanted vary tremendously in the before and after shots.

Even writing words on the outside of a test tube had an effect on the water crystals. The words "I love you" generated crystals that were clear, pristine, and gorgeously shaped, while the words "You make me sick, I'm going to kill you" created a demonlike form in a brown, muddy color. Considering that our bodies are 70 percent water, imagine the impact that negative thinking and speaking can have on our own and our families' well-being.

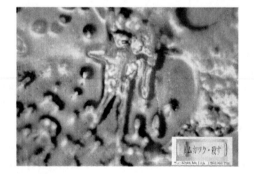

I love you   You make me sick, I'm going to kill you

Swiss medical doctor Hans Jenny has provided us with dramatic images of the impact of sound on matter, available in his book *Cymatics: A Study of Wave Phenomena and Vibration*. The word *cymatics* comes from the Greek *kyma*, meaning "wave." Dr. Jenny performed many of his experiments by putting substances such as sand, fluids, and powders on a metal plate. The plate was attached to an oscillator (a vibrator), controlled by a frequency generator capable of producing a broad range of vibrations. By turning a dial on the frequency generator, Dr. Jenny would cause the plate to vibrate at different frequencies, and what started out as an inert blob of sand or water would transform into an animated, pulsating form as soon as the plate or membrane was excited by vibration. Even if someone brushed the sand on the plate and disturbed its shape, within seconds it would reorganize into its original form—all as a result of the vibrations it was receiving.

Dr. Jenny then constructed the tonoscope to make the human voice visible without any electronic apparatus as an intermediate link. This yielded the amazing possibility of being able to see the physical image of the vowel, tone, or song a human being produced directly. Not only could you hear a melody, you could see it. Using the tonoscope, Jenny noticed that when the vowels of the ancient languages of Hebrew and Sanskrit were pronounced, the sand took the shape of the written symbols for these vowels. *As we speak, so does it become.*

In his introduction to *Cymatics,* John Beaulieu, ND, PhD, writes that metaphorically, our physical body, emotions, and thought processes are like wave forms that are organized by underlying vibrational fields. Our denser physical body is animated by the subtler vibrations of our emotions and thoughts. This vibrational field is known as an energy field in energy medicine, and it is the entire field, rather than just a symptom, that a practitioner looks at when evaluating a patient.

> In the vibrational field it can be shown that every part is, in the true sense, implicated in the whole.
>
> —DR. HANS JENNY

"Vibrational therapies" such as music, sounds, movements, scents, and so on support a shift in the field, and as the person shifts into resonance with a more coherent field, his or her symptoms may disappear as a more harmonious pattern emerges. "The result will be a new energetic field in which the old symptoms can no longer exist," writes Beaulieu. "This is a 'transformation' as opposed to 'fixing a part.' The old energy field will still be available, yet we will now have developed the ability to shift into a new field."[10]

After my car accident, when I was recovering from skin graft surgery on my back, a friend of mine who's a chiropractor, holistic practitioner, and Native American flute player offered to do a sound healing, a "tonal attunement" as he called it. I had no idea what that meant, but I went to his office and followed him and his partner into a small room. There was a futon on the floor in the center of the room, images of wildlife on the walls, and candlelight flickering in the shadows. My only task was to lie down, close my eyes, and relax.

For the next hour, I visited nirvana as they shrouded me in sound, beginning with the deep drone of the Australian aboriginal didjeridoo. During the session, they also used Native American flutes, gongs, Tibetan bowls and prayer chimes, drums, and rattles. At one point, both of them placed their didjeridoos on my belly and droned away, creating overtones to shift my frequency and open whatever channels were blocked by the trauma. They used the rattles, they said later, to ruffle up my energy field and get me back to my original resonance with the earth. When I left their office, I knew something had shifted, but I didn't know until later that it was my own frequencies that had changed, as they rebalanced with the heavens, reconnected with the source.

It's clear from an abundance of research, and from our own personal experience with music, that sound has an ability to alter our state. Our ears are gateways to sacred happenings, receivers of holy messages and vital secrets. Aside from enabling us to heal ourselves through the vibrations of sound, our ears give us the capacity to hear each other into being. As I hear your stories and you hear mine, ideas arise, understanding occurs, and the fragments of our lives arrange themselves into a whole that we can make sense of.

Our stories contain the answers to each other's questions. What I cannot find in searching through the riches and rubble of my own life may become apparent to me in the witnessing of yours. It's through our stories that we begin to name ourselves, to say who we are under all the social trappings, and to emerge from those trappings like a butterfly from a chrysalis. We are midwives, in a way, to each other's rebirth.

When we ask someone to be our sounding board, we are asking to be heard, knowing that in that process we will come to a greater clarity about what we believe. Our listeners are the ones who help us shape our consciousness, experience our wisdom, and hone our skills in bringing it forward. And when we listen to others, this is the gift we offer them. When we feel heard, we feel healed; we feel that we matter, that our thoughts and emotions are worthy of regard. In the presence of authentic listening, only love abides. And if we lived in a world where each of us truly listened to each other's deepest concerns, only peace would abide, for listening is a state of suspended judgment. Listening is tuning in to our common frequency, hearing the beat of our global heart.

Listening is a sacramental act. It is an outward sign of love that brings grace and light to the moment of sharing. When we open our ears attentively, carefully to another's sounds, we open our hearts to a deeper resonance, and beneath the conversation,

The vocal nourishment that the mother provides to her child is just as important to the child's development as her milk.

—DR. ALFRED TOMATIS

179

between the lines, there is a great, wild flurry of energy that feeds our cells and heals our wounds. As St. Francis said, "It is in giving that we receive." And in listening we find ourselves, right there in the voice of the other.

REFLECTION

Reflect for a moment on the people you prefer to spend time with. What is it about their behavior that draws you to them? Do you have a sense that they listen to you better than others in your life? Do they reflect you back to yourself in a way that is helpful and clarifying to you? Do you do the same for them?

EXERCISE

Read these ten questions and see if you're giving people a good reason to listen to you.

1. **Are you being negative?** Nobody enjoys being in the presence of negative energy. Whining and complaining are two of the surest ways to turn off your listener. Try listening to yourself as you speak. Pay attention to your tone of voice. If you are whining, stop it. For one week, try turning your complaints into requests and see if you notice a difference in how your ideas are received.

2. **Do you share opinions, but not your inner self?** When's the last time you were in the presence of a powerful speaker? What do you remember about what the speaker said? Chances are, whoever was talking was sharing some personal story, illustrating a point with an anecdote. Listeners get engrossed in a conversation when the speaker actually shares something meaningful about his or her life. Rich communication never occurs by accident. It takes

intention and attention. Think of the most engaging conversationalist you know. Next time you hear that person, listen for how much of him- or herself the speaker really shares. Try sharing something personal next time you're in a conversation with someone who's important to your life. Trust him or her enough to admit a fear of yours, to tell a story from your childhood, or to share a vision you have for the future. We are all waiting to have these conversations, but no one wants to go first. Try going first.

3. **Are you planning what you want to say while others speak, instead of listening?** This one always backfires. It's a dead giveaway. People know when you're doing it because your responses to their speaking are usually inappropriate, and communication breaks down rapidly. No one listens back to someone who hasn't listened to them. Instead of spouting off your opinions immediately after a person has spoken, ask them something about what they just said. Pay attention to their speaking, and they will pay more attention to yours.

4. **Do you live up to your word?** Did you ever know someone who was always going to do this and always promising to do that and never came through? Did you stop listening to that person after a while? The world is full of dreamers and planners, but it's people's actions, not their dreams, that inspire us. Open up and share something you've accomplished that you're proud of. If you have something you want to accomplish, ask for support. People will not take us seriously if they see we do not take our own words and commitments seriously.

5. **Have you created an environment for listening?** It is not easy to listen to someone in a room where televisions and radios are in competition with humans. If real communication is important to you, try turning off the

tube and finding a commercial-free FM station that plays music conducive to conversation. Classical music stimulates the alpha waves in our brains, allowing for more creativity to be stimulated.

6. **Do you speak as a victim of circumstances or as a creator of possibilities?** People who speak as if the world were out to get them have a difficult time finding listeners. No one wants to get pulled into the emotional quicksand that a "victim" seems to be buried in. Consider how you respond as a listener to other people's tales of woe. Do you tire quickly in that context? Do you get depressed and feel burdened? Energy is contagious. If you speak as the one who's designing your life, rather than as a victim of other people's actions, you will empower yourself and others.

7. **Does your listener know the value of your relationship with her or him?** Establishing a background of trust and relatedness is critical to communication. The better sense a person has of you and of your commitment to the relationship, the more open she or he will be to your speaking. If what needs to be communicated is difficult or risky, it often helps to begin by stating what's at stake for you and how important honesty is to the relationship.

8. **Do you inquire about what may be important to your listener or do you mostly talk about yourself?** One way to ensure that your listener is with you is to include her or his interests in your conversation. The next time you have coffee with your neighbor or sit next to your coworker in the cafeteria, initiate a conversation about something you know that person is interested in. If she's a ski enthusiast, ask her about her favorite places to ski. If he's into computer games, strike up a conversation about an article

you read on the subject. People listen up and open up when you show a genuine regard for something they're interested in.

9. **If people listened to you like you listen to others, would you be satisfied?** Most of us have a person in our life who plays the role of listener when we really need to talk about something. If you have such a person, consider what particular skills this person has at listening. Why did you pick her or him as your sounding board? What is it that makes you trust her or him? What body language does this person exhibit when you speak that lets you know she or he is with you? Is it helpful to have people give you advice when you share something difficult, or would you prefer they just listen and let you sort things out in their presence? Can you be present to someone's pain without trying to solve all her or his problems? Observe how you listen the next time someone shares something difficult and see if you can refrain from offering advice and platitudes.

10. **Are you complaining to the wrong people?** It doesn't help anyone to complain to people who have no power to change things. If something is wrong, find out who's in charge and take your concern to the right person.

WRITING EXERCISE

Put on a piece of soothing music and close your eyes. Starting with your first memory, go forward in time, reflecting on events that were upsetting to you. As you come to each one, bring your attention back to the music and feel it washing over all your cells. Feel the vibrations of the music making contact with every fiber of your being, caressing it, balancing it. Be aware that the music is healing your body and releasing its blockages, freeing the energy that's been frozen in place. Let yourself relax into this mystery and breathe deeply, sending your love to every cell. Forgive yourself and everyone else who comes to mind as you journey, knowing that everything that ever occurred in your life is part of the trajectory that brought you here, to this moment of grace, to this healing, to this threshold to a new life.

When your forgiveness is complete, begin to give thanks to everyone in your life who did what they did to get you here. In your journal, write down the names of those you are forgiving and what you're forgiving them for. Make your list as complete as possible, so you will not need to revisit this. If you could not forgive everyone, forgive yourself for that, and consider getting help from someone who can help you release that energy.

Seeing Our Way Clear

Listen, O Beloved!
I am the reality of the world,
The center of the circle.
I am the part and the whole.
I am the will holding Heaven and earth in place.
Only so you may see me.

—Ibn al-'Arabi

A mother walks in to find her five-year-old daughter feverishly coloring on a white sheet of paper.

"What are you coloring?" she asks.

"I'm drawing a picture of God," says the girl.

"Oh, honey, no one knows what God looks like," says the mom.

"They will when I get done with this drawing," replies the girl confidently.

Children have no fear of blasphemy. They know what they know and they share it with everyone—until someone scares them out of the habit of authenticity.

A while ago, I was asked to give a short talk at the opening reception at a hospital where four doctors were exhibiting their photographs. The woman who invited me to speak did so because I wrote a book titled *God Is at Eye Level: Photography as a Healing Art,* and she thought it was a nice link. A few days before the opening, she called to give me a heads-up. "A couple of the doctors are upset because they don't want anyone bringing religion into the picture, and they say their photography has nothing to do with healing. You might want to be careful about what you say," she warned.

I arrived at the reception early enough to view all the photographs and was stunned at how moved I was by each body of work. One was a series of black-and-white images from the same Himalayan mountain range I had trekked in a decade earlier. One group was color landscapes from my favorite place in this country, Canyon de Chelly on the Navajo reservation in Arizona. One was an array of dazzling close-ups of flowers, and another was a series of vibrant murals and portraits from a Hispanic barrio in south San Diego. Every photograph in the exhibition spoke to my heart, aroused my emotions, caused me joy, and reconnected me to the whole.

When I started to talk, I looked out at the doctors, their arms crossed, their faces stern and inanimate. I was mindful of speaking only about my own process of photographing, not wanting to make any of them uncomfortable. I spoke about photography as my way of grounding myself in the present, about how it's the most healing thing I do, because it roots me in the now, and when I'm there, truly present to just what's before me, I feel a oneness with life. I'm untouched and unfettered by anything past or future—no regrets, no fears, no anxieties—just a kinship with what's at hand. I spoke of my belief that the Divine dwells in the present moment, and when I'm there, I'm safe and I know it.

I spoke about the process of photographing others and what intimacy and communion emerge as we take our roles as seer

The eye with which I see God is the same eye as that with which God sees me. My eye and the eye of God are one eye, one vision, one knowledge, and one love.

—MEISTER ECKHART

and seen, giver and receiver, lover and beloved. I spoke about the power photographs have had in the course of my life— to open my heart, to alter my thinking, to bring me to prayer, to tears, to action. Like mysticism, photography, for me, has led to a direct and unmediated experience of the holy. In those moments, with my camera in hand, the world is my altar, and I am the servant of unity, looking for signs of the one in the many.

I shared my reactions to each of the doctor's photographs, commenting on how they awakened my senses, conjured up memories, ignited my imagination and joy. Their images made me feel connected to my world, in awe of its mystery, in love with its flowering. And this, to me, was a sacred thing, a holy event, because it brought me home and fastened me to the Creator like a button in a buttonhole.

As I spoke, I watched the doctors move forward in their seats. I saw their faces soften, their eyes widen. They never knew the power of their work, the healing potential of their images, but when I spoke of it, they resonated and opened to a new possibility. After my talk, each one came up to me independently, took me aside, and said how proud they felt, how happy they were that someone sensed the spirit in their work and brought it to light. In their own words, they each said the same thing: I can't talk about God in my work. I feel it, but I can't say it, and I'm glad you did.

Their own voices had been silenced by the culture that contained them. They were like the mother who said, "Honey, no one knows what God looks like." And my talk was like the drawing of the little girl. We *all* know what God looks like.

> Make visible what, without you, might never have been seen.
> —ROBERT BRESSO

187

God looks like the dawn and the unfolding day. God looks like the grocery store clerk, the kindergartner, the image in the mirror. God looks like Easter Sunday, the first day of spring, a Passover seder, the birth of a baby, September 11. God looks like the redwood, the iris, the antelope, the forest fire, the AIDS patient, the parched riverbed. There is not one thing our eyes encounter that is not God, including our own flesh and blood. We are one with the source, and the whole spectacular universe is God unveiled, transcendent *and* immanent, around us *and* within us.

Every spiritual tradition points to this, and yet somehow we have a notion that it is blasphemous to speak of it. We're afraid to mention the holy one within in our daily conversations, though it is that which is the breath by which we speak, the eyes by which we see. "The Self is hidden in the hearts of all, as butter lies hidden in cream," says the Upanishads. "Wheresoever you turn, there is the face of God," says the Qur'an. Jesus says, "Whoever sees anything at all is looking into the eyes of the Only One Who Is." The Sufi mystic Ibn al-'Arabi writes, "The existence of all created things is His existence. Thou dost not see, in this world or the next, anything beside God." And the poet Hafiz writes in his poem "We Might Have to Medicate You":

> *Resist your temptation to lie*
> *By speaking of separation from God.*

Where is God himself but in the part of him he set forth forever in your brother's holiness, that you might see the truth about yourself, set forth at last in terms you recognized and understood?

—*A Course in Miracles*

Otherwise,
We might have to medicate
You.
In the ocean
A lot goes on beneath your eyes.

Listen,
They have clinics there too
For the insane
Who persist in saying things like:

"I am independent
from the
Sea,

God is not always around

Gently
Pressing against
My body."[1]

We are intricately entwined with the Divine in ways that cannot be spoken of, but the reality is not to be denied. We do not have to seek after God. There is no journey to take, no text to pore over, nothing to learn in the matter. As the Lankavatara Sutra reminds us, "These teachings are only a finger pointing to the Noble wisdom ... they are intended for the consideration and guidance of the discriminating minds of all people, but they are not Truth itself, which can only be self-realized within one's own deepest consciousness." It is through us, through our consciousness, that the divinization of humanity and all the earth is occurring. By learning to see, by becoming alert and awake, we feel the call and presence of the unmanifest asking for, and guiding us into, the kind of creative action that gives birth to this process. Everything takes form according to the consciousness that shapes it. Since we create in our own image, in order for our creations to be light-filled, inspired, magnificent, so must our self-image be. What comes out of us is only as brilliant, as loving as our images of ourselves. To give gold, we must mine the gold within.

The treasure is in us, of us. And if we think not, then our thoughts deceive us. It is like trying to solve a problem with a mindset that *is* the problem. We cannot be healed until we accept that we *are* healed. We cannot sense the Divine until we feel its presence in our own cells and devote our highest love to the life within. How we see ourselves has everything to do with how we see others and how we see God. The great Jesuit psychologist and retreat director Anthony deMello said, "If you have to have an image of God, make sure it's an image of the kindest, most loving person you know, because you are going to become your image of God."

When we drop our illusions of separateness and the biases of programmed thinking that obscures our mystical interconnectedness, the transcendent dimensions of our lives begin to emerge. It is like the day when a child first discovers how to make meaning from words. Suddenly a whole new world erupts as each letter is perceived, not as a singular thing, but as an important part of a whole thought. Perhaps each of us is a

What is within is also without. What is without is also within. He who sees difference between what is within and what is without goes forevermore from death to death.

—THE VEDAS

Where one stands determines what one sees.

—SANDRA SCHNEIDERS

letter, the world is a word, the universe is a sentence, and God is the meaning. Until we each fully manifest our letterhood, the meaning will be hidden, like the butter in the cream.

The Kabbalah says that "we receive the light, then we impart the light. Thus we repair the world." The repair part gets done when we *impart* the light. That means we have to show up. We have to shine. We have to let the great one within loose in the world by speaking our thoughts, sharing our feelings, revealing the inner. Our energy is a force that has an effect on other energies. There are six billion people on earth, and we are each a particular and individualized expression of an underlying field of awareness. Gregg Braden writes in *The Isaiah Effect,* "As one of us pioneers a new creative solution to the seemingly small challenges of our individual lives, we become a living bridge for the next person who finds himself or herself faced with the same challenge, and the next, and so on."

It is through our eyes that we perceive the world, and through our eyes that we project our inner selves outward. "The eyes are the windows to our souls," said Shakespeare, letting light in, letting light out. Jacob Liberman, author of *Light, Medicine of the Future,* writes, "As each of us becomes whole, we radiate light—light from within—unimpeded by our self-imposed emotional and physical blocks. The medicine of the future *is* light. We are healing ourselves with that which is our essence."[2]

According to Liberman, who has doctorates in optometry and vision science, our eyes contain 137 million photoreceptors and more than one billion parts. They function as an index of

In all ten directions of the Universe,
There is only one truth.
When we see clearly, the great teachings are the same. —RYOKAN

What we are looking for is Who is looking.
—ST. FRANCIS OF ASSISI

191

what is occurring in the body and mind. An examination of the eyes can inform us of approximately three thousand different conditions pertaining to our physical health. The human body is a living photocell that is energized by sunlight, our main nutrient. The eyes are the channel through which this light enters into us.

The German philosopher Wolfgang Goethe and his protégé Rudolph Steiner did extensive studies on the effect that color has on our lives, claiming that colors give rise to the feelings that lead to our actions. The Greek philosopher Pythagoras was using color therapy five hundred years before the birth of Jesus. Reds, oranges, and yellows tend to energize us, while blues, greens, and indigos calm us. Research in hospitals has proven that patients in rooms with windows looking out on nature tend to heal faster and require fewer drugs. Returning to the green Northeast from the dusty brown of southern California always makes my eyes smile. Returning to nature has proven to be a healing and creative act for artists of all kinds, from Georgia O'Keeffe to Annie Dillard to Thoreau and Emerson.

A recent *New York Times* article on the subject of reading addressed the impact that Ralph Waldo Emerson had on Walt Whitman. When Whitman first picked up the work of Emerson, he was working as a carpenter, framing houses in Brooklyn. He'd been a journalist for a while and had written some lackluster fiction, but it didn't appear that he was going anywhere with it. Then he read Emerson, who altered everything he ever thought about authority. Purportedly, he

When the eyes see what they have never seen before, the heart feels what it has never felt.

—Baltasar Gracian

described it like this: "I was simmering, simmering, simmering. Emerson brought me to a boil." When Whitman exploded into the world, it was the beginning of one of the most fabulous transformations in the history of literature. This is the effect we have on each other. We may not have the brilliance or breadth of Emerson or Whitman, but we do fuel each other as they did. Just telling how we see things leads to another seeing things in a different way.

When I sit in conversation with a friend, I'm not listening for solutions. I'm listening for perceptions, insights, ideas. And when I speak, I tell stories with as many details, as much nuance as I can, so the listener gets a good strong visual. Communion with others is not about answers. It's about our questions. We only have to know the questions and wrestle with them. Lay them on the table. Let our thoughts collide over them, like the collisions of right brain and left, positive and negative, sperm and egg—life-giving unions that re-pair the poles. If we remain silent, we forsake our selves, like lonely children hiding in our rooms. "Not to transmit an experience is to betray it," says Elie Wiesel. We are agents of evolution, not its observers. Our brains have grown, our consciousness has expanded, and we are more aware of our quantum connections than ever before. In Emerson's words, "We lie in the lap of immense intelligence, which makes us receivers of its truth and organs of its activity." We have come to the point in evolution where our own role in the matter is becoming clearer. Each of us is here to do something particular—and whatever meaning our lives have will rise up from our response to that challenge.

When you look for God, God is in the look of your eyes.

—RUMI

193

As Rumi says in his poem "The Far Mosque":

The place that Solomon made to worship in,
called the Far Mosque, is not built of earth
and water and stone, but of intention and wisdom
and mystical conversation and compassionate action.

Every part of it is intelligence and responsive
to every other. The carpet bows to the broom.
The door knocker and the door swing together
like musicians. This heart sanctuary does
exist, but it can't be described. Why try!

Solomon goes there every morning and gives guidance
with words, with musical harmonies, and in actions,
which are the deepest teaching. A prince is just
a conceit until he does something with generosity.[3]

The age of light is coming to term, and we are its mothers and midwives. Each voice is essential in this borderland. Every thought materializes with enough intensity, and every prayer is answered if it is imagined to be, embodied as if so. We are pregnant with what we are praying for. In Neil Douglas-Klotz's translation of Jesus's words from the original Aramaic, the new reading is, "All things that you ask straightly, directly ... from inside my name, you will be given. So far you have not done this. Ask without hidden motive and be surrounded by your answer. Be enveloped by what you desire, that your gladness be full."[4]

Our vision and faith calls tomorrow toward us. The answers already exist. Peace is already present. They are the future, waiting to be drawn down into our awareness through the power of our prayer and longing. But we must express this desire, let its energy surge through our bodies, fueling our cells and rising up for release into the world, into the ears of God, into the physical realm of our own experience. When Gandhi said, "We must be the change we want to see in the world," this is what he meant. Peace is only a concept until it is materialized through the concrete and particular expressions of our selfhood. Until we express peace, it will not exist as a prevailing reality.

But how will others see us, what will they think of us if we dare to self-express? That thought plagued my father and kept him silent most of his life. He worried desperately what the neighbors would think, what his coworkers would think, what the relatives would think, and as a result very few people entered into the beautiful mind and heart of this dear child of God. He died from a heart attack at the age of sixty, and I always wondered if he'd only opened his heart more, expressed it more, might he have lived longer?

A friend once said to me, "What people think of me is none of my business." Good bumper sticker, I thought. If we could act without this fear, drawing our life lines like the child drawing God, with no reservation or hesitancy, our energy would flow so smoothly and effortlessly through our bodies that health problems would disappear. The symphony within would play of its own accord, our vibrations would be in sync with the music of the cosmos, and we, in our most natural, healthy state, would resonate with every other living thing.

> When no one is looking and I want to kiss God, I just lift my own hand to my mouth.
>
> **—HAFIZ**

We forfeit so much of our life letting this concern about others' opinions drive us, when in reality, everyone is going to view us through their own lens anyway. We live in a holographic world where no one sees the same thing from the same place, physically or emotionally. Every image is a mirror of ourselves, and what we see is not something about the other, but something about who *we* are. One action will draw criticism from one, praise from another, so to act from anywhere but our own center is just silly. Inauthentic action is exhausting and time-consuming. If I believed in sin, I'd put it in the cardinal sin category.

When I was recovering from my accident, I was full of anxiety and fear. I was also in grave danger of infection, due to the seriousness of my burns. I decided to reach out to everyone I knew and ask for help, for prayers and emotional support. I sent e-mails to hundreds of friends around the country sharing my fears and vulnerabilities. I knew they could help me heal, and I needed their help desperately. Every few weeks, I e-mailed the whole group and let them know how I was improving, thanking them for all their prayers and candles. The response to this was interesting. I got hundreds of cards and e-mails from people thanking me for asking, telling me how *my* asking for help helped *them* ask for help. Seeing a strong, independent, creative woman confess to fear and helplessness gave them permission to accept and acknowledge their own need for help. Not only did I get better in the process, but a lot of us got better.

And still there was one voice in the crowd admonishing me for making a big drama out of the whole thing. Her perception

Inner vision is perhaps the greatest change catalyst that the world has ever known.

—DIARMUID O'MURCHU

196

was that I was making a public scene, drawing attention to myself, and somehow that was selfish or self-centered. How she saw me had nothing to do with me. It was all about her and her style of bearing pain.

I learned from that experience never to think I could make the same impression on any two people. The only thing I can do is be true to the core of me, act with as much honor as I can, and remember that how people see me is something I have no control over. I'm aware that my actions and my creations have a power and that I can have an intention to direct that power, visualize its impact in positive ways, and send my energy out on a wave of love from the center of my heart—and still, when it reaches the others, what they do with it is up to them.

My job as a teacher is to create an occasion for people to come together, to convene the circle, elicit the questions, and share images and metaphors from the stories of my life. Since the field that draws me is visual and mythic, it follows that my focus and feelings will be rooted there. People who care about such things will be drawn to me, and the energy that we create will be a synthesis of our personal holdings. We will bring to light what we feel, believe, and hope for, aided by the heart-opening arts of music, photography, and poetry. We will not ask ourselves *what is wrong, who is to blame?* We will ask ourselves *what does the world we want to be a part of look like?*

Doris Lessing wrote in *A Small, Personal Voice,* "One must have a vision to build toward, and that vision must spring from the nature of the world we live in.... What is the choice before us? It is not merely a question of preventing an evil, but of

> Wakefulness is a state of non-illusion where you see things not as you are but as they are.
>
> —ANTHONY DEMELLO

197

strengthening a vision of a good which may defeat the evil." This is what we do when we focus our attention, call on our intuition, draw forth images and ideas from the inner realms. We are opening ourselves to and strengthening our vision of a world that now exists only in a potential state.

We *are* the cocreators, the prophets, the mystics, but we have been taught the opposite for so long that we don't believe it, don't dare act on it. If we want to live powerfully, we must drop our notions of weakness. If we want to live in beauty, we must drop what is not beautiful from our minds. If we want to live in truth, we must question every belief we cling to and write our own creeds. To know and experience union, we have to give up our learned dualities and lean into the essence of everything around. There is *not* the sacred and the profane, the earthly and the heavenly, the sinners and the saved. There is only God, infusing and infused into everything.

The other day, I was photographing tide pools at the ocean's edge. The waves crashed onto the shore, ruffled their way across the rocks, and swirled and bubbled into the shallow sandstone pools beneath my feet. I hovered over a patch of moss-covered rock and photographed a piece of the action. When the photos were developed, I was stunned. Every single tiny bubble I caught in my lens reflected back an image of myself. *Everything I looked at looked back at me and contained me.*

All life is a mirror to us, reflecting who we are back to ourselves. The act of seeing is the act of recognizing our common ground—the life force that holds us all together on this plane.

Whoever does not see God in every place does not see God in any place.

—Rabbi Elimelech

In order to see, you have to stop being in the middle of the picture.

—Sri Aurobindo

To contemplate is "to make a temple of." It is time for the undoing of *us and them,* time to lose the shoddy thinking that separates spirituality from action, creativity from divinity, sacred from secular. It is time for a great labor and groan and push into an era of illumined experience, where the sense of oneness flows like honey through the common soul. This will come when we begin to *speak* our knowing, when we come out as creators and mystics and light-bearers, when we take our place as priests and priestesses concelebrating the sacraments of compassion and unity on the altars of our city streets. As shapers of this culture, let us take back the light—singing *yes* to life, *yes* to change, *yes* to the one, the oneness, the wonder. We are the dawn, the light of the world—our voices like candles, our love like the sun.

WALKING MEDITATION

Go for a walk some place in nature. Imagine your eyes as extensions of the universe. Rather than focusing on what is in front of you, keep your eyes aimed at infinity and let everything else fall out of focus. As you walk, consider the possibility that your eyes are the eyes through which God is seeing, glancing into the world God created. Imagine a divine force moving into the world *through* your eyes. Notice how this feels.

EXERCISE

Walk around your house and stop at each painting, photograph, poster, or sculpture you encounter on your walls and bookshelves. Spend a moment with each piece and reflect on what it means to you. Why is it there? How does it feed you? What memories does it evoke? Does it add light to your life? A sense of well-being? If it doesn't contribute something positive to you, replace it with something that does.

EXERCISE

Pay attention to what draws your eye during the day. Notice what images and what kinds of people attract you, what cityscapes or landscapes appeal to you. At the end of each day, share what you noticed with someone in your life, giving the details as fully as you can, commenting on why and how it had an impact on you. As you begin to share your observations, notice how your vision changes, how your focus sharpens. Observe how you are affected and altered by the things you notice.

EXERCISE

Imagine that everything in your life, every person you encounter, truly is a mirror to you. When you are in the presence of people who are difficult, see if you can distinguish what they are mirroring to you. Can you find yourself in their behavior? Are they acting out in a way that you don't allow yourself to act out? What is the real reason you are upset with that person? What upsets you about your own behavior?

WRITING EXERCISE

At the end of the day, sit quietly, take a few deep breaths, and give some thought to the images your eyes took in during the day. Imagine that it was God who was looking through your eyes, and in your journal, write this phrase and complete it with images: "God saw through my eyes today and this is what God saw ..."

A Cell in the Right Brain of God

The world is God's body. God draws it ever upward.
The only worthwhile joy is to release some infinitesimal
quantity of the absolute, to free one fragment of being,
forever. Living well is cooperating as one individual
atom in the final establishment of a world.

—Teilhard de Chardin

It's good to have an image, something to root us when we lose our ground, something to hold on to when our memories fragment and leave us doubting. As a visual thinker, I rely on images for my understanding of the world and my place in it. When people speak to me, their words come at me like pictures across the sound waves. Marion Woodman says that "the images on which we feed govern our lives." I'm fed by an image of myself as a cell in the right brain of God. It makes me feel like I'm part of a wondrous whole, spirited forth in the service of creativity, a neuron traversing divine dendrites, receiving signals from the sacred heart of being itself.

Whenever I speak to groups of people, I know that my job is to feed them stories. No matter what information I'm trying to communicate, it'll never take unless I wrap it up in a package of images, convey it in a way that touches the emotions, my own included. No matter how many times I tell some stories, there are a few that always bring tears to my eyes, and I cry my way right through the telling. It's our nature to cry when we're in the presence of truth. When something gets revealed that has a meaning big enough to hold all of us in it, true enough to remind us that underneath all our differences and opinions, there's something mysterious and beyond words holding us together, then that thing is worth our tears.

Once I went to visit a friend's mother in the hills of Kentucky. I was on a cross-country trip interviewing people about their values. The woman, Babe, was sitting on her porch when I pulled up to the homestead where she lived with her eighty-seven-year-old brother, Arthur. Babe and I sat on the porch for hours, telling stories, mining our lives for tales that revealed our common bonds. I was going to spend the night, then leave in the morning for the deeper South.

When we went inside, she took me into the living room, "Arthur's room," she called it. There was a huge coffee table covered with right-wing political literature, pamphlets from the John Birch Society, magazines that represented a kind of thinking that was as far from mine as I could imagine. I was glad Arthur wasn't around. I didn't need to meet him. I already knew everything I needed to know about him, just looking at his reading materials. We were as opposite as two people could be.

Babe and I ate supper together, and just as we were finishing up, in walked Arthur. When Babe introduced me and told him I was interviewing people across the country, he asked when I wanted to interview him. I gulped and hesitated, trying to figure out how I could avoid it, when he said, "Meet me on the front porch tomorrow morning at eight." Trained for politeness, I agreed.

The next morning, he was sitting out there with his hat on and his walking stick in hand. "Come on," he barked, and he headed off into the yard. He started telling me about the lumber business he used to own, what kind of trees were on the property, how he knew the land like the back of his hand. The he stopped in his tracks and pointed at a tree with his walking stick. "Look over there at that walnut tree," he said. "Can you tell me how in the world that tree spits out those walnuts that are so hard I can't crack 'em with my hands? Even them chipmunks have to crack 'em on a rock just to get 'em open. What power's loose in the world that can make that happen year after year?"

We walked a bit further, then he stopped again, pointing his stick at the nearby garden. "Look over there at those rows of corn. Why, I just planted those seeds a while ago, and now look, row after row of perfect stalks, with the silkiest golden tassels you ever did see. And do you know what you're gonna find when you pull off those tassels and husk those ears? You're gonna find row after row of golden kernels, all lined up perfect. You tell me, girl, what power's loose in this world that can make that happen?"

I was amazed. This was a man who was supposed to be my opposite. A man I didn't want to talk with. A man I'd boxed into the category "other" and written off as a person to avoid. And now he was ushering me around his land, opening his heart, revealing his love affair with the earth we were walking on. We walked for two hours, through the woods, down to the creek, across the meadows, and all the while Arthur spoke of the birds, the flowers, the maples, the oaks, as if they were miracles of life going unnoticed. My listening was a cavern for his secrets, a temple for his sacred thoughts. My questions drew the light from his deepest places. My laughter met his gruffness and turned it into joy. We were yin and yang, Arthur and I, and on that two-hour walk we fell in love.

He insisted I stay, and every day for a week we'd spend hours on the land, as he talked of trees and nature and his troubled life. Once he confessed to me his life-long dream of standing in the middle of a sequoia forest. "I waited too long, it'll never happen now, but that's something I dreamed of since I was a boy."

"Arthur, it's not too late," I said. "You can still get there."

"No, it's too late," he insisted. "My own damn fault. I just waited too long."

After that, when I was on the road, I'd always look for postcards with pictures of trees. "Dear Arthur," I'd write. "It's not too late. There's still time. Get to the redwoods! Love, Jan." I must have sent him dozens of cards.

Months went by, and I finally made it back to my home in Syracuse. When I collected my mail, what a surprise to find a postcard from Arthur, from the Sequoia National Park. "Dear Jan, If it hadn't been for you, I'd never have made it. These trees make me cry like a baby. What power's loose in this world? I love you, Arthur."

He died a couple of months after that, but he often comes to mind when I encounter people who seem poles apart from where I am. Recently, at a party in Hollywood, I sat down next to a total stranger and started a conversation. The host of the party had a twenty-something son who was a musician living in New York. He was in the process of putting together an eclectic group of musicians and singers who would use instruments from around the world and operatic voices to tell their stories with a unique soundscape. I said to the stranger, "Isn't it wonderful about Mitch putting this group together? He's so creative. I think it's a great idea, and I sure hope he's successful."

The guy turned his whole body toward me and was so close I could see the veins in his neck popping. "Fuck art for art's sake! If it doesn't sell tickets and make money, I'm not interested. That kid's not going to go anywhere without money behind him. I've been in the music industry long enough to know art isn't worth a dime, and I don't give a damn about it."

I felt like I'd been bitten by a crocodile. I wanted to run away immediately, just to get out of his reach. He felt like a black hole, and I didn't want to get sucked in. I said to him, "As an artist, I do believe in art for art's sake. I know the power of art, and I'll never stop making it, and money doesn't have one thing to do with it, as far as I'm concerned." Then I got up and walked away, looking for someone I knew so I could vent about what a jerk he'd been.

I was practically breathless when I ran into Mitch's girlfriend. "You're not going to believe what just happened ..." Even as I told her the story, in the back of my mind was a voice saying "old behavior, old behavior." But I had been so affronted, so bewildered by this man's outburst, that I felt compelled to get it out of me, blaming him for my upset. Her pat response about how only insecure people treat others like that didn't help one bit, so I went in search of another confidante. Just as I rounded the corner and called to my friend Heather, I saw the man sitting alone near the bar, smoking a cigarette. As Heather asked, "What's up?" I heard a deeper voice from below, "Haven't you learned anything? Are you going to keep repeating your old habits?" An image of Arthur came to mind. "Nothing," I said to Heather. "I'm going to go over and talk to that guy."

I sat down next to him, smiled, and asked him what he did in the music industry. He acted as if nothing had happened at all. He talked a little bit about how he was a drummer in Detroit for a while, then moved to Los Angeles and became an agent, and what a cutthroat business it was, and then he got quiet. "You know what really turns me on? Reading. I can't stop reading," he said. "It's all I want to do. I was just reaching for the Currier and Ives book on the coffee table when you walked in." I saw an image of an addict ready to shoot up, being interrupted by someone walking into the room. "I read three books on Eisenhower just this week. Why Eisenhower, I'll never know." We went on to talk about politics, Bush, the Iraq war, and there was not one thing we agreed on, but I loved my time with him. I loved our differences. It was the strangest thing. What we had to say seemed totally irrelevant, compared to the newness that was rising up as we both opened and stretched toward the "other."

In technical terms, what I was experiencing with Arthur and this man at the party is called *limbic resonance*. Even though our thoughts were disparate, on some level we were emotionally attuned to each other. What we were feeling was more important than what we were thinking. Researchers at the Institute of HeartMath (IHM) have learned that when two people are at a conversational distance, the electromagnetic signal generated by one person's heart can influence the other person's brain rhythms. If I have love or compassion or fear in my heart, it actually gets registered in the brain waves of the person I'm sitting next to. Vibrationally, we are connected to each other in profound and mysterious ways. When people touch—even a simple handshake—there is a surprisingly large exchange of subtle electromagnetic information being transferred. Researchers at IHM seated two people four feet apart and instructed them to just sit quietly and not think of anything or do anything specific. They simultaneously monitored one person's heart rate (ECG) and the other person's brain waves (EEG). Neither person registered an energy exchange.

However, in the second part of the experiment, the two people were asked to hold hands. The data showed that when people touch or are in close proximity, one person's heartbeat signal is registered in the other person's brain waves. More refined techniques have since been developed by IHM that indicate there is an energy exchange that occurs up to five feet away from the body even without touching.

We've also learned that it takes about six seconds for emotions to flood through our system and dissipate. That gives us six seconds to manage anger, six seconds to create compassion, six seconds to act reflectively from the limbic brain, rather than reflexively from the fight-or-flight reptilian brain. If we pause for six seconds before expressing our emotions, we can actually choose a response that is true to our heart and consistent with who we are. If you do an Internet search for "six seconds" you can find an abundance of websites that are dedicated to bringing emotional intelligence into practice in schools, families, organizations, and communities.

The only way to tempt happiness into the mind is by taking it into the body first.

—MARY OLIVER

If I had waited six seconds after my initial upset with the man at the party, I wouldn't have needed to find someone to dump all my negative energy on. I would have remembered the cost of that action, maybe seen an image of myself pouring a bucket of ashes over someone's head, which is just what I did, on an energetic level, when I shared the story of the man's insensitivity. It was totally unnecessary for me to do that. It contributed nothing to anyone and was simply an exhibition of old-habit thinking on my part.

Our thoughts and emotions have incredible power, and what we do with them matters significantly. Because we're all connected on a quantum level, vibrationally and energetically, our thoughts and feelings can bring healing or harm to ourselves and others. We know from the experiments done with Buddhist monks in Japan that we can purify water with the power of our minds. We know from an experiment performed in Washington, D.C., by the Maharishi University that a critical mass of meditators can influence the crime rate in a metropolitan city, and from Dr. Larry Dossey's work that medical patients who are prayed for heal faster. Many studies have found that just 1 percent of a population practicing Transcendental Meditation (TM) is sufficient to bring about a significant reduction in crime, sickness, and accidents, a phenomenon researchers call the Maharishi effect.

Experiments were carried out in the Middle East during the Lebanon war that demonstrated that groups of TM meditators were able to produce a 34 percent reduction in war intensity and a 76 percent reduction in war deaths. In 2003, the highly respected *Journal of Offender Rehabilitation* devoted all four quarterly issues entirely to studies demonstrating that the TM program is effective in treating and preventing criminal behavior, as well as reducing international conflicts and terrorism.

Peter Tompkins and Christopher Bird offer fascinating accounts of the physical, emotional, and spiritual connections between plants and humans in their book *The Secret Life of Plants*. One experiment performed by a medical director and chemist involved a male subject who had brought a philodendron he had nursed from a seedling and cared for tenderly. The two scientists attached a polygraph to the plant and asked the owner a series of questions, instructing him to give false answers to some of them. The plant had no trouble indicating through the galvanometer which questions were answered falsely.

To see if a plant could display memory, six blindfolded polygraph students drew folded strips of paper from a hat. One of them contained instructions to root up, stamp on, and thoroughly destroy one of the two plants in a room. The criminal was to commit the crime in secret. No one knew his identity, and only the second plant would be a witness. When the surviving plant was attached to a polygraph, the students paraded before it one by one. The plant gave no reaction to five of them, but when the actual culprit approached, the meter went wild. There is mind in all matter.

Even robots have been documented responding to the power of thought. In one experiment, a robot was sent into a room full of baby chicks in bright daylight. All its movements were random. Knowing that the chicks prefer well-lit rooms, the researchers then turned off all the lights, leaving the chicks in the dark, and sent the robot back in, this time carrying a light. The robot spent a significant amount of time near the chicks; its former random movements were now affected by the chicks' desire for its light.

It is impossible to deny our capacity to affect reality with the power of our minds. Doesn't it make you wonder why we aren't *using* this power? Imagine what we might be able to accomplish as a nation if we decided to counter terrorism with consciousness, if we actually committed to creating an invincible moral force by focusing our minds on our oneness with the "other," offsetting every thought of violence with a more powerful feeling of peace. Imagine how it might feel to be part of a country that outlawed war, as it once outlawed slavery, segregation, and sex discrimination.

According to scientific research, we already have what it takes physiologically to accomplish such things. If there were a massive campaign directed at every

American that informed us, in simple terms, of our power to create peace by choosing to think and feel and act peacefully, we could, as a nation, bring an end to terrorism. We know that believing is seeing. We know that our feelings have an impact on others' thoughts and that our thoughts influence the world of matter. And we know the impact of a national campaign. In my own life, my behaviors have been conditioned by campaigns from as far back as Smokey the Bear when I learned that "only YOU can prevent forest fires." Then there was the antilitter campaign of the 1960s that was so successful I've not been able to throw any litter on the ground since. And what about the "no drinking and driving" campaign, and the seat belt campaign? They have all influenced millions of Americans and caused measurable changes in our behavior. So it's not such an outlandish thought after all. It's just not profitable. So the revolution in consciousness proceeds at a slow pace, growing mind by mind, heart by heart. But we can each speed up the pace by practicing mindfulness on a daily basis.

Our world was turned upside down on September 11, 2001, and we cannot right it with old thinking and old behavior. We cannot look to the past for answers. They do not live there. We must *imagine* ourselves forward, envision the world we want to create, and feel the new reality in every cell of our beings to bring it about—for it is our feelings, our heartfelt emotions, that will inspire the new choices, open our minds to the new solutions. The question is not *what is wrong and how can we fix it?* The question is *what does the world we want to live in look like?*

Until we get a picture of it in our minds, we cannot manifest it. If we see it and desire it fully, imagine it fearlessly, hold to it wholeheartedly, despite criticism or opposition from others, then we create the possibility for its being. We become the vessels for its expression, and through us the new will arrive, enfleshed, incarnated. The Second Coming is the coming into consciousness, and it is happening all around us. One by one, people are opening to the Divine within, stepping into their roles as prophets and peacemakers, stepping out of old conditioning and becoming catalysts for conversations of consequence. There is a mass conversion under way as millions of us acknowledge our place in the body of God and devote our lives to the cocreation of a world that works for everyone. As we see it, feel it, and believe it, so is it becoming.

Physicist Max Planck wrote, "All matter originates and exists only by virtue of a force which brings the particles of an atom to vibration and holds this most minute solar system of the atom together.... We must assume behind this force the existence of a conscious and intelligent mind. This mind is the matrix of all matter." The *who* that we are is one with this very matrix. We are the vessels through which the Divine operates, just as a light bulb is a vessel for electricity. The force comes through us, taking whatever shape we give it. Whether one is a terrorist or a piano tuner, a murderer or a mystic, the very same force is behind each individual, holding the atoms and cells together, unifying us in the web of existence.

When Einstein reached the conclusion that "something deeply hidden had to be behind things," this is what he was talking about. When the Indian mystic Sri Aurobindo wrote, "That within us which seeks to know and to progress is not in the mind but something behind it which makes use of it," he, too, was referring to the great consciousness of which we are a part and to whom we belong. God is making use of our bodies and minds to be manifest. We are part of the mosaic of God. As the poet Hafiz writes: "God said, 'I am made whole by your life. Each soul, each soul completes me.'"

Adoration is the essential preparation for action.

—EVELYN UNDERHILL

210

When our souls materialize bodies to do their work in this world, from the very beginning we are led to believe that we are our bodies. But we are *not* our bodies. We are their observers, their caretakers. We are the mind behind their movements, the eye behind their seeing. The cells in our bodies completely replace themselves every seven years, but our consciousness, connected to the source, maintains its perfect wholeness throughout eternity. Our cells come and go, but our memory of the ocean stays the same. When I was under the crashed car, facing death, I knew I was in for another journey, that even though my body wasn't going to survive, the *real* me was going home, returning to my source. While I waited for death, I had no fear, present as I was to the merging at hand.

Western science has caught up with Eastern spirituality and validated that the outer world of atoms and elements mirrors the inner world of our thoughts and emotions. Jean E. Charon, a theoretical physicist at the University of Paris, has said that electrons and photons themselves are microcosms and that they are equipped with mechanisms of memory and thinking. When two electrons that were once connected are separated from each other, even as far as the ends of the earth, an adjustment to the spin of one causes a *simultaneous* change in the spin of the other. At the quantum level, instantaneous actions occur at a distance.

Quantum nonlocality or nonseparability is asking us to completely revise our ideas about objects. According to Victor Mansfield in *Synchronicity, Science, and Soul-Making,* we can no longer consider objects as independently existing entities that

They say that Sufis don't pray, because they know that *everything* is God.

—Coleman Barks

211

can be localized in well-defined regions of space-time. They are interconnected in ways not even conceivable in classical physics. Physicist Menas Kafatos writes: "Nature has shown us that our concept of reality, consisting of units that can be considered as separate from each other, is fundamentally wrong." Quantum nonlocality proves that particles that once interacted together remain in some sense parts of a system that responds as one entity to further interactions.

Since the entire universe originated in a flash of light known as the big bang, the existence of quantum nonlocality points toward a profound cosmological holism and suggests that if everything that ever interacted in the big bang maintains its connection with everything it interacted with, then every particle in every star and galaxy that we can see "knows" about the existence of every other particle, according to physicist John Gribbin. Since our own bodies are fundamentally composed of these elements, then we can include ourselves in this profound holism. Every particle in our being is mystically connected to, intimately tuned in to every particle in everyone else's being. When Jesus said, "What you do for the least of these, you do for me as well," he wasn't just speaking metaphorically. Nor was the poet who wrote, "Every man's death diminishes me."

A Hasidic saying gives us a wonderful image of this concept: The tree, upon seeing the ax enter the forest, notices its wooden handle, and says, "Look, one of us." Or as Coleman Barks so poetically puts it, "All the particles of the world are in love and looking for lovers. Pieces of straw tremble in the presence of amber." This is the magic and the science of our nonlocal

> The severed particle trembles at the approach of the rest.
> —TEILHARD DE CHARDIN

world, unfolding every day, in front of our eyes, countless miracles and mysteries in every human and heavenly body.

On the subatomic level, research has shown that our DNA exerts an influence over matter, shaping protons into wave patterns through some kind of invisible force. And we can influence our DNA. With the power of our mind, we can cause our own DNA to relax and unwind, allowing us to access more of its codes. In one study, human placental DNA was placed in a container to measure changes; twenty-eight vials of it were given to twenty-eight researchers who were trained in generating and feeling feelings. Researchers found that the DNA changed shape according to the feelings of the researchers.

In another study, leukocytes (white blood cells) were harvested for DNA and placed in chambers to be measured for electrical charges. The donor, who sat in another room, was subjected to emotional stimulation, such as war images, sexual erotica, and humor. When the donor exhibited emotional peaks and valleys, measured by electrical responses, so did the DNA *at the same time*. This was also true when researchers separated the donor by fifty miles. *What power is loose in the world?*

The IHM website (www.heartmath.org) has an astonishing array of experiments that demonstrate these phenomena, proving that with mindfulness, openness, and commitment, we can enter deeper levels of consciousness and expand the realm of our imagination. Creativity is not a gift that some people have and others don't. It's a mode of mindfulness, a byproduct of attunement. We are creative by nature, and every choice we make is a brushstroke on the canvas of our lives. Every feeling we have shapes the very contours of our reality.

We create the events of our lives with the power of our combined thoughts and emotions. As Neale Donald Walsch puts it, "The universe makes multiple copies of our thoughts." What we experience on Tuesday is the result of what we thought and felt on Monday. The lives we enter into are creations of our own making, issuing forth from the images and words we form in our own imaginations. Just as the

Buddhist monks brought a stagnant pond back to life through meditative power, so can we, with the power of our thoughts, affect change in our own bodies, which are 70 percent water and susceptible to thought. If we would only love our bodies, *exactly as they are,* if we would adore them and nourish them with unstinting reverence, they would transform before our very eyes. But if we hate them, speak badly of them, abuse them, they will take on the form of that hatred.

With this great brain of ours—the most complex entity, for its size, known in all the universe—we are shaping our bodies, our families, our communities, and the world. As Krishnamurti reminds us, "The inward strife projected outwardly becomes the world chaos. War is the spectacular result of our everyday life." It is our responsibility, our burden, and our privilege to contribute to the outcome of the evolution still to come. We create peace by thinking peace, feeling peace, removing conflict from our daily lives, and loving ourselves as we love God, who *is* our self, flowing through our bodies every minute of the day.

All day long our cells are constantly chattering, and our brain is in on the conversation, according to neuroscientist Candace Pert, author of *Molecules of Emotion.* She writes that "consciousness is contained in every cell."[1] When an organ is transplanted from one body to another, the cellular memories come right along with it. In May 1988, Claire Sylvia received the heart of an eighteen-year-old male who had been killed in a motorcycle accident. Soon after the operation, Sylvia found herself acting more masculine and strutting down the street

You must be your own lamps, be your own refuges. Take refuge in nothing but yourself.

—BUDDHA

(which, being a dancer, was not her usual manner of walking). She began craving green peppers and beer, which she had never liked before. Sylvia even began having recurring dreams about a man named Tim, who she felt was her donor, and who, as it turns out, was. When she met Tim's family, she learned that all her new cravings and behaviors closely mirrored his.

An eight-year-old girl who received the heart of a murdered ten-year-old began having nightmares in which she relived the crime. Her dreams helped police solve the murder. In other stories, a shy, reserved woman developed a more assertive personality, and a male recipient strangely picked up his donor's musical taste. Every cell is a carrier of information no matter where it goes. Cells are consciousness enclosed within a membrane, as we are consciousness enclosed within a body. The Sufi mystic Ibn al-'Arabi said, "If thou know thine own existence thus, then thou knowest God; and if not, then not." Consciousness is the ground of being. It is divine thought, and we are its thinking. There is nowhere to look and not find consciousness, not encounter God. Quantum physics is coming up with such mind-bending and bizarre discoveries that the global brain is expanding exponentially. Everyday ideas we once held as true are put out to pasture, replaced by pronouncements that make our heads spin. The brilliant and renowned endocrinologist Deepak Chopra tells us that we are thoughts that have learned to create a physical machine, that our body is a three-dimensional picture of what we are thinking. In *Quantum Healing,* he writes, "At the very instant that you think, 'I am happy,' a chemical message translates your emotion, which has no solid existence whatsoever in the material world, into a bit of matter so perfectly attuned to your desire that literally every cell in your body learns of your happiness and joins in."[2] Consciousness is what allows us to talk to fifty trillion cells in our body at the same time in their own language. We're having a personal Pentecost every day of our lives.

Our body and brain are the physical manifestation of our immaterial mind. The mind is like the symphony, and the body and brain are the instruments and players. In Candace Pert's words: "Every second a massive information exchange is occurring in the body and each messenger system has its own unique tone—a signature tune. These tunes rise and fall, wax and wane, bind and unbind. If we could hear this body music with our ears, the sum of the sounds would be the music we call emotions."

Our raw emotions are striving to be expressed in the body. They're always moving up and down the chakras and the spinal cord, carrying information on a cellular level, communicating through a psychosomatic network with every system in our body, and seeking a final release and integration through the brain. They're like seedlings burrowing through the soil in search of the sun. If they are stunted in their journey, denied expression, there is no flow, no growth, no vitality. Releasing our emotions is part of the process of unmanifest consciousness becoming manifest. It's through the expression of our emotions that we, as incarnate versions of the Divine, allow the Great Beloved to flow through us and become present in our world.

It is this very flow of energy and emotional release that keeps us healthy and happy, but our brain, attempting to prevent overload, is cautious about what information it allows into the cortex. So the brain comes up with rationalizations ("You shouldn't feel this way"; "Be careful, you shouldn't hurt anybody"; "Your feelings aren't as important as someone else's") to push the energy down, creating a struggle, dis-ease, in the body. "Emotion is not generated by the brain, but by the cells themselves. The cellular level, where emotions are instigated, is also where unexpressed emotions are stored. The catharsis of illness

Consciousness is the ground of all being and our self-consciousness is That consciousness.

—AMIT GOSWAMI

216

expresses the sudden, overwhelming release of information that has been trapped in our bodies," says Pert. If we do not express our emotions and keep the energy flowing through systems, we are setting ourselves up for emotional and physical distress.

After my accident, I was besieged with inner voices that tried to keep me from expressing my emotions about the incident. My dominating cortex kept saying to my cells, "Get over it, you lived didn't you?... There are a lot of people suffering more than you.... You shouldn't have to go to therapy to get over this. Just stop thinking about it." As a result, my emotions had nowhere to go, and my body's vital energy was blocked, leading to major anxiety and sleeplessness. I couldn't heal fully till I released my emotional pain, but cognitive therapy, talk therapy, wasn't effective in the least. It was like letting the fox guard the chicken coop. My brain was the problem, not the solution.

I needed to find a bodyworker, a bioenergetics therapist, to guide me through the process, so my emotions had a chance to come out without fear of judgment from the brain. In a safe environment, I let my wounded back talk to me. I let my body tell me what it felt like to receive such a shock, to be on the edge of death, to experience several caregivers who were less than compassionate. And once my feelings had a safe place to be released, my terror, my sadness, and my anger dissipated. Then I was back in balance, and my body could heal itself. It's like the Dead Sea and the Sea of Galilee. They're both fed by the same river Jordan, only one is stagnant while the other is full of life. The reason is that the Sea of Galilee lets the river go, while the Dead Sea has no outlets. I couldn't heal until I began to let my feelings go.

Part of our cultural heritage is the belief that some emotions are good and some are bad, so we try to suppress the ones we think are bad. How many of us have been told, "If you don't have something good to say, don't say anything at all"? If we're ever going to access our highest consciousness, express our creativity, and keep the flow of divine mind coursing through us, we have to let go of these inherited beliefs. Anger, fear, and sadness are as healthy as joy, peace, and courage. Suppressing any of these leads to trouble, as Freud acknowledged when he described depression as anger redirected against oneself.

Carl Jung called emotion the chief source of consciousness. "There is no change from darkness to light or from inertia to movement without emotion," he wrote. Our inability to feel our "negative" emotions often leads to strokes, heart attacks, and other organic problems. According to Elaine de Beauport in *The Three Faces of Mind*, our feelings are exercise for the organs of the body just as swimming or running is exercise for the muscles of the body. "We need to practice feelings consciously at least twenty minutes every day to gradually build our emotional strength."

We may need to do some remedial work in the *expression* of some emotions, but it's a scientific fact that we hurt ourselves terribly when we fail to let our emotions surface. Research shows that more heart attacks occur on Monday mornings than any other day of the week and that death rates peak during the days after Christmas for Christians and after Chinese New Year for the Chinese. The state of our emotions affects whether or not we succumb to viral infections. The immune systems of cancer patients have been shown to be much stronger for people in touch with their emotions.

When the biochemicals of our emotions are flowing freely through our bodies, what we feel is happiness. Bliss is our default mode. To sustain it, what we have to do is allow the

When you work in interior work, the work is not done by method, but by intensity.   —KABIR

218

flow, all the while knowing we're culturally conditioned not to do so. Until we get in the habit, it feels as if we're going against the grain, and we *are*. We're taking back authority over our own lives. We're forging an identity that's integrated, dynamic, energetically charged. We're unfolding and liberating our creative imagination, firing more neurons, sparking more ideas. We're opening ourselves to the light of the world, and selfish as it may seem, it is an act as honorable and humble as prayer.

The English novelist Aldous Huxley believed that each of us is potentially mind at large, capable of remembering all that has ever happened to us and of perceiving everything that is happening everywhere in the universe. In *The Doors of Perception,* he writes that since we're animals concerned mostly with survival issues, that vast cosmic mind has to be funneled through the reducing valve of our brain and nervous system. The subtle vibrational energy gets integrated into our cellular matrix by passing through a step-down system of transformers known as our chakras. For a variety of reasons, most of us are only receiving a trickle of the kind of consciousness that will help us stay alive on the planet.

Huxley writes: "Some of us are born with a bypass that circumvents this reducing valve—some acquire temporary bypasses through spiritual practice, hypnosis, drugs—we receive something more than, and above all, something different from the carefully selected utilitarian material which our narrowed, individual minds regard as a complete or sufficient picture of reality." When I read this, I saw a literal image of a funnel going into my brain, and I was excited to think about my own potential to expand or bypass the reducing valve.

The hardware for omniscience is installed in our brains.

—JOAN BORYSENKO

219

This is what our spiritual practice is all about. My own practice is simply an hour of silence in front of a candle every morning. I say a couple of formal prayers, because I love the sound of them, but mostly I'm just in the presence of the beloved, attentive and thankful. When I'm with people, I try to speak as if my words are the blueprint for the future I'm summoning. And during the day, since I'm usually alone and in silence as I work, there is plenty of opportunity to connect, to feel my communion with God. I feel a tremendous oneness, which both comforts and inspires me to create work that reflects this experience.

Writing books is one way to communicate it, but I think music, images, and storytelling are even more powerful channels because they arouse the emotions, open people up for transformation *in the heart*—and that's the source, the wellspring of change. Thoughts make us consider, but feelings make us *move*. Our culture is so brain-heavy that we're way out of balance. I think that's why the sacred feminine is coming back. We can't live without her any longer. We've grown ourselves outward, through science, technology, and medical advances, and now it's time to deepen, to grow inwardly, to use our magnificent brains in the service of soul, both as individuals and as members of a human race that's on a very precipitous edge.

We all know this on some level. We feel it in our bones; we wake up aching, longing for something to change. We know there's something missing, that there's more to life than consumption, money, and material comforts, but we can't put the pieces together. We've been so trained to think of ourselves as

Our call in life is to right action, not right doctrine. Speculation on how God works has not served us.

—DIARMUID
O'MURCHU

separate that it's nearly impossible to imagine ourselves as cellularly connected, not only to each other, but to God as well. Until we can imagine that vividly and feel the joy of being part of a communion of saints, we can't possibly open our reducing valves enough to let in the consciousness that will unfold our next steps.

The physicist David Bohm believes that the way we think of the totality is crucial for the overall order of the human mind itself. In *Wholeness and the Implicate Order,* he writes that if we think of the totality as constituted of independent fragments, then that is how our minds will operate, but "if we can include everything coherently and harmoniously in an overall whole that is undivided, unbroken, and without a border (for every border is a division or break) then our minds will tend to move in a similar way, and from this will flow an orderly action within the whole." Even amoebas, in times of famine, come together and practice being multicellular.

We're like caterpillars getting close to the great transformation. In preparation for its metamorphosis, the caterpillar eats one hundred times its weight, falls asleep, and then forms a chrysalis. When the imaginal cells of the new begin to form themselves, the immune system of the caterpillar tries to fight them off. The immune system fails, and the caterpillar cells become the soup that nurtures the life of the butterfly.

I think we're going through a similar process. We're in a massive consumption phase now, and many of us are asleep, napping in the chrysalis. Since we're all at different stages, some of us are feeling the invasion of the new and are resisting it with all our might. We don't want to give up what we know and have. Even though we're participating in a civilization that keeps millions of people starving while a small percentage own most of the wealth, we don't want the upset that fixing that might cost us. Even though most of our institutions are failing us, we don't have enough moral outrage to fuel a change in course. We've stuffed ourselves—those of us who can— and we're sleeping now. It's just too bad about the others.

We have to tune out our emotions to sustain this thinking, because if we let ourselves really *feel* our oneness with those people who have nothing because of this imbalance, then we'd have to do something. We'd have to bear the weight of our complicity. We'd have to feel the sorrow, the hunger, the angst, and the terror of the ones left behind. We'd have to cry, we'd have to forgive ourselves, and we'd have to act in different ways. So instead we become like the cortex that comes up with all the rationalizations for not letting in the emotions. We live half-lives, buying more and more to make ourselves feel better, as if joy were something that comes from outside instead of bubbling up from within as a reward for being true. No, if we are to find real meaning, feel real joy, it will come on the wings of a fully engaged life, a life in the service of the many, rooted in the heart, and fueled by passion. It will come when we remember that giving is receiving, and the more we give of ourselves, the more meaning, joy, and fulfillment will come our way.

Just as the DNA of a caterpillar contains the blueprint of the butterfly, so do our bodies contain the answer to every question haunting us now. As we become more embodied, more attuned to the web of energy we're all a part of, we bring about our own transformation from caterpillar to butterfly. Evolution is not a blind, accidental, improvising process. It is a continuation of creation. We are not remote observers but vital participants in the action, and when we fully embrace the power within us, dare to *be* the Divine we now only call on, we'll unleash every code in our DNA and fashion a world of grandeur and grace.

The trouble with trying to change the world is that weeks can go by and nothing happens.

—Rev. Carol Carnes

Geneticists are discovering "unused" sections of DNA, masked by histones and activated by nonhistone proteins, which are thought to contain the blueprint of the future. If histones have been masking these sections of DNA, perhaps we are the nonhistones (the "her tones," the sound of the sacred feminine) that are arriving to activate the proteins and nourish the imaginal cells of the new. This is all an inner process. There is nothing needed that is outside us. This is the time for work within, for self-discovery and self-expansion. The frontier to explore is the frontier of our own beings.

Recent brain research has focused on the prefrontal neocortex, which neurologist Paul MacLean refers to as "angel lobes," attributing to them our higher human virtues of love, compassion, and empathy, as well as our advanced intellectual skills. It turns out that we have a significant amount of brain space that is not committed to any specific function, referred to by scientists as "uncommitted cortex." Perhaps that is where God is resting, waiting for us to commit ourselves to the greatest collaboration we could ever imagine—the design and creation of a world that meets the needs of every living creature. It's like the blank page, the empty palette, the music awaiting the dance. *What shall we do with our uncommitted cortex?*

Since we're all bound together energetically, all one with and in the mind of God, the work will ultimately be a mosaic, composed of the parts that each of us brings. As Virginia Woolf said, "Masterpieces are not single and solitary births; they are the outcome of many years of thinking in common, of thinking by the body of the people, so that the experience of the mass is behind the single voice." All we have to do is our part. The final masterpiece will emerge as each of us rises to the task and responds to the questions: *What in the world do I truly love? What is moving from my center to the world at large?*

The path to that answer takes us right to the heart, the threshold to our inner wisdom. It is what Rumi refers to in this poem, "Two Kinds of Intelligence":

There are two kinds of intelligence: One acquired,
as a child in school memorizes facts and concepts
from books and from what the teacher says,
collecting information from the traditional sciences
as well as from the new sciences.

With such intelligence you rise in the world.
You get ranked ahead or behind others
in regard to your competence in retaining
information. You stroll with this intelligence
in and out of fields of knowledge, getting always more
marks on your preserving tablets.

There is another kind of tablet, one
already completed and preserved inside you.
A spring overflowing its springbox. A freshness
in the center of the chest. This other intelligence
does not turn yellow or stagnate. It's fluid,
and it doesn't move from outside to inside
through the conduits of plumbing-learning.

This second knowing is a fountainhead
from within you, moving out.[3]

Living creatively means diving into this fountainhead, this overflowing spring, and letting its freshness source and sustain us. Our souls have conjured these bodies to do their work in the world, and just as a pitcher of water floats in the river—water within, and water without—so do we hold within the very Divine to whom we belong. Ours is a holographic universe, and in every part, the whole is contained. The answers to our questions are in every cell, waiting to be expressed in the flow of our feelings. It is not intellect we need to fix our lives, our relationships, our broken world—it is insight, inner sight.

Lao-tzu says, "Why scurry about looking for the truth? It vibrates in everything and every not-thing, right off the tip of your nose. Can you be still and see it in the mountain? The pine tree? Yourself? Don't imagine that you'll discover it by accumulating more knowledge. Knowledge creates doubt, and doubt makes you ravenous for more knowledge. You can't get full eating this way." To live imaginative and inspired lives doesn't take genius, money, or luck. It takes time, the courage to go within, and the commitment to a daily practice of communion with the beloved so we can ignore the voices of the small and petty and preserve our magnitude amid waves of mediocrity. It takes verve and stamina and rebellious originality. The great poet Mary Oliver says, "In order to be the person I want to be, I must strive hourly against the drag of others."

It takes a tremendous amount of self-love to stay true to our path. A short time ago I was talking with two women, both of whom are mothers, artists, and professional women in their early thirties. We got on the subject of self-image, and when I asked how they rated their self-love on a scale of one to ten, one said six and the other seven. Their focus is on their shortcomings, because their ears are more often tuned to the outer world than their own inner sanctuaries. What they're hearing about themselves from critical partners and a culture whose goal is to

> Those who don't feel this life pulling them like a river, those who don't drink dawn like a cup of springwater or take in sunset like supper, those who don't want to change, let them sleep. —RUMI

225

promote insecurity is shaping their emotional world more than their own self-knowing.

That's why we need time alone, every day, to reroot ourselves in the soil of God. In *The Pregnant Virgin,* Jungian therapist Marion Woodman writes: "When society deliberately programs itself to a set of norms that has very little to do with instincts, love or privacy, then people who set out to become individuals, trusting in the dignity of their own soul and the creativity of their own imagination, have good reason to be afraid. They are outcasts." Any of us who are trying to live creatively, simply, compassionately are at risk of being outcasts. *But so what?* There is freedom there. There is fluidity, spontaneity, and the deep joy of knowing we're true to our essence, true to the soul who took on this body to perform its task.

There is nothing to seek, for we have within us the entire world. Through the tops of our heads, the heavens enter, and through the soles of our feet come the powers of earth—forces divine and forces mortal, roiling in our blood, our organs, our bones, fusing and forging the new from the old. Our research is done and all that is left is to tune our ear to the great below, hear the beat of our throbbing heart, and press on through each challenge calling "yes" and "thanks."

Strange as it sounds, there is only one of us, and each of us is a cell in that great holy one. Each of us is a carrier of sacred wisdom, a prophet announcing the world to come, a mystic bewildered by the God in our bed. We are part of an ongoing new creation that is unfolding through and in and with our bodies. Through our senses, we experience the miracle of the Divine

We're not afraid of the unknown. We're afraid of the known coming to an end.

—ANTHONY deMELLO

226

indwelling every day, in our own beings, and in everything that exists around us. The world is our altar, our communion table, our laboratory, our stage.

And these bodies of ours, these are our souls' sacred vessels, the instruments through which the Great Beloved sings, laughs, labors, and loves. We are the eyes through which God sees, the mind through which God ponders, the hands through which God touches. As we dwell as cells in the body of God, God dwells in us as our vital force, pushing outward, awaiting release, prompting communion, awareness, and joy.

To love ourselves is an act of faith, a sacrament of acknowledgment, a gesture of solidarity with the holy one within. It is the first and most important step, for we can only love others as we love ourselves. No matter what you were ever told about loving yourself, remember now that your body is the materialization of divine energy. Love it extravagantly, cherish it, adore its mystical workings and miraculous potential. Look beyond the surface as you peer into your mirror, and thank the one within for this chance to be alive, to be of use, and to be a cocreator of this magnificent experience called life.

REFLECTION

Take some time to ponder the words of Dag Hammarskjöld: "In our era, the path to holiness necessarily passes through the world of action." Does this ring true for you? What are the elements of a holy life? What actions are you taking to bring your faith into the world?

EXERCISE

If you're in an emotional situation, try using the analytical part of your brain—the cortex—for six seconds before you respond. The cortex handles math, language, complex visual or auditory processing, and other "high order" thinking. To get an effective pause, you'll make the cortex work hard on one of those tasks by thinking. This pause gives you time to choose a constructive response to your emotions, so you can express the emotions you feel in a way that is compassionate and consistent with your goals. For more info on this, see the website at www.6seconds.org.

Even though this technique sounds easy, it takes practice and discipline. But the rewards are well worth it. Here are a few six-second suggestions:

- Remember six of the Seven Dwarfs in alphabetical order.
- Name six foreign capitals.
- Count to six in a foreign language.
- Visualize six details of a beautiful place.
- Conjugate six Latin verbs.
- Feel six breaths of air filling your lungs and imagine what it looks like.
- Name six emotions you are feeling.

If you get to the point where your six-second pause becomes routine, you may need to change your assignment to keep the cortex working.

WRITING EXERCISE

Look through the quotes in this chapter and select one you resonate with. The reason you resonate with it is that, on some deep level, you sense its truthfulness. Your body agrees with its essence. In order for this to be true, you must have had an actual experience that led you to know this. See if you can go back to the event that led to your knowledge of this truth. How old were you? What were you doing? Who was there? Where were you? What could you see, hear, taste, smell, feel? Using the quote as an epigraph at the beginning of the essay, write the story of how you learned that truth.

Notes

1: A Deep Step into God

1. Coleman Barks, *The Essential Rumi* (San Francisco: HarperSanFrancisco, 1995), 191.

2: Love of the Dance

1. Diarmuid O'Murchu, *Quantum Theology: Spiritual Implications of the New Physics* (New York: Crossroad Publishing, 1998), 40.
2. Malidoma Patrice Somé, *Ritual: Power, Healing, and Community* (Portland, Ore.: Swan Raven, 1993), 107.
3. Jane Roberts, *The "Unknown" Reality,* vol. 1 (Englewood Cliffs, N.J.: Prentice Hall, 1997).
4. Oliver Davies, trans., *Meister Eckhart: Selected Writings* (New York: Penguin Books, 1994).
5. *Peace Pilgrim: Her Life and Work in Her Own Words* (Santa Fe: Ocean Tree Books, 1982). To receive a free copy of Peace Pilgrim's book, visit www.peacepilgrim.net, or write Friends of Peace Pilgrim, 43480 Cedar Avenue, Hemet, CA 92344.

3: The Whole World in Our Hands

1. Daniel Ladinsky, *Love Poems from God: Twelve Sacred Voices from the East and West* (New York: Penguin Compass, 2002), 106.
2. Mae-Wan Ho, "The Entangled Universe," *Yes! A Journal of Positive Futures* (Spring 2000).
3. Visit www.alexgrey.com for more information on Alex Grey's work.
4. Robert Bly, *The Kabir Book* (Boston: Beacon Press, 1977), 4.
5. Joseph Chilton Pearce, *The Biology of Transcendence: A Blueprint of the Human Spirit* (Rochester, Vt.: Park Street Press, 2002), 2.

4: No Holding Back

1. Interview with Anodea Judith by Jordan S. Gruber in February 1999, posted online at www.enlightenment.com/media/interviews/judith.html.
2. Alain Daniélou, *Yoga: The Method of Re-integration* (Whitefish, Mont.: Kessinger Publishing, 2003).
3. Richard Gerber, MD, *A Practical Guide to Vibrational Medicine: Energy Healing and Spiritual Transformation* (New York: HarperCollins, 2000).
4. Rosalyn L. Bruyere, *Wheels of Light: Chakras, Auras, and the Healing Energy of the Body* (New York: Simon & Schuster, 1994).
5. Susan Lark's website is very informative: www.drlark.com.
6. Ken Dychtwald, *Bodymind* (New York: J. P. Tarcher, 1986), 154.
7. Neil Douglas-Klotz, *Prayers of the Cosmos: Meditations on the Aramaic Words of Jesus* (San Francisco: Harper & Row, 1990).

5: Sexuality and the Sacred

1. Marija Gimbutas interview, posted online at www.levity.com/mavericks/gimbut.htm.
2. Elinor Gadon, *The Once and Future Goddess: A Sweeping Visual Chronicle of the Sacred Female and Her Reemergence in the Cult* (San Francisco: HarperSanFrancisco, 1989).
3. Tom Robbins interview, posted online at www.1giantleap.com.
4. Sue Monk Kidd, *Dance of the Dissident Daughter: A Woman's Journey from Christian Tradition to the Sacred Feminine* (San Francisco: HarperSanFrancisco, 1996), 219.
5. Howard Clinebell, *Ecotherapy: Healing Ourselves, Healing the Earth* (New York: Haworth Press, 1996).
6. Daniel Ladinsky, trans., *The Gift: Poems by Hafiz, the Great Sufi Master* (New York: Penguin, 1999), 160.
7. Jan Phillips, *All the Way to Heaven*. CD available at www.janphillips.com.
8. Pierre Teilhard de Chardin, *The Divine Milieu: An Essay on the Interior Life* (New York: Harper & Row, 1957).
9. O'Murchu, *Quantum Theology,* 191.
10. Audre Lorde, *Sister Outsider: Essays and Speeches* (Freedom, Calif.: Crossing Press, 1984).

6: The Hourglass Dress

1. Ladinsky, *Love Poems from God,* 203.
2. Lisa Sarasohn, *The Woman's Belly Book: Finding Your True Center for More Energy, Confidence, and Pleasure* (Novato: New World Library, 2006). Also, "From Ancient Spiritual Practice to the Unified Field: The Body's Center as the Center of Consciousness," *Consciousness Research Abstracts.* (1996); also, http://honoringyourbelly.com/inspiration/articles/unified_field.html.
3. Gadon, *The Once and Future Goddess.* Also see "The Goddess Ungirdled: How I Learned to Love My Belly and Found the Sacred Feminine Within," *SageWoman.* (Spring 1996): 9; also at http://honoringyourbelly.com/inspiration/articles/goddess_ungirdled.html.
4. Omraam Mikhaël Aïvanhov, *Man's Subtle Bodies and Centres: The Aura, the Solar Plexus, the Chakras* (London: Cygnus Books, 2000).
5. Lisa Sarasohn, *The Woman's Belly Book: Finding Your True Center for More Energy, Confidence, and Pleasure* (Novato: New World Library, 2006).
6. Karlfried Graf Dürckheim, *Hara: The Vital Center of Man* (1987; repr., Rochester, Vt.: Inner Traditions, 2004). Also see "The Goddess Ungirdled: How I Learned to Love My Belly and Found the Sacred Feminine Within," *SageWoman.* (Spring 1996): 8; also at http://honoringyourbelly.com/inspiration/articles/goddess_ungirdled.html. Also, http://www.innertraditions.com/isbn/1-59477-024-7
7. Barry Kapke, "Hara (Pt II): Working from the Center," *Massage & Bodywork* (August/September 2001).
8. Myra Shapiro, *I'll See You Thursday* (St. Paul: Blue Sofa Press, 1996).

7: The Heart of the Matter

1. Reports from the Institute of HeartMath can be found at www.heartmath.org.
2. Helen Schucman, *A Course in Miracles* (Tiburon, Calif.: Foundation for Inner Peace, 1975).
3. Pearce, *The Biology of Transcendence,* 59.
4. Kabir Helminski, ed. and trans., *The Pocket Rumi Reader* (Boston: Shambhala, 2001). More information can be found at www.sufism.org.
5. Ladinsky, *Love Poems from God,* 112.
6. Pir Vilayat Inayat Khan, *Awakening: A Sufi Experience* (New York: Penguin Putnam, 1999), 168.
7. In the original Aramaic, which was the language spoken at the time, the reference was to the creative force, which was thought of as feminine. All the translations we have inherited from

the Greek, Hebrew, and Latin texts match the mindsets of the interpreters and have mis-shaped our consciousness for two millennia.

8. Thomas Berry, *The Great Work: Our Way into the Future* (New York: Random House, 1999).
9. Dychtwald, *Bodymind,* 154.
10. Danah Zohar and Ian Marshall, *SQ: Spiritual Intelligence, the Ultimate Intelligence* (London: Bloomsbury Publishing, 2000), 148.
11. Pierre Teilhard de Chardin, *The Heart of Matter* (New York: Harcourt and Brace, 1976), 53, 35.

8: Praising Our Own Geography

1. Sandy Supowit, "One Morning in the Bathroom Mirror," in *Halves of Necessity* (Austin: Plain View Press, 1999), 93.
2. Susan Brownmiller, *Femininity* (New York: Ballantine, 1994).

9: Claiming Our Voice

1. Audre Lorde, *Sinister Wisdom,* no. 7, posted online at www.sinisterwisdom.org.

10: Let's Hear It for the Ears

1. Deepak Chopra, MD, *Perfect Health* (New York: Harmony Books, 1991).
2. Jonathan Goldman, *Healing Sounds: The Power of Harmonics* (Rochester, Vt.: Healings Arts Press, 2002), viii. More information can be found at www.healingsounds.com.
3. Bijal P. Trivedi, "Was Maya Pyramid Designed to Chirp Like a Bird?" *National Geographic Today* (December 6, 2002).
4. Ani Williams's website offers information on sound healing: www.aniwilliams.com.
5. These planetary sounds can be heard at www.body-mind.com/bmrpg2aaSP.html.
6. Isadora Duncan, *My Life* (New York: W. W. Norton, 1998).
7. Sarah Anderson, ed., *Heaven's Face Thinly Veiled: A Book of Spiritual Writing by Women* (Boston: Shambhala, 1998), 26.
8. Don Campbell, *The Mozart Effect: Tapping the Power of Music to Heal the Body, Strengthen the Mind, and Unlock the Creative Spirit* (New York: HarperCollins, 2001), 104.
9. Masaru Emoto, *Messages from Water* (Tokyo: Hado Publishing, 1999), 73.
10. Hans Jenny, *Cymatics: The Study of Wave Phenomena and Vibration* (Berkeley: Macromedia Press, 2001).

11: Seeing Our Way Clear

1. Ladinsky, *The Gift,* 217.
2. Jacob Liberman, *Light, Medicine of the Future: How We Can Use It to Heal Ourselves Now* (Santa Fe: Bear & Co., 1991), xxii.
3. Barks, *The Essential Rumi,* 191.
4. Douglas-Klotz, *Prayers of the Cosmos,* 86–87.

12: A Cell in the Right Brain of God

1. Candace Pert, *Molecules of Emotion: The Science behind Mind-Body Medicine* (New York: Scribner, 1997).
2. Deepak Chopra, MD, *Quantum Healing: Exploring the Frontiers of Mind/Body Medicine* (New York: Bantam, 1989).
3. Barks, *The Essential Rumi,* 178.

Acknowledgments

To my Creator, for loving me into existence.

To my mom, for bringing me into this world and showing me how to live without fear.

To my partner, Annie, for the presence of your being and the gifts of your wisdom and support.

To my spiritual sisters in San Diego, for your singing, your reiki, your massages, and all your stories, which fuel me for the journey.

To my spiritual sisters and brothers around the country, for inviting me into your lives and giving us the opportunity to learn from each other.

To Daniel Ladinsky, Coleman Barks, and Kabir Helminski for your exquisite translations of the mystics and your extraordinary generosity in sharing them.

To Alex Grey, for your visionary paintings, which help us to see what the eyes cannot.

To Judi Beach, Pene Bourk, Toni Farkas, Myra Shapiro, and Sandy Supowit, for letting me share your beautiful poems and stories with others.

To Hannelore Hahn, for creating the International Women's Writing Guild and to all my IWWG sisters around the world.

To Joseph Chilton Pearce, for taking the time to talk with me about the heart.

To Robin and Cody, for creating the Prophets Conferences and giving me the opportunity to share my work there.

To Maura Shaw, Sarah McBride, and Kate Mueller, for your fabulous editorial skills and support.

Inspiration

Finding God Beyond Religion: A Guide for Skeptics, Agnostics & Unorthodox Believers Inside & Outside the Church
By Tom Stella; Foreword by The Rev. Canon Marianne Wells Borg
Reinterprets traditional religious teachings central to the Christian faith for people who have outgrown the beliefs and devotional practices that once made sense to them.
6 x 9, 160 pp, Quality PB, 978-1-59473-485-4 **$16.99**

Fully Awake and Truly Alive: Spiritual Practices to Nurture Your Soul
By Rev. Jane E. Vennard; Foreword by Rami Shapiro
Illustrates the joys and frustrations of spiritual practice, offers insights from various religious traditions and provides exercises and meditations to help us become more fully alive.
6 x 9, 208 pp, Quality PB, 978-1-59473-473-1 **$16.99**

How Did I Get to Be 70 When I'm 35 Inside?: Spiritual Surprises of Later Life
By Linda Douty
Encourages you to focus on the inner changes of aging to help you greet your later years as the grand adventure they can be.
6 x 9, 208 pp, Quality PB, 978-1-59473-297-3 **$16.99**

Journeys of Simplicity: Traveling Light with Thomas Merton, Bashō, Edward Abbey, Annie Dillard & Others
By Philip Harnden
Invites you to consider a more graceful way of traveling through life. PB includes journal pages to help you get started on your own spiritual journey.
5 x 7¼, 144 pp, Quality PB, 978-1-59473-181-5 **$12.99**
5 x 7¼, 128 pp, HC, 978-1-893361-76-8 **$16.95**

Perennial Wisdom for the Spiritually Independent: Sacred Teachings—Annotated & Explained
Annotation by Rami Shapiro; Foreword by Richard Rohr
Weaves sacred texts and teachings from the world's major religions into a coherent exploration of the five core questions at the heart of every religion's search.
5½ x 8½, 336 pp, Quality PB Original, 978-1-59473-515-8 **$16.99**

Saving Civility: 52 Ways to Tame Rude, Crude & Attitude for a Polite Planet *By Sara Hacala*
Provides fifty-two practical ways you can reverse the course of incivility and make the world a more enriching, pleasant place to live.
6 x 9, 240 pp, Quality PB 978-1-59473-314-7 **$16.99**

Spiritually Healthy Divorce: Navigating Disruption with Insight & Hope *By Carolyne Call*
A spiritual map to help you move through the twists and turns of divorce.
6 x 9, 224 pp, Quality PB, 978-1-59473-288-1 **$16.99**

Who Is My God? 2nd Edition
An Innovative Guide to Finding Your Spiritual Identity *By the Editors at SkyLight Paths*
Provides the Spiritual Identity Self-Test™ to uncover the components of your unique spirituality.
6 x 9, 160 pp, Quality PB, 978-1-59473-014-6 **$15.99**

Or phone, fax, mail or e-mail to: SKYLIGHT PATHS Publishing
Sunset Farm Offices, Route 4 • P.O. Box 237 • Woodstock, Vermont 05091
Tel: (802) 457-4000 • Fax: (802) 457-4004 • www.skylightpaths.com
Credit card orders: (800) 962-4544 (8:30AM–5:30PM EST Monday–Friday)
Generous discounts on quantity orders. SATISFACTION GUARANTEED. Prices subject to change.

Children's Spirituality

Adam & Eve's First Sunset: God's New Day *By Sandy Eisenberg Sasso; Full-color illus. by Joani Keller Rothenberg*
A lesson in hope and faith—and that there are some things beyond our control—for every child who worries about what comes next.
9 x 12, 32 pp, Full-color illus., HC, 978-1-58023-177-0 **$17.95*** For ages 4 & up

Because Nothing Looks Like God *By Lawrence Kushner and Karen Kushner; Full-color illus. by Dawn W. Majewski*
Invites parents and children to explore the questions we all have about God.
11 x 8½, 32 pp, Full-color illus., HC, 978-1-58023-092-6 **$17.99*** For ages 4 & up
Also available: **Teacher's Guide** 8½ x 11, 22 pp, PB, 978-1-58023-140-4 **$6.95**

But God Remembered: Stories of Women from Creation to the Promised Land
By Sandy Eisenberg Sasso; Full-color illus. by Bethanne Andersen
A fascinating collection of four different stories of women only briefly mentioned in biblical tradition and religious texts.
9 x 12, 32 pp, Full-color illus., Quality PB, 978-1-58023-372-9 **$8.99*** For ages 8 & up

Does God Hear My Prayer? *By August Gold; Full-color photos by Diane Hardy Waller*
Introduces preschoolers and young readers to prayer and how it helps them express their own emotions.
10 x 8½, 32 pp, Full-color photo illus., Quality PB, 978-1-59473-102-0 **$8.99** For ages 3–6

For Heaven's Sake *By Sandy Eisenberg Sasso; Full-color illus. by Kathryn Kunz Finney*
Heaven is often found where you least expect it.
9 x 12, 32 pp, Full-color illus., HC, 978-1-58023-054-4 **$16.95*** For ages 4 & up

God in Between *By Sandy Eisenberg Sasso; Full-color illus. by Sally Sweetland*
A magical, mythical tale that teaches that God can be found where we are.
9 x 12, 32 pp, Full-color illus., HC, 978-1-879045-86-6 **$16.95*** For ages 4 & up

God's Paintbrush: Special 10th Anniversary Edition *By Sandy Eisenberg Sasso; Full-color illus. by Annette Compton*
Invites children of all faiths and backgrounds to encounter God through moments in their own lives.
11 x 8½, 32 pp, Full-color illus., HC, 978-1-58023-195-4 **$17.95*** For ages 4 & up

Also available: **God's Paintbrush Teacher's Guide**
8½ x 11, 32 pp, PB, 978-1-879045-57-6 **$8.95**

God's Paintbrush Celebration Kit: A Spiritual Activity Kit for Teachers and Students of All Faiths, All Backgrounds
9½ x 12, 40 Full-color Activity Sheets & Teacher Folder w/ complete instructions, HC, 978-1-58023-050-6 **$21.95**
Additional activity sheets available:
8-Student Activity Sheet Pack (40 sheets/5 sessions), 978-1-58023-058-2 **$19.95**
Single-Student Activity Sheet Pack (5 sessions), 978-1-58023-059-9 **$3.95**

I Am God's Paintbrush (A Board Book) *By Sandy Eisenberg Sasso; Full-color illus. by Annette Compton*
5 x 5, 24 pp, Full-color illus., Board Book, 978-1-59473-265-2 **$7.99** For ages 0–4

It's a … It's a … It's a Mitzvah *By Liz Suneby and Diane Heiman; Full-color Illus. by Laurel Molk*
Join Mitzvah Meerkat and friends as they introduce children through lively illustrations and playful dialogue to the everyday kindnesses that mark the beginning of a Jewish journey and a lifetime commitment to *tikkun olam* (repairing the world).
9 x 12, 32 pp Full-color illus., HC, 978-1-58023-509-9 **$18.99***

* A book from Jewish Lights, SkyLight Paths' sister imprint

Bible Stories / Folktales

Abraham's Bind & Other Bible Tales of Trickery, Folly, Mercy and Love
By Michael J. Caduto
New retellings of episodes in the lives of familiar biblical characters explore relevant life lessons.
6 x 9, 224 pp, HC, 978-1-59473-186-0 **$19.99**

Daughters of the Desert: Stories of Remarkable Women from Christian, Jewish and Muslim Traditions
By Claire Rudolf Murphy, Meghan Nuttall Sayres, Mary Cronk Farrell, Sarah Conover and Betsy Wharton
Breathes new life into the old tales of our female ancestors in faith. Uses traditional scriptural passages as starting points, then with vivid detail fills in historical context and place. Chapters reveal the voices of Sarah, Hagar, Huldah, Esther, Salome, Mary Magdalene, Lydia, Khadija, Fatima and many more. Historical fiction ideal for readers of all ages.
5½ x 8¼, 192 pp, Quality PB, 978-1-59473-106-8 **$14.99** Inc. reader's discussion guide

The Triumph of Eve & Other Subversive Bible Tales
By Matt Biers-Ariel
These engaging retellings of familiar Bible stories are witty, often hilarious and always profound. They invite you to grapple with questions and issues that are often hidden in the original texts.
5½ x 8¼, 192 pp, Quality PB, 978-1-59473-176-1 **$14.99**
Also available: **The Triumph of Eve Teacher's Guide**
8½ x 11, 44 pp, PB, 978-1-59473-152-5 **$8.99**

Wisdom in the Telling: Finding Inspiration and Grace in Traditional Folktales and Myths Retold
By Lorraine Hartin-Gelardi
6 x 9, 192 pp, HC, 978-1-59473-185-3 **$19.99**

Religious Etiquette / Reference

How to Be a Perfect Stranger, 5th Edition: The Essential Religious Etiquette Handbook
Edited by Stuart M. Matlins and Arthur J. Magida
The indispensable guidebook to help the well-meaning guest when visiting other people's religious ceremonies. A straightforward guide to the rituals and celebrations of the major religions and denominations in the United States and Canada from the perspective of an interested guest of any other faith, based on information obtained from authorities of each religion. Belongs in every living room, library and office. Covers:
African American Methodist Churches • Assemblies of God • Bahá'í Faith • Baptist • Buddhist • Christian Church (Disciples of Christ) • Christian Science (Church of Christ, Scientist) • Churches of Christ • Episcopalian and Anglican • Hindu • Islam • Jehovah's Witnesses • Jewish • Lutheran • Mennonite/Amish • Methodist • Mormon (Church of Jesus Christ of Latter-day Saints) • Native American/First Nations • Orthodox Churches • Pentecostal Church of God • Presbyterian • Quaker (Religious Society of Friends) • Reformed Church in America/Canada • Roman Catholic • Seventh-day Adventist • Sikh • Unitarian Universalist • United Church of Canada • United Church of Christ

"The things Miss Manners forgot to tell us about religion."
—*Los Angeles Times*

"Finally, for those inclined to undertake their own spiritual journeys ... tells visitors what to expect."
—*New York Times*

6 x 9, 432 pp, Quality PB, 978-1-59473-294-2 **$19.99**

The Perfect Stranger's Guide to Funerals and Grieving Practices: A Guide to Etiquette in Other People's Religious Ceremonies
Edited by Stuart M. Matlins
6 x 9, 240 pp, Quality PB, 978-1-893361-20-1 **$16.95**

The Perfect Stranger's Guide to Wedding Ceremonies: A Guide to Etiquette in Other People's Religious Ceremonies
Edited by Stuart M. Matlins
6 x 9, 208 pp, Quality PB, 978-1-893361-19-5 **$16.95**

Spirituality

The Passionate Jesus: What We Can Learn from Jesus about Love, Fear, Grief, Joy and Living Authentically
By The Rev. Peter Wallace Reveals Jesus as a passionate figure who was involved, present, connected, honest and direct with others and encourages you to build personal authenticity in every area of your own life.
6 x 9, 208 pp, Quality PB, 978-1-59473-393-2 **$18.99**

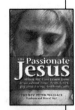

Gathering at God's Table: The Meaning of Mission in the Feast of Faith
By Katharine Jefferts Schori A profound reminder of our role in the larger frame of God's dream for a restored and reconciled world. 6 x 9, 256 pp, HC, 978-1-59473-316-1 **$21.99**

The Heartbeat of God: Finding the Sacred in the Middle of Everything
By Katharine Jefferts Schori; Foreword by Joan Chittister, OSB Explores our connections to other people, to other nations and with the environment through the lens of faith. 6 x 9, 240 pp, HC, 978-1-59473-292-8 **$21.99**

A Dangerous Dozen: Twelve Christians Who Threatened the Status Quo but Taught Us to Live Like Jesus
By the Rev. Canon C. K. Robertson, PhD; Foreword by Archbishop Desmond Tutu
Profiles twelve visionary men and women who challenged society and showed the world a different way of living.
6 x 9, 208 pp, Quality PB, 978-1-59473-298-0 **$16.99**

Decision Making & Spiritual Discernment: The Sacred Art of Finding Your Way
By Nancy L. Bieber Presents three essential aspects of Spirit-led decision making: willingness, attentiveness and responsiveness. 5½ x 8½, 208 pp, Quality PB, 978-1-59473-289-8 **$16.99**

Laugh Your Way to Grace: Reclaiming the Spiritual Power of Humor
By Rev. Susan Sparks A powerful, humorous case for laughter as a spiritual, healing path.
6 x 9, 176 pp, Quality PB, 978-1-59473-280-5 **$16.99**

Bread, Body, Spirit: Finding the Sacred in Food *Edited and with Introductions by Alice Peck*
6 x 9, 224 pp, Quality PB, 978-1-59473-242-3 **$19.99**

Claiming Earth as Common Ground: The Ecological Crisis through the Lens of Faith
By Andrea Cohen-Kiener; Foreword by Rev. Sally Bingham
6 x 9, 192 pp, Quality PB, 978-1-59473-261-4 **$16.99**

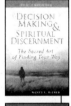

Creating a Spiritual Retirement: A Guide to the Unseen Possibilities in Our Lives *By Molly Srode*
6 x 9, 208 pp, b/w photos, Quality PB, 978-1-59473-050-4 **$14.99**

Creative Aging: Rethinking Retirement and Non-Retirement in a Changing World *By Marjory Zoet Bankson*
6 x 9, 160 pp, Quality PB, 978-1-59473-281-2 **$16.99**

Keeping Spiritual Balance as We Grow Older: More than 65 Creative Ways to Use Purpose, Prayer, and the Power of Spirit to Build a Meaningful Retirement *By Molly and Bernie Srode*
8 x 8, 224 pp, Quality PB, 978-1-59473-042-9 **$16.99**

Hearing the Call across Traditions: Readings on Faith and Service *Edited by Adam Davis; Foreword by Eboo Patel*
6 x 9, 352 pp, Quality PB, 978-1-59473-303-1 **$18.99**

Honoring Motherhood: Prayers, Ceremonies & Blessings *Edited and with Introductions by Lynn L. Caruso*
5 x 7¼, 272 pp, Quality PB, 978-1-58473-384-0 **$9.99**; HC, 978-1-59473-239-3 **$19.99**

The Losses of Our Lives: The Sacred Gifts of Renewal in Everyday Loss *By Dr. Nancy Copeland-Payton*
6 x 9, 192 pp, HC, 978-1-59473-271-3 **$19.99**

Renewal in the Wilderness: A Spiritual Guide to Connecting with God in the Natural World *By John Lionberger*
6 x 9, 176 pp, b/w photos, Quality PB, 978-1-59473-219-5 **$16.99**

Soul Fire: Accessing Your Creativity *By Thomas Ryan, CSP*
6 x 9, 160 pp, Quality PB, 978-1-59473-243-0 **$16.99**

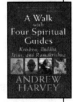

A Spirituality for Brokenness: Discovering Your Deepest Self in Difficult Times *By Terry Taylor*
6 x 9, 176 pp, Quality PB, 978-1-59473-229-4 **$16.99**

A Walk with Four Spiritual Guides: Krishna, Buddha, Jesus, and Ramakrishna *By Andrew Harvey*
5½ x 8½, 192 pp, b/w photos & illus., Quality PB, 978-1-59473-138-9 **$15.99**

Prayer / Meditation

Men Pray: Voices of Strength, Faith, Healing, Hope and Courage
Created by the Editors at SkyLight Paths
Celebrates the rich variety of ways men around the world have called out to the Divine—with words of joy, praise, gratitude, wonder, petition and even anger—from the ancient world up to our own day.
5 x 7¼, 192 pp, HC, 978-1-59473-395-6 **$16.99**

Honest to God Prayer: Spirituality as Awareness, Empowerment, Relinquishment and Paradox
By Kent Ira Groff
For those turned off by shopworn religious language, offers innovative ways to pray based on both Native American traditions and Ignatian spirituality.
6 x 9, 192 pp, Quality PB, 978-1-59473-433-5 **$16.99**

Sacred Attention: A Spiritual Practice for Finding God in the Moment
By Margaret D. McGee
Framed on the Christian liturgical year, this inspiring guide explores ways to develop a practice of attention as a means of talking—and listening—to God.
6 x 9, 144 pp, Quality PB, 978-1-59473-291-1 **$16.99**

Women of Color Pray: Voices of Strength, Faith, Healing, Hope and Courage
Edited and with Introductions by Christal M. Jackson
Through these prayers, poetry, lyrics, meditations and affirmations, you will share in the strong and undeniable connection women of color share with God.
5 x 7¼, 208 pp, Quality PB, 978-1-59473-077-1 **$15.99**

Living into Hope: A Call to Spiritual Action for Such a Time as This
By Rev. Dr. Joan Brown Campbell; Foreword by Karen Armstrong
6 x 9, 208 pp, HC, 978-1-59473-283-6 **$21.99**

Praying with Our Hands: 21 Practices of Embodied Prayer from the World's Spiritual Traditions
By Jon M. Sweeney; Photos by Jennifer J. Wilson; Foreword by Mother Tessa Bielecki; Afterword by Taitetsu Unno, PhD
8 x 8, 96 pp, 22 duotone photos, Quality PB, 978-1-893361-16-4 **$16.95**

Secrets of Prayer: A Multifaith Guide to Creating Personal Prayer in Your Life   By Nancy Corcoran, CSJ
6 x 9, 160 pp, Quality PB, 978-1-59473-215-7 **$16.99**

Three Gates to Meditation Practice: A Personal Journey into Sufism, Buddhism, and Judaism   By David A. Cooper
5½ x 8½, 240 pp, Quality PB, 978-1-893361-22-5 **$18.99**

Prayer / M. Basil Pennington, OCSO

Finding Grace at the Center, 3rd Edition: The Beginning of Centering Prayer
With Thomas Keating, OCSO, and Thomas E. Clarke, SJ; Foreword by Rev. Cynthia Bourgeault, PhD A practical guide to a simple and beautiful form of meditative prayer.
5 x 7¼, 128 pp, Quality PB, 978-1-59473-182-2 **$12.99**

The Monks of Mount Athos: A Western Monk's Extraordinary Spiritual Journey on Eastern Holy Ground
Foreword by Archimandrite Dionysios
Explores the landscape, monastic communities and food of Athos.
6 x 9, 352 pp, Quality PB, 978-1-893361-78-2 **$18.95**

Psalms: A Spiritual Commentary   *Illus. by Phillip Ratner*
Reflections on some of the most beloved passages from the Bible's most widely read book.
6 x 9, 176 pp, 24 full-page b/w illus., Quality PB, 978-1-59473-234-8 **$16.99**

The Song of Songs: A Spiritual Commentary   *Illus. by Phillip Ratner*
Explore the Bible's most challenging mystical text.
6 x 9, 160 pp, 14 full-page b/w illus., Quality PB, 978-1-59473-235-5 **$16.99**; HC, 978-1-59473-004-7 **$19.99**

Spirituality / Animal Companions

Blessing the Animals
Prayers and Ceremonies to Celebrate God's Creatures, Wild and Tame
Edited and with Introductions by Lynn L. Caruso
5¼ x 7¼, 256 pp, Quality PB, 978-1-59473-253-9 **$15.99**; HC, 978-1-59473-145-7 **$19.99**

Remembering My Pet
A Kid's Own Spiritual Workbook for When a Pet Dies
By Nechama Liss-Levinson, PhD, and Rev. Molly Phinney Baskette, MDiv; Foreword by Lynn L. Caruso
8 x 10, 48 pp, 2-color text, HC, 978-1-59473-221-8 **$16.99**

What Animals Can Teach Us about Spirituality
Inspiring Lessons from Wild and Tame Creatures
By Diana L. Guerrero
6 x 9, 176 pp, Quality PB, 978-1-893361-84-3 **$16.95**

Spirituality & Crafts

Beading—The Creative Spirit
Finding Your Sacred Center through the Art of Beadwork *By Rev. Wendy Ellsworth*
Invites you on a spiritual pilgrimage into the kaleidoscope world of glass and color.
7 x 9, 240 pp, 8-page color insert, 40+ b/w photos and 40 diagrams Quality PB, 978-1-59473-267-6 **$18.99**

Contemplative Crochet
A Hands-On Guide for Interlocking Faith and Craft *By Cindy Crandall-Frazier; Foreword by Linda Skolnik*
Illuminates the spiritual lessons you can learn through crocheting.
7 x 9, 208 pp, b/w photos, Quality PB, 978-1-59473-238-6 **$16.99**

The Knitting Way
A Guide to Spiritual Self-Discovery *By Linda Skolnik and Janice MacDaniels*
Examines how you can explore and strengthen your spiritual life through knitting.
7 x 9, 240 pp, b/w photos, Quality PB, 978-1-59473-079-5 **$16.99**

The Painting Path
Embodying Spiritual Discovery through Yoga, Brush and Color *By Linda Novick; Foreword by Richard Segalman*
Explores the divine connection you can experience through art.
7 x 9, 208 pp, 8-page color insert, plus b/w photos, Quality PB, 978-1-59473-226-3 **$18.99**

The Quilting Path
A Guide to Spiritual Discovery through Fabric, Thread and Kabbalah *By Louise Silk*
Explores how to cultivate personal growth through quilt making.
7 x 9, 192 pp, b/w photos and illus., Quality PB, 978-1-59473-206-5 **$16.99**

The Scrapbooking Journey
A Hands-On Guide to Spiritual Discovery *By Cory Richardson-Lauve; Foreword by Stacy Julian*
Reveals how this craft can become a practice used to deepen and shape your life.
7 x 9, 176 pp, 8-page color insert, plus b/w photos, Quality PB, 978-1-59473-216-4 **$18.99**

The Soulwork of Clay
A Hands-On Approach to Spirituality *By Marjory Zoet Bankson; Photos by Peter Bankson*
Takes you through the seven-step process of making clay into a pot, drawing parallels at each stage to the process of spiritual growth.
7 x 9, 192 pp, b/w photos, Quality PB, 978-1-59473-249-2 **$16.99**

Women's Interest

Birthing God: Women's Experiences of the Divine *By Lana Dalberg; Foreword by Kathe Schaaf*
Powerful narratives of suffering, love and hope that inspire both personal and collective transformation.
6 x 9, 304 pp, Quality PB, 978-1-59473-480-9 **$18.99**

On the Chocolate Trail: A Delicious Adventure Connecting Jews, Religions, History, Travel, Rituals and Recipes to the Magic of Cacao *By Rabbi Deborah R. Prinz*
Take a delectable journey through the religious history of chocolate—a real treat!
6 x 9, 272 pp, 20+ b/w photographs, Quality PB, 978-1-58023-487-0 **$18.99***

Women, Spirituality and Transformative Leadership: Where Grace Meets Power
Edited by Kathe Schaaf, Kay Lindahl, Kathleen S. Hurty, PhD, and Reverend Guo Cheen
A dynamic conversation on the power of women's spiritual leadership and its emerging patterns of transformation.
6 x 9, 288 pp, HC, 978-1-59473-313-0 **$24.99**

Spiritually Healthy Divorce: Navigating Disruption with Insight & Hope *By Carolyne Call*
A spiritual map to help you move through the twists and turns of divorce.
6 x 9, 224 pp, Quality PB, 978-1-59473-288-1 **$16.99**

New Feminist Christianity: Many Voices, Many Views *Edited by Mary E. Hunt and Diann L. Neu*
Insights from ministers and theologians, activists and leaders, artists and liturgists who are shaping the future. Taken together, their voices offer a starting point for building new models of religious life and worship.
6 x 9, 384 pp, Quality PB, 978-1-59473-435-9 **$19.99**; HC, 978-1-59473-285-0 **$24.99**

Bread, Body, Spirit: Finding the Sacred in Food *Edited and with Introductions by Alice Peck*
6 x 9, 224 pp, Quality PB, 978-1-59473-242-3 **$19.99**

Dance—The Sacred Art: The Joy of Movement as a Spiritual Practice *By Cynthia Winton-Henry*
5½ x 8½, 224 pp, Quality PB, 978-1-59473-268-3 **$16.99**

Daughters of the Desert: Stories of Remarkable Women from Christian, Jewish and Muslim Traditions
By Claire Rudolf Murphy, Meghan Nuttall Sayres, Mary Cronk Farrell, Sarah Conover and Betsy Wharton
5½ x 8½, 192 pp, Illus., Quality PB, 978-1-59473-106-8 **$14.99** Inc. reader's discussion guide

The Divine Feminine in Biblical Wisdom Literature: Selections Annotated & Explained
Translation & Annotation by Rabbi Rami Shapiro; Foreword by Rev. Cynthia Bourgeault, PhD
5½ x 8½, 240 pp, Quality PB, 978-1-59473-109-9 **$16.99**

Divining the Body: Reclaim the Holiness of Your Physical Self *By Jan Phillips*
8 x 8, 256 pp, Quality PB, 978-1-59473-080-1 **$18.99**

Honoring Motherhood: Prayers, Ceremonies & Blessings *Edited and with Introductions by Lynn L. Caruso*
5 x 7¼, 272 pp, Quality PB, 978-1-58473-384-0 **$9.99**; HC, 978-1-59473-239-3 **$19.99**

> **Next to Godliness:** Finding the Sacred in Housekeeping *Edited by Alice Peck*
> 6 x 9, 224 pp, Quality PB, 978-1-59473-214-0 **$19.99**
>
> **ReVisions:** Seeing Torah through a Feminist Lens *By Rabbi Elyse Goldstein*
> 5½ x 8½, 224 pp, Quality PB, 978-1-58023-117-6 **$16.95***
>
> **The Triumph of Eve & Other Subversive Bible Tales** *By Matt Biers-Ariel*
> 5½ x 8½, 192 pp, Quality PB, 978-1-59473-176-1 **$14.99**
>
> **White Fire:** A Portrait of Women Spiritual Leaders in America *By Malka Drucker; Photos by Gay Block*
> 7 x 10, 320 pp, b/w photos, HC, 978-1-893361-64-5 **$24.95**

Woman Spirit Awakening in Nature: Growing Into the Fullness of Who You Are *By Nancy Barrett Chickerneo, PhD; Foreword by Eileen Fisher*
8 x 8, 224 pp, b/w illus., Quality PB, 978-1-59473-250-8 **$16.99**

Women of Color Pray: Voices of Strength, Faith, Healing, Hope and Courage *Edited and with Introductions by Christal M. Jackson*
5 x 7¼, 208 pp, Quality PB, 978-1-59473-077-1 **$15.99**

* A book from Jewish Lights, SkyLight Paths' sister imprint

Spiritual Practice

Fly-Fishing—The Sacred Art: Casting a Fly as a Spiritual Practice *By Rabbi Eric Eisenkramer and Rev. Michael Attas, MD; Foreword by Chris Wood, CEO, Trout Unlimited; Preface by Lori Simon, executive director, Casting for Recovery*
Shares what fly-fishing can teach you about reflection, awe and wonder; the benefits of solitude; the blessing of community and the search for the Divine. 5½ x 8½, 160 pp, Quality PB, 978-1-59473-299-7 **$16.99**

Lectio Divina—The Sacred Art: Transforming Words & Images into Heart-Centered Prayer
By Christine Valters Paintner, PhD
Expands the practice of sacred reading beyond scriptural texts and makes it accessible in contemporary life.
5½ x 8½, 240 pp, Quality PB, 978-1-59473-300-0 **$16.99**

Writing—The Sacred Art: Beyond the Page to Spiritual Practice *By Rami Shapiro and Aaron Shapiro*
Push your writing through the trite and the boring to something fresh, something transformative. Includes over fifty unique, practical exercises. 5½ x 8½, 192 pp, Quality PB, 978-1-59473-372-7 **$16.99**

Conversation—The Sacred Art: Practicing Presence in an Age of Distraction
By Diane M. Millis, PhD; Foreword by Rev. Tilden Edwards, PhD
Cultivate the potential for deeper connection in every conversation. 5½ x 8½, 192 pp, Quality PB, 978-1-59473-474-8 **$16.99**

Pilgrimage—The Sacred Art: Journey to the Center of the Heart *By Dr. Sheryl A. Kujawa-Holbrook*
Explore the many dimensions of the experience of pilgrimage—the yearning heart, the painful setbacks, the encounter with the Divine and, ultimately, the changed orientation to the world. 5½ x 8½, 240 pp, Quality PB, 978-1-59473-472-4 **$16.99**

Dance—The Sacred Art: The Joy of Movement as a Spiritual Practice *By Cynthia Winton-Henry*
5½ x 8½, 224 pp, Quality PB, 978-1-59473-268-3 **$16.99**

Giving—The Sacred Art: Creating a Lifestyle of Generosity *By Lauren Tyler Wright*
5½ x 8½, 208 pp, Quality PB, 978-1-59473-224-9 **$16.99**

Haiku—The Sacred Art: A Spiritual Practice in Three Lines *By Margaret D. McGee*
5½ x 8½, 192 pp, Quality PB, 978-1-59473-269-0 **$16.99**

Hospitality—The Sacred Art: Discovering the Hidden Spiritual Power of Invitation and Welcome
By Rev. Nanette Sawyer; Foreword by Rev. Dirk Ficca
5½ x 8½, 208 pp, Quality PB, 978-1-59473-228-7 **$16.99**

Labyrinths from the Outside In, 2nd Edition: Walking to Spiritual Insight—A Beginner's Guide
By Rev. Dr. Donna Schaper and Rev. Dr. Carole Ann Camp
6 x 9, 208 pp, b/w illus. and photos, Quality PB, 978-1-59473-486-1 **$16.99**

Practicing the Sacred Art of Listening: A Guide to Enrich Your Relationships and Kindle Your Spiritual Life *By Kay Lindahl*
8 x 8, 176 pp, Quality PB, 978-1-893361-85-0 **$16.95**

Recovery—The Sacred Art: The Twelve Steps as Spiritual Practice *by Rami Shapiro; Foreword by Joan Borysenko, PhD*
5½ x 8½, 240 pp, Quality PB, 978-1-59473-259-1 **$16.99**

Running—The Sacred Art: Preparing to Practice *By Dr. Warren A. Kay; Foreword by Kristin Armstrong*
5½ x 8½, 160 pp, Quality PB 978-1-59473-227-0 **$16.99**

The Sacred Art of Chant: Preparing to Practice *By Ana Hernández*
5½ x 8½, 192 pp, Quality PB, 978-1-59473-036-8 **$16.99**

The Sacred Art of Fasting: Preparing to Practice *By Thomas Ryan, CSP*
5½ x 8½, 192 pp, Quality PB, 978-1-59473-078-8 **$15.99**

The Sacred Art of Forgiveness: Forgiving Ourselves and Others through God's Grace *By Marcia Ford*
8 x 8, 176 pp, Quality PB, 978-1-59473-175-4 **$18.99**

The Sacred Art of Listening: Forty Reflections for Cultivating a Spiritual Practice *By Kay Lindahl; Illus. by Amy Schnapper*
8 x 8, 160 pp, b/w illus., Quality PB, 978-1-893361-44-7 **$16.99**

The Sacred Art of Lovingkindness: Preparing to Practice *By Rabbi Rami Shapiro; Foreword by Marcia Ford*
5½ x 8½, 176 pp, Quality PB, 978-1-59473-151-8 **$16.99**

Thanking & Blessing—The Sacred Art: Spiritual Vitality through Gratefulness *By Jay Marshall, PhD; Foreword by Philip Gulley*
5½ x 8½, 176 pp, Quality PB, 978-1-59473-231-7 **$16.99**

About SKYLIGHT PATHS Publishing

SkyLight Paths Publishing is creating a place where people of different spiritual traditions come together for challenge and inspiration, a place where we can help each other understand the mystery that lies at the heart of our existence.

Through spirituality, our religious beliefs are increasingly becoming a part of our lives—rather than *apart* from our lives. While many of us may be more interested than ever in spiritual growth, we may be less firmly planted in traditional religion. Yet, we do want to deepen our relationship to the sacred, to learn from our own as well as from other faith traditions, and to practice in new ways.

SkyLight Paths sees both believers and seekers as a community that increasingly transcends traditional boundaries of religion and denomination—people wanting to learn from each other, *walking together, finding the way.*

For your information and convenience, at the back of this book we have provided a list of other SkyLight Paths books you might find interesting and useful. They cover the following subjects:

Buddhism / Zen	Hinduism / Vedanta	Prayer
Catholicism	Inspiration	Religious Etiquette
Children's Books	Islam / Sufism	Retirement
Christianity	Judaism	Spiritual Biography
Comparative Religion	Kabbalah	Spiritual Direction
Current Events	Meditation	Spirituality
Earth-Based Spirituality	Midrash Fiction	Women's Interest
Enneagram	Monasticism	Worship
Global Spiritual Perspectives	Mysticism	
Gnosticism	Poetry	

Or phone, fax, mail or e-mail to: SKYLIGHT PATHS Publishing
Sunset Farm Offices, Route 4 • P.O. Box 237 • Woodstock, Vermont 05091
Tel: (802) 457-4000 • Fax: (802) 457-4004 • www.skylightpaths.com
Credit card orders: (800) 962-4544 (8:30AM–5:30PM EST Monday–Friday)
Generous discounts on quantity orders. SATISFACTION GUARANTEED. Prices subject to change.